**IMPLEMENTING
SUSTAINABLE
URBAN TRAVEL
POLICIES**

National Reviews

EUROPEAN CONFERENCE OF MINISTERS OF TRANSPORT

EUROPEAN CONFERENCE OF MINISTERS
OF TRANSPORT (ECMT)

The European Conference of Ministers of Transport (ECMT) is an inter-governmental organisation established by a Protocol signed in Brussels on 17 October 1953. It is a forum in which Ministers responsible for transport, and more specifically the inland transport sector, can co-operate on policy. Within this forum, Ministers can openly discuss current problems and agree upon joint approaches aimed at improving the utilisation and at ensuring the rational development of European transport systems of international importance.

At present, the ECMT's role primarily consists of:

– helping to create an integrated transport system throughout the enlarged Europe that is economically and technically efficient, meets the highest possible safety and environmental standards and takes full account of the social dimension;

– helping also to build a bridge between the European Union and the rest of the continent at a political level.

The Council of the Conference comprises the Ministers of Transport of 43 full member countries: Albania, Armenia, Austria, Azerbaijan, Belarus, Belgium, Bosnia-Herzegovina, Bulgaria, Croatia, the Czech Republic, Denmark, Estonia, Finland, France, FYR Macedonia, Georgia, Germany, Greece, Hungary, Iceland, Ireland, Italy, Latvia, Liechtenstein, Lithuania, Luxembourg, Malta, Moldova, Netherlands, Norway, Poland, Portugal, Romania, the Russian Federation, Serbia and Montenegro, Slovakia, Slovenia, Spain, Sweden, Switzerland, Turkey, Ukraine and the United Kingdom. There are six Associate member countries (Australia, Canada, Japan, Korea, New Zealand and the United States) and one Observer country (Morocco).

A Committee of Deputies, composed of senior civil servants representing Ministers, prepares proposals for consideration by the Council of Ministers. The Committee is assisted by working groups, each of which has a specific mandate.

The issues currently being studied – on which policy decisions by Ministers will be required – include the development and implementation of a pan-European transport policy; the integration of Central and Eastern European Countries into the European transport market; specific issues relating to transport by rail, road and waterway; combined transport; transport and the environment; sustainable urban level; the social costs of transport; trends in international transport and infrastructure needs; transport for people with mobility handicaps; road safety; traffic management; road traffic information and new communications technologies.

Statistical analyses of trends in traffic and investment are published regularly by the ECMT and provide a clear indication of the situation, on a trimestrial or annual basis, in the transport sector in different European countries.

As part of its research activities, the ECMT holds regular Symposia, Seminars and Round Tables on transport economics issues. Their conclusions serve as a basis for formulating proposals for policy decisions to be submitted to Ministers.

The ECMT's Documentation Service has extensive information available concerning the transport sector. This information is accessible on the ECMT Internet site.

For administrative purposes the ECMT's Secretariat is attached to the Organisation for Economic Co-operation and Development (OECD).

Publié en français sous le titre :
Transports urbains durables : la mise en œuvre des politiques
EXAMENS NATIONAUX

Further information about the ECMT is available on Internet at the following address:
www.oecd.org/cem
© ECMT 2003 – ECMT *Publications are distributed by:* OECD *Publications Service,*
2, rue André Pascal, 75775 PARIS CEDEX 16, France.

Foreword

Following publication of the joint ECMT and OECD report *Urban Travel and Sustainable Development* in 1995, Ministers of Transport asked for a review of the implementation of urban transport policies in the light of the recommendations made. This review was undertaken over the period 1998-2001 resulting in a summary report to Ministers that can be consulted on the web at *www.oecd.org/CEM/topics/council/cmpdf/2001/CM0113e.pdf* and a series of published reports including a survey of urban travel trends and policy developments in cities across the ECMT and OECD regions, and in-depth reviews on implementing urban sustainable travel policies in the Netherlands and Hungary. The present report presents the results of eleven "self-reviews" by national governments on progress towards sustainable urban travel policies and opens with a synthesis of the experience reported in these countries. The synthesis report draws also on developments reported in the peer reviews and cities survey.

Table of Contents

Synthesis Report

National Reviews by Country

SYNTHESIS REPORT

1. Socio-economic, Institutional and Environmental Contexts

1.1. Key trends as identified five years ago and today

The 1995 joint ECMT/OECD report *Urban Travel and Sustainable Development* noted the following general trends:

Key urban trends

- About three-quarters of the population of OECD/ECMT countries now live in urban areas. Settlement patterns are becoming more complex characterised by a continuous "suburbanisation" of the population and of jobs.
- Travel by car has increased in almost all countries and at a rate which, fifty years ago, would not have been thought possible. This has been due to long-term annual increases of 2 to 3% in national wealth, a general lowering in the real costs of using a car and the emergence of more car dependent life-styles.
- Trip length both by car and public transport has increased as activities have become more dispersed. Suburb-to-suburb journeys have shown the fastest growth. At the same time there has been a shift from walking and cycling to motorised modes.
- Car ownership has conferred on a large and increasing public a freedom to travel anywhere at any time and enabled jobs, shops and services to relocate to peripheral areas. It has also allowed more people to enjoy living in more spacious surroundings.
- Industry has not been slow to take advantage of the freedom offered by road transport. The ease with which goods can be transported between almost any locations has allowed innovations such as "just-in-time" production and a reduction in warehousing facilities. Firms of all kinds have, at the same time, tended to move to edge-of-town sites to exploit the increased personal mobility of their car-owning customers and employees.

- Innovations in logistics, coupled with increases in the consumption of goods, have caused road freight traffic to grow at nearly 5% per annum over the last 20 years, even faster than car traffic (3.3% per annum).

Costs of key trends

- All these changes have been associated with economic growth, but they have not been without their costs:

- Almost all large towns and cities are congested in the central and inner areas for much of the day and along the main arteries at peak times. Many are becoming increasingly congested in the suburbs at certain times of the day.

- Fringe areas of cities are difficult and costly to serve by public transport.

- Those without access to a car are becoming increasingly isolated from jobs and services.

- Deaths and injuries on urban roads occur in unacceptable numbers, do untold damage to those who are bereaved or maimed and create an atmosphere of fear.

- Inner and many outer parts of cities are dominated by road traffic. Road noise affects to a serious extent almost half the urban residents in most countries.

- Air pollution is present in almost all parts of cities. Exhaust emissions, in addition to contributing to photochemical smog, are associated with a wide range of health problems.

- Not all the effects of traffic are local. Photochemical smog and acid rain are regularly exported from cities to their surroundings and even to adjacent countries and carbon dioxide is emitted whenever fossil fuels are burnt.

Compared with the earlier period, the national governments reporting in 2000/2001 revealed some differences in developments over the last 5 years, with some new patterns emerging. It was also possible to obtain much more information from countries in transition in the current review. The results reported are described in the following sections.

1.1.1. Did urban populations continue to grow? Did sprawl continue to expand with degradation of an inner ring of suburbs?

In America the classic trend towards sprawl appears to continue. Despite the phenomenon being most marked on the American continent, sprawl has become a major feature of developments in eastern Europe in the last decade. In western Europe some reversal in the trend appears to be emerging with residents and to a smaller extent employers being attracted back to city centres.

The USA reports widespread growth in urban populations and faster growth in consumption of land around urban areas, with a trend towards lower density residential and business land use. In many of the older cities of the north-east and Midwest, city centre populations are stable or declining whilst the suburbs are growing.

Finland reports continued growth in urban populations. Norway reports the classic pattern of business and residents moving out of city centres into the suburbs creating sprawl in the 1970s and 1980s but notes an emerging change of preference for higher density housing closer to the city centres in the 1990s. In Switzerland the share of total population in the largest urban regions has decreased slightly in recent years. There is some evidence, however, of the inner most city areas becoming more attractive, partly as a result of successful transport policies and resulting reductions in nuisance, with an influx of returning wealthy citizens. This new trend is also noted in France, where the population of Paris has been stable for over a decade, but at the same time the inner suburbs grow and the outer suburbs have grown dramatically. In most cities peripheral areas have shown the strongest growth in employment opportunities, but the Swiss cities have also maintained or even increased employment in the city centres.

There are important differences in the development of degraded inner suburbs. Switzerland has avoided this effect successfully and, with Finland, reports that current development plans put a strong emphasis on providing attractive living spaces in the inner areas. Some cities that have suffered very widespread degradation, such as London, have made successful, if limited, inroads in reversing the trend.

Both Finland and the USA report that sprawl is one of the main concerns of urban citizens, often viewed with more disquiet even than traditional urban fears such as crime.

1.1.2   Did car ownership and use continue to grow?

Car ownership and use have almost universally continued to grow on a strongly increasing trend, with growth particularly in the suburban areas and in concentric movements between suburbs and between cities in heavily populated regions. Car ownership still tends to be lowest in city centres where public transport is available and parking space is at a premium; it is highest in suburban areas poorly served by public transport. The costs of car ownership have continued to decline relative to incomes in the countries surveyed. Though the costs of car use rose in some countries with increases in fuel taxation in the late 1990s, the United Kingdom is the most striking example, costs in real terms are now universally below historic highs. In the USA costs have continued to fall from levels already well below Europe. At the same time the average quality of passenger cars has improved in terms of comfort, durability and accessories, creating additional value for buyers and attraction for use over public transport.

1.1.3. Did ridership on public transport continue to fall?

Trends vary markedly. Some of the biggest cities show strong growth in ridership linked to the economic growth of the last 5 years, London is especially striking. In the second largest city in Europe, Paris, the trend is for stability. In Switzerland rail ridership has grown strongly with improved services but the pattern with local buses varies greatly between cities.

In Finland the volume of passengers using public transport is stable although its share has declined slightly to around 20% of total passenger traffic. Norway saw a decline in ridership in its main cities in the first half of the 1990s partly reversed in the second half in response to investment in public transport systems. Oslo accounted for much of the growth in ridership which reached 20% of total passenger traffic.

In eastern Europe ridership levels have declined with increases in car ownership but are still on average far above western European levels. The Czech Republic reports an "enormous shift" from public transport to cars in the last decade, down from 75% of total urban passenger traffic (90% of peak traffic) at the beginning of the 1990s to 60% at the end of the decade. The decline flattened out in the second half of the 90s with currently a "stagnation" in ridership. The Czech review expresses fears that there is little scope to attract passengers back to public transport either through price or improving the quality of service.

In the USA mass transit accounts for only 4% of trips but ridership grew by 5% during the 1990s. Buses, the most widespread system, saw ridership decline slightly whilst light rail/tram systems increased between 15 and 20%, rail rapid transit ridership increased by 10% and commuter rail ridership increased by 17%.

1.1.4. Trends in pedestrian and bicycle trips

The share of pedestrians and bicycle trips varies very much among European cities, while it is extremely low in the USA (6.5% of local trips, 0.5% of p-km). The number of cycling journeys for distances up to 7 km is highest in the Netherlands. Bicycle traffic increased slightly in the Netherlands to 25% of trips on a nationwide scale or 7% of total p-km. Very high levels of walking and cycling are also reported in Hungary: walking in Budapest accounts for 25% of all trips undertaken.

Most countries probably show a tendency for people to replace short distance trips on foot or by bicycle with travel by car or on public transport trips for reasons of convenience. This trend of a reduction of the share of non-motorised movements is reported in the reviews of Norway and Switzerland.

1.1.5. Trends in congestion

Congestion is notoriously difficult to measure, and the yardsticks used vary greatly from study to study – even within a single country. If there is a general trend it appears to be slightly contradictory. Commuting and leisure journeys by car have lengthened, the number of short trips substituting for walking have increased, average speeds have risen whilst congestion is encountered more frequently. The trend is revealed in the statistics reported in the US review and repeated in many countries.[1] In some urban regions it is reported to occur for increasingly long periods as well as more frequently, for example in the Randstad. In others, for example Paris, it appeared to decline slightly in the 1990s.

In many cities the location of the worst congestion has changed, moving from city centre areas to suburban radial access corridors and particularly to concentric suburb-to-suburb routes. Congestion varies also as a result of historic transport investment levels with marked differences between some neighbouring countries, *e.g.* France and the United Kingdom. In Italy congestion is viewed clearly as the most critical problem by urban citizens.

Eastern Europe also presents mixed trends. In the wealthier cities, rapid growth in car ownership and use has resulted in severe congestion, most notably in Prague and central Moscow. Car traffic and parking management measures already widely developed in cities with longer experience of a high degree of motorisation can probably be deployed to good effect. It is difficult to predict what the residual level of congestion might be.

Finland reports success in avoiding congestion in Helsinki through provision of public transport that accounts for 70% of peak hour passenger traffic. Switzerland reports success in managing traffic in its capital city, Zurich, achieved through a mix of "homeopathic restraint" on access to the city centre, through managing traffic lights, restricting parking capacity and using traffic calming measures. It has also extended bus and tram networks, provided separate lanes for them and given buses and trams priority at junctions, resulting in excellent public transport services. Many of Switzerland's other cities show similar patterns. This is despite expansion of suburban areas little different from patterns in many other mid-sized European towns where congestion is often much worse.

1.1.6. Was there progress in terms of traffic safety?

Two major trends can be distinguished with regard to road safety:

- In western Europe the trends in traffic accidents were uncoupled from trends in car traffic. The Netherlands, Italy and Switzerland report real improvements, whilst Italy mentions pedestrians, bicycles and powered two wheelers as the main risk groups.

- In some CEECs the number of traffic accidents is increasing in proportion to increases in car traffic (Czech Republic). The poor condition of cars and roads is responsible together with insufficient safety awareness and education of drivers. In Hungary the situation is in flux with perspectives for the coming years unclear.

Norway and Finland report fluctuating trends in the number of accidents and fatalities. In Norway, whilst the number of accidents and of injured persons decreased from 1995 to 2000 by 4% from an already low base, the number of people killed in traffic accidents increased by 11%.

1.1.7. Were policies against air pollution, noise and CO_2 emissions successful?

Russia reported continuing poor performance in regard to both air pollution and noise. Several of the other reviews highlighted progress in improving air quality, reducing noise exposure and reducing accidents as an important part of the responses to policies aimed at improving sustainability. Air quality is reported to have improved significantly in Finland, Switzerland and the USA and to be generally good in Norway. Even in these countries, however, there are negative notes. The USA amongst others reports that gains from improved vehicle technologies and fuels and retirement of grossly polluting vehicles have been partly offset by increased vehicle use and changes in consumer preference towards sport utility vehicles and mini vans with lower fuel economy. Despite the overall improvement, Switzerland reports continued widespread excedence of ambient limits for particulates in urban areas and for NO_x close to major road arteries. This pattern may well be true for other cities too.

Norway reports some improvement in regard to noise. Noise nuisance in Switzerland has tended to shift from local roads to highways, where it should generally be possible to use noise walls to reduce nuisance in the future. Even if the problem is less widespread on more minor roads, dealing with nuisance here is more difficult due to the expense of noise walls relative to traffic flow. Several countries recorded recent progress but noted concerns for the future (e.g. the Netherlands). Noise reduction is a priority area for future attention in most of the countries reviewed.

Greenhouse gas emissions were mentioned only in the US review, where it was noted that no institutional responsibilities have been defined. This lack of focus on CO_2 emissions at the urban level probably reflects a view that climate change is a national, rather than local urban issue. The fact that measures taken to address urban issues, including many air pollution, congestion and traffic management measures and especially measures that influence driving style and vehicle maintenance, also have an important impact on CO_2 emissions[2] does not yet appear to have been assimilated. There is clearly a role for national climate change programmes to make inroads in shaping urban transport policies – or perhaps conversely for national programmes to take fuller account of the actions taken at the local level in urban areas.

1.2. Political and economic frameworks

There are several dimensions to political and economic frameworks that are relevant to traffic trends and urban travel policy measures.

1.2.1. *West and East*

The most marked distinction is between Western countries and Central and Eastern European countries. The west has undergone several decades of relatively coherent economic development with relatively smooth growth of traffic and time for coping with its negative side effects. In the Central and Eastern European countries, however, a sharp increase in motorisation took place during a transition period that is only ten years old. Poland reports on the especially high value individuals assign to owning a car, and suggests that most people are not at all prepared to accept constraints on car use.

While the share of public transport has fallen in western countries over a period of several decades and in many has now stabilised or even improved, the collapse of public transport in Central and Eastern European countries is considered dramatic by their governments (Czech report), even if modal shares are still much higher than in the West. A special situation has to be faced in Russia and some of the other CIS countries where socio-economic conditions are poor and the outlook for improvement uncertain. In Russia, motorisation is still at a low level due to relative incomes and prices and at the same time resources are extremely short for renewing public transport fleets.

Urban transport in Central and Eastern European countries suffers in general from structural institutional change. National governments have very rapidly delegated responsibility for local transport to local governments, without allocating corresponding financial means to this level of government. In Poland this shift has been accompanied by strong increases in fares, but the revenues that result are not enough to cover repairs and fleet renewal. Only recently has a new law reinstated some support to local governments from national resources, for example compensation for lost revenues resulting from national schemes for reduced fares for a growing number of disadvantaged social groups.

1.2.2. *Europe and the* USA

The most drastic difference between traffic in Europe and traffic in the USA stems from differences in fuel prices. Particularly low levels of fuel taxation have assisted the development in the USA of extreme urban sprawl, very high shares of car traffic and correspondingly high CO_2 emissions. Dependency on cars is so high that even general awareness of the problem is low, and the political possibilities for managing the situation extremely limited.

1.2.3. Differences within Western Europe

Until a few years ago major distinctions could be observed with regard to the degree of centralisation or decentralisation of government powers related to urban policies. On the one side stood for instance France, with a high degree of centralisation, and on the other Switzerland. These differences are, however, narrowing, at least so far as the allocation of responsibilities is concerned. There is, in Western Europe, a clear shift towards decentralising responsibilities towards regional and local levels.

More difficulties are faced with allocating corresponding financial resources. Switzerland is probably the only case where each level of government (local, cantonal, federal) has its own substantial tax raising powers. Such allocation of economic resources has a strong influence on policy making. In the opposite situation, top down transfers may be accompanied by stronger political influence from central government.

Earlier deficits in local involvement in decision making in some states (especially France) have also been reduced by considerable efforts to promote participatory processes and consultation between the interests of public authorities, economic actors and local populations.

Notes

1. See also Round Table 110 *Traffic Congestion in Europe*, ECMT, Paris 1999.
2. See for example ECMT/ACEA/OICA Turin Conference on Smart CO_2 Reductions, *ibid*.

2. National Experience in Policy Development

2.1. The Capacity of Local and Regional Governments to Make Policy and Invest in Transport Systems

This has emerged as an important issue in strategies to improve transport policy in urban areas. In many western European countries decentralisation has played an important role in providing resources for investment in public transport systems and for a balance in overall transport infrastructure investments that best serves local needs. In the USA there is a strong trend towards devolution in transport decision making, from Federal to State, metropolitan area and local levels. State and local governments have wide discretion to invest federal transport funds to meet local priorities (sometimes in competition with longer term, more global environmental priorities).

In eastern Europe the last decade has seen withdrawal of central government from local and regional policy making but this has not been accompanied by a transfer of resources or powers to raise finance locally. More recently the granting of powers to charge for parking has led to this becoming an important source of municipal finance in some cities in Central and Eastern Europe. At the other end of the scale, some Swiss cities face difficulties in raising sufficient resources for road maintenance and for the high level of public transport services they provide because unlike Federal or Cantonal levels of government they have no revenue raising powers other than local income and property taxes. A high level task force has been established to find solutions for this and other urban travel problems.

In Germany the system of Federal government generally seeks to assign power and responsibility to the lowest competent level of government and responsibility for urban and transport planning, matched with financial resources is vested in municipal and regional authorities.

Norway also reports a particularly strong tradition in all aspects of empowering local and regional governments to take responsibility for urban transport infrastructure and of ensuring good co-operation between authorities at different levels of government. However there are problems with the allocation of responsibilities for roads and especially bus operations. Bus services are purchased by county governments, with competition for resources between rural and urban areas in the county. Difficulties in co-ordinating policy result in stalemate where typically each level of administration, municipal, county and national, blames the others for lack of progress. A national committee has been established to re-examine the distribution of tasks between different levels of government, including in the transport sector, and the Ministry of Transport is preparing pilot projects involving new models for the organisation of transport authorities in cities. The aim is to improve the co-ordination of both road infrastructure and public transport investments and management with land use planning.

Financing for public transport in Norway has changed markedly. Transfers from the national to county governments earmarked for expenditure on transport were introduced at the beginning of the 1980s. In 1983 deficit funding of bus and ferry companies was replaced by contracts determining grant levels. In 1986 earmarking ended and counties were free to spend according to priorities both inside and outside transport and a year later counties were given the power to set fare levels. Since then government subsidies for transport have steadily diminished, falling 42% in real terms in the decade to 1997. Several companies in the largest cities now operate without subsidy. An initial fall in ridership that followed seems to have been successfully reversed through a wide range of measures to strengthen public transport and improve quality of service.

Like Norway, the Netherlands reports problems in integrating local and regional policies for example in relation to parking pricing and application of planning guidance, however, action is being taken to address the problems identified. Increased decision and funding powers at local and regional levels is a key feature of current transport policy.

Switzerland reports in some cases a pattern of political tension between Canton (county) government and the government of its chief city – often of opposing political colour. Stalemate has normally been overcome by a mature tradition of public consultation and negotiation, though the process can take years. The Federal Government took action in the late 1980s to improve co-operation between the different levels of government through planning laws and air quality protection laws that require joint regional plans for air pollution.

Finland reports highly effective decentralisation of decision and funding powers but notes a consequent frustration that national government finds it increasingly difficult to influence local policies. Norway has addressed this problem through its Planning and Building Act under which the Government sets national objectives and municipal and county authorities develop solutions on the basis of local conditions and potential. The USA has addressed these kinds of problems through the Transportation Act for the 21st Century (TEA-21) which defines a participatory planning framework that States and local areas are expected to follow and encourages balance between economic, environmental and social equity goals and an integrated approach to decision making.

France reports a different tradition of effective integration. Urban transport planning is primarily the responsibility of the local Communes but in many cases they have delegated their powers to collective inter-communal organisations. Various arrangements evolved and in 1999 the Government legislated to simplify the forms of co-operation and at the same time increased transfers from the budget to groupings of communes. As a result most urban areas now are organised into such groupings. The Paris region accounts for half of the urban population and is different in that the state plays a much greater role in transport and spatial planning. Central government is responsible for both the strategic transport plan and the urban mobility plan of the Paris region.

Italy reports a sustained movement to decentralise decision making and financial responsibility for transport, giving more power to the Regions, Provinces and Municipalities. In 1997 Provinces and Municipalities overtook central government as the main source of funds for transport. Transparency and integration of transport planning at the local level and between local and regional levels has been improved through the introduction of biennial Urban Traffic Plans (which are not linked to financing) and more recently with Urban Mobility Plans which are designed to attract finance from central government for long term investments.

Poland has replaced central planning with decentralised policy making for urban transport and land use planning but the local and regional authorities are severely under-funded for their transport responsibilities. As a result maintenance and renewal of tram and other public transport systems has been reduced to levels that will result in sharply rising operating costs and therefore increased funding problems in the future. Short term reductions achieved in operating deficits appear likely to prove a false economy. Russia reports similar funding difficulties with a vacuum in political authority for public transport services following the withdrawal of central government. Nevertheless, it notes good co-operation between local and regional levels of government.

Common to all eastern European countries, the Czech review reports on the complete reorganisation of local and regional government. In many countries there have been several waves of reorganisation since the end of central planning, partly reflecting power struggles between democratic forces and vestiges of the earlier regimes. This has complicated planning and financial arrangements for transport and the environment and has delayed the transfer of powers to authorities best placed to serve the geographic dimensions of urban areas.

2.2. Integration of transport and other policies

2.2.1. Integrated transport and environment policy making

Although integrated policy making is fundamental to sustainable development, few countries treated the issue explicitly in their reviews, possibly because they see integration more as a national issue. At the local level the main element is increasing integration of land use and transport planning to promote sustainable mobility and this is dealt with below.

Switzerland reports strong and efficient policy linkage. Like the USA it highlights the importance of a federal clean air act in requiring local governments to draw up regional plans to combat air pollution, with a major role for transport policies. Noise and CO_2 policies are also well integrated with transport policies in Switzerland. In Finland the integration of environmental policies into transport policy is also achieved with the help of a national environmental programme judged to provide a practical tool for environmental management of transport policy.

In the United Kingdom, merger into one Ministry of former Departments of Transport and the Environment (including regional planning) had profound effects on policy. Although environment and transport now find themselves in separate ministries the legacy of integrated policy making remains in much transport policy making, at least for the time being. Merging Transport with Public Works in France has improved integration with a similar merger in Italy. Poland reported promising developments in local government, particularly in a set of progressive large and medium sized cities. Without addressing the issue directly, it is clear from the Russian review that lack of policy integration is a handicap to developments.

2.2.2. Integration of transport and land use planning

Most of the countries reviewed report recent initiatives to improve the integration of land use planning with transport policy. The Netherlands has perhaps the strongest tradition in this area but reported some difficulties in ensuring that standards are applied evenly by neighbouring municipal authorities, with instances of competition to attract business developments through derogations to planning codes.

Norway also has a strong tradition in this area and is examining the possibility of adopting a Dutch type ABC zoning system. For more than a decade Norway has searched for satisfactory arrangements for planning transport and land use at a regional level. The Plan and Building Act provides the framework for national goal setting that is reflected in local and county planning. However the administrative separation between county and municipal government can frustrate integrated planning of transport services in and around urban areas. Some promising experiments involving the largest cities failed due partly to the lack of a formal relationship with the established planning processes. The search for improved arrangements continues.

In Switzerland, land use and transport planning are integrated effectively at the regional level in the Cantonal master plans. At a federal level, sectoral land use plans are developed by the Ministries responsible in close collaboration with the Federal Office of Spatial Development with sectoral plans, for example covering railways and public transport. In Finland, transport system plans have been drawn up for most urban areas taking full account of land use development plans.

In France, procedures for drawing up collective urban mobility plans (PDU) were introduced in 1982 and made obligatory for cities over 100 000 in 1996. The plan for Paris was completed at the end of 2000. These plans seek to co-ordinate transport and land use planning in order to promote a sustainable balance between mobility and accessibility on the one hand and health and environmental protection on the other hand. The law requires that they seek to improve safety (particularly for pedestrians), reduce car traffic, promote walking and cycling, optimise use of the roads and parking space, improve the organisation of freight deliveries and ensure that employers encourage their personnel to use public transport and car sharing. The law also requires the introduction of integrated tariffs and ticketing for public transport. The first achievements of the plans produced to date has been to raise awareness in the public and their local representatives of the issues involved and also to create new links between the many actors involved. The success or otherwise of the plans will be assessed after 5 years. Italy is also developing urban mobility plans along similar lines.

France reports problems not so much with integrating land use policy with transport planning but ensuring coherence with social policies towards housing. Interest free loans are available to lower income families seeking to purchase a house. No conditions in respect of sustainable development of urban areas are attached to these loans and they favour the development of low-density estates on the outskirts where public transport is entirely lacking. More generally much still needs to be done to improve co-operation with private property developers. The price of land for property development is lower on the periphery, but the cost to local tax payers of providing transport and other services is highest in these areas. Orientating housing and business developments towards inner suburbs and around nodes served by public transport in the outer suburbs, through financial incentives or other means, might alleviate the problem.

German cities have begun to put an emphasis on mixed development, preserving areas where housing, employment and social services exist in close proximity, developing other activities in single use areas such as housing estates and ensuring that green field developments include a mix of housing, employment, services and leisure facilities.

Portugal cites some success, notably in the city of Evora, in developing integrated local traffic and land use plans, redirecting car traffic away from the centre

19

of the city and enhancing public transport services, including with park and ride systems, financed partly through the introduction of parking charges in the centre. Ultimately the intention is to introduce a cordon charge for entering the city centre by car.

Several countries report measures to limit or suspend development of out of town shopping and commercial developments with a strong preference to site such developments inside existing urban areas and avoid the generation of unmanageable new transport demand. Some of the measures taken appear so inflexible that they may bear a risk of backlash if as a result municipalities and businesses come to believe that economic development is stifled. Finland reports restrictions that though not absolute result in practice in a ban on development outside town centres whilst Norway has suspended developments for 5 years while a long term policy is developed.

Poland reports widespread uncontrolled and unmanageable out of town developments as one of the major forces driving urban areas away from sustainable development.

The USA reports insufficient co-ordination of transport and land use planning. Transport is the responsibility of the States, regional transportation planning agencies and transport providers, whilst zoning and other land use planning issues are the responsibility of the cities and counties. TEA-21 provides direction for better co-ordination but there are opportunities for further improvement. There could also be better integration of energy policy goals. The Civil Rights Act and Environmental Justice Orders have provided legal recourse for citizens, specifically minority and low-income groups, concerned with adverse impacts from federally funded transport investments. State and local planners face major challenges in responding to this new, legal, equity dimension to transport decision-making. The Swiss review also raises the importance of social and regional equity issues in transport policy assessments.

2.2.3. Assessment procedures

Effective cost benefit appraisal methodologies and procedures for informing decision making are an important aspect of developing more integrated transport, land-use and local economic policy. France has made extensive use of cost benefit appraisals for transport investment projects and the results have been important in shaping overall policy. Tools for policy appraisal have been developed but are employed little. All projects over EUR 83 million require both an *ex ante* evaluation and two *ex post* evaluations, one year and then three to five years after completion. Evaluations are made on the basis of cost benefit assessment of quantities that can be expressed in monetary terms. Time savings generally dominate the results masking other economic factors and environmental aspects. The French review lists many important factors that are not taken into account and identifies a resulting bias towards road projects, and particularly those that engender urban sprawl. Multi-criteria analysis is viewed as the answer to some of the present shortcomings.

Norway has recently introduced improved cost-benefit assessment procedures but encounters difficulties in comparing results across modes. The Dutch Ministry of Transport has recently developed guidelines for the systematic use of cost-benefit analysis: these have now to be implemented.

The Czech review reveals that integration of transport and land use planning is still in its earliest stages. Guidelines are being drawn up in central government but the application at a local level will be on an "if possible" basis for some time to come. The government hopes that environmental impact assessment and strategic environmental assessment procedures will play a significant part in containing environmental impacts in urban areas in the future. Curiously, none of the other countries in the survey reported developments in environmental impact assessment methodologies or procedures, perhaps indicating that transport ministries see these tools as essentially the responsibility of environment ministries.

2.3. Public transport policy in urban regions

The funding of local and regional authorities was partly addressed in the first section of Chapter 2. The availability of resources for funding public transport operations and infrastructure investments is examined in more detail here together with more technical aspects of policy towards public transport that are also important.

2.3.1. Improvement of the public transport system

The main feature of the transport systems of many Swiss cities is the excellence of public transport – tram, bus and surface rail. The emphasis in Swiss cities has been in improving the frequency of service and the spatial coverage of public transport systems, ensuring a maximum of the population are close to bus and tram stops. Improving the performance of existing systems, for example through introduction of telematic control and information systems (giving users real-time information on bus and tram arrival times) has been given priority over heavy investments in new fixed infrastructure such as metro systems.

Italy reports successes from improving the quality of bus services with IT solutions, giving buses priority at traffic lights and providing passengers with accurate information on arrival/departure times at bus stops. Dedicated bus lanes are an important tool in cities in almost all the countries surveyed, with the increasing use also of prioritised traffic lights to favour buses and trams at junctions. Germany also reports widespread application of such telematic control systems.

21

Many of the larger French cities including Paris enjoy excellent public transport systems, with heavy metro systems not confined to the capital, and a recent emphasis on sophisticated tramways. The Netherlands too is characterised by a dense and well co-ordinated public transport network – rail, tram and bus – throughout the Randstad, even if recent capacity problems on the railways have tarnished its image.

In all these countries integrated ticketing and passes valid on all modes plays an important role in increasing the attractiveness of public transport. Integrated ticketing has also been developed in Prague and some other Czech cities and also recently in some Finnish municipalities. The Netherlands has the longest running system, the *"Strippen card"*, with additional passes to be introduced when responsibility for services are regionalised in 2003 and a smart card system under development. Italy also reports success from simplifying tariffs and ticket purchase.

High frequencies of service characterise France, the Randstad and Switzerland, and under the Swiss *Rail and Bus* 2000 initiative, which is first and foremost a major investment program designed to improve inter-city linkages, integrated time-tabling has been applied nation-wide in preference to an emphasis on high speed inter-city connections. As a result, convenient no-wait connections enable people to travel from many villages to any city in the country on public transport in reasonable time. Finland has also put the emphasis in recent years on improving quality of service by improving punctuality and creating "travel chains" of interconnecting services that provide a competitive alternative with the car.

Germany places an emphasis on competitive tendering of services in urban rail and bus operations as a way of not only cutting costs but also of improving services and enhancing the quality and environmental performance of buses. The Federal Environment Ministry runs a pilot project to show higher environmental standards can be achieved through competition, promoting the performance of low floor busses that meet the strictest emission noise standards.

Park and ride systems have been introduced in a number of medium sized UK cities, in Lisbon and some other Portuguese cities and in the Czech Republic. In Switzerland they have not been successful on a large scale but most suburban railway stations have small areas reserved for park and ride.

2.3.2. *Fares and financing of public transport*

In the Paris region integrated planning of all the public transport services is assured by a "syndicate" of the region's eight Departments together with the Regional government. The syndicate selects and co-ordinates the public and private service providers, sets tariffs and service levels and co-ordinates timetables. An earmarked tax for public transport was introduced in 1971 and subsequently extended to other urban areas down to 10 000 inhabitants. It is levied on companies employing more than 9 people within the urban perimeter and is the major source of funding for public transport. EUR 2 billion are collected annually in the Paris region with a further EUR 1.4 billion in other towns and cities. Public transport in Paris is funded roughly one third each from the fare box, the earmarked transport levy on companies, and general taxation (70% from central government 30% from the Departments). Bus services in the centre, metro and rail services are all monopolies with competition for bus contracts only in the suburbs. In the French provinces central government contributions to funding public transport has played a major role in modernising networks and particularly in developing new tramways. Technical as well as financial support was provided by the State. Underground metros attract support up to 20% and surface tramways and buses 35% up to limits of EUR 7.6 million and 3.8 million respectively. Support for provincial urban areas is set to rise to EUR 150 million per annum, half destined for tramways, buses, metros etc, and half for other elements in urban mobility plans.

Under the Local Authority Transport Infrastructure Financing Act the German Government provided DM 3.28 billion (EUR 1.7 billion) in 2001 to finance State government support to public transport in cities. The money can be spent on vehicles as well as infrastructure. Subject to providing partial matching finance the States are free to allocate 80% of this support according to their own priorities. Since 1996 the funding of all local and regional rail passenger services has been entirely a responsibility of the States. The services provided and the level of fares are determined in negotiation between the states and the transport operators they designate.

Norway allocates EUR 110 million to rail per annum, something over half for urban rail, and EUR 353 million for local buses, a third to urban areas. Public funding for the running costs of public transport companies has been reduced 42% in the last decade, with an initial decline in ridership partly reversed by an emphasis on improved quality of service.

Finland reports a slight decline in government funding for public transport from EUR 470 million in 1992 to EUR 400 million recently. Funding consists of purchase of transport services, purchase of fare reductions and funding of experiments for development of transport services. Indirect support is also provided through reimbursement of travel expenses by the municipalities for some groups, for example school children.

In Switzerland, fare policy for public transport is based on a so-called half-price pass that allows people who travel frequently to benefit. Almost half of the population has this kind of pass. Some 20% of the population have either a General System Pass (that can involve local bus and tram services as well as all railways and regional buses) or another form of monthly or annual season ticket. A large part of the pricing policy of public transport operators is, however, a function of sophisticated

23

marketing policies. Many forms of "combi-tickets" are issued that allow travel free of charge or travel at reduced cost to large events (such as football games, rock concerts) or ski resorts. Revenues are recouped from the resort or event organiser under contract. Special price arrangements can also be made with employers for commuters.

The Czech Republic reports municipal expenditure on transport in the four largest cities of EUR 412 million in 1999, 70% of which went to mass transit systems. This represents a sixth to a third of total municipal spending and compares quite favourably with for example Finland or Norway despite the large difference in per capita incomes. In addition central government contributes to the cost of purchasing buses and trams, modification of tram infrastructure and construction of the Prague underground.

The US Department of Transportation allocates over EUR 3.3 billion a year to urban public transport for routine capital expenditure and maintenance. This is complemented by other Federal programs that fund capital expenditure, including for new rail projects. States and local governments provide grants to pay operating deficits and for some capital purchases using a range of revenue sources including sales, gas, and income taxes. Public transport is promoted by more than 500 urban public transport operators using a range of fare strategies. Metropolitan areas can use the transport planning process to select public transport and other projects for funding under the TEA-21 Congestion Management and Air Quality Program or through the transfer of Federal funds from the highway program.

Reducing the costs of public transport is important for all the governments involved in the survey. The Netherlands reports some success in developing effective incentive structures in a very gradual program of introducing competitive tendering for bus services provided by private sector operators. Experience in some other countries (Germany, Sweden, UK) suggests the process could be speeded up. Italy shows a similar pattern, with the law providing for contracting out of services through competitive tendering since 1997 but so far only just under half of all public transport are utilities undergoing the transformation. Poland also reports some success in developing effective incentive structures in its extensive tram systems, although against a background of under-funding that threatens productivity in the longer term.

The Netherlands is the only country to discuss cost recovery targets for public transport. Bus and tram systems currently cover only 35-40% of their total costs and efforts to raise this to 50% are underway. Passenger rail services cover 100% of the capital and running costs of train operations (fulfilling the current target) whilst making no contribution to infrastructure costs for rail, although charging for infrastructure use at short run marginal costs is being introduced.

Poland discusses fares policy, reporting systems that are too complicated and that encourage illegal fare-dodging. Hungary reports on the general problem in transition economies that, although local government is nominally responsible for fares policy, in fact it has little freedom and depends on annual negotiations with the Ministry of Finance to cover revenue shortfalls and to finance discretionary fares. Hungary also details the problems encountered in co-ordinating public transport in cities where a number of different companies operate local and inter-urban buses, rail and metro services. Integrated ticketing initiatives have repeatedly failed due to an inability to agree on how to share responsibilities for deficits between the operators.

2.4. Car restraint policies

2.4.1. Parking policies

Parking policies are one the most important and widely used instruments employed in promoting a more sustainable urban environment. The Tokyo metropolitan government has long practised a regulatory policy of requiring proof of a rented or owned off-road parking space for the purchase of private cars. In Europe, Switzerland has perhaps developed the instrument to the greatest degree. Charging used in all of the country's main cities (which only medium-sized on a European scale) and policies to reduce, or at least stabilise, the number of public parking spaces available in central urban districts and restrict the number of private parking lots in new buildings have been employed for a number of years. In the latest stage, negotiations are underway with large property owners to begin charging for and reducing the number of existing residential parking spaces in some urban locations.

Germany has experimented with a more radical approach, designing residential areas with parking places provided only for car sharing, disabled access and visitors. The Bremen-Hollerland settlement is the leading example of such "car-free" housing.

Parking charges have been developed on a wide scale in the Dutch Randstad with attention paid to co-ordinating availability and pricing between inner and outer urban areas and between neighbouring municipalities. More needs to be done to improve regional co-ordination but the issue is being addressed.

Whilst parking charges and limitation of the number of parking spaces available in specific areas are central to most large cities policies, enforcement varies extremely widely. In London, for example, privatisation of enforcement with effective incentive structures resulted in a sharp increase in the effectiveness of enforcement in the late 1980s. Enforcement is virtually instantaneous in the most central areas of the city. In Paris at the other extreme enforcement is insufficient to

25

prevent ubiquitous contravention of the parking regulations, with parking on pavements and on crossings a constant problem for pedestrians.[1]

Significant progress is reported in Budapest in improving the management of traffic through the introduction of parking charges differentiated by zone and providing off-street paid parking spaces. There is still some way to go, however, to resolve problems with matching the supply and demand for parking space and in reducing the nuisance caused by uncontrolled on-street parking.

2.4.2. Traffic management

Making the most effective use of existing infrastructure is the cornerstone of current Swiss transport policy. Traffic management through careful co-ordination of traffic light networks is reported to have played an important role in managing road capacity and influencing access to sensitive central urban areas. For the future, attention will focus on intelligent traffic management systems to maximise use of existing road capacity in preference to expanding capacity through construction. Germany reports a long tradition of balancing the use of roads by different users to achieve a more environmentally rational transport system, using traffic calming measures beginning with pedestrianisation of city centres and followed by creating wider vehicle-restricted areas for pedestrians, cyclists or public transport and 30 km/h "home zones".

There have been some very promising developments in the combination of parking policies, traffic light control and intelligent traffic management systems in Italy, for example in Turin.[2] Italy has been through several phases of experiment in trying to tackle congestion with traffic management measures, beginning in the 1970s with the closure of small areas to traffic. In the 1980s the emphasis was on day time bans of traffic from some city centres and on alternate traffic circulation according to license plate numbers. More recently wider areas of restricted access to cars have been designated together with extensions to pedestrianised areas, mainly in the historic centres of cities. Congestion persists, however, and experiments with cordon pricing are poised to begin. Rome introduced a cordon charge in October 2001, roughly matched to the morning peak but only covering a relatively small central area. It has been very effective in controlling unauthorised access to the historic centre of the city but the scheme would have to cover a wider area and charge higher fees to have an impact on congestion.

Pollution alert systems have been introduced in Athens, Paris and a number of US cities. When weather forecasts predict poor air quality (usually high levels of ozone) car drivers are encouraged not to drive. These systems generally rely mainly on voluntary compliance even where vehicle identification and enforcement procedures have been set up. In Paris the Ministry of Environment acknowledges that in its current phase the system chiefly aims to raise awareness among drivers and is thus not strictly enforced. In Athens, where odd-even license plate numbering is used as the basis for enforcement, the system has been undermined by wealthier households purchasing a second, usually old and relatively dirty, vehicle with an appropriate licence plate number.

Poland and Russia expressed a particular interest in monitoring trends in car technologies linked to formulating policies for restricting access to city centres to cleaner cars.

2.4.3. *Economic instruments*

The Netherlands and Norway report significant development of economic instruments to promote development of more sustainable urban travel patterns. The Dutch Government has developed its mix of road user charges over the last decade to increase differentiation of fixed charges according to environmental criteria and variabilise charging through a relative increase in fuel taxation. It believes this has made a significant contribution to sustainable development in urban areas as well as at the national level. The Government has been developing plans for urban/interurban road pricing for a decade. There have been difficulties in gaining political acceptance.

Norway uses cordon charging on urban roads to raise resources for infrastructure investments, primarily in roads. These tolls are differentiated in some cities to manage peak traffic but the overall level of charges is linked to investment costs as opposed to congestion costs. A proposal to introduce a legal framework for introducing road congestion pricing schemes is before parliament. The main purpose of such schemes would be to regulate traffic in order to reduce congestion and improve the local environment. If the framework is adopted, congestion pricing might replace some existing toll rings when these expire, but local authorities would not be permitted to operate traditional tolls and congestion pricing simultaneously on the same roads.

Italy has adopted a legal framework for introducing electronic control of access to town centres and several cities have begun to develop cordon pricing systems. There were delays to implementation due to legal challenges to their introduction. Technically, the system in Bologna is ready for operation and the system in Rome became operational in October 2001, although not currently configured to have much impact on congestion (see above).

There is some experience with various forms of road pricing in the USA. Time of day tolls for bridges and tunnels are widespread and there is some construction of new highway lanes with limited access for "high" occupancy vehicles and drivers prepared to pay a charge for single occupancy access. These initiatives are primarily for financing rather than congestion management purposes.

The Czech review reports active interest in developing economic instruments to ensure transport users pay the full costs of infrastructure use and hopes they will play a significant part in containing the environmental impacts of transport in urban areas in the future.

Germany reports a change in the fiscal environment to avoid promoting private car use for commuting trips over other modes. In January 2001 the basis for tax refunds for journeys to work was changed from mileage driven to a distance based flat rate regardless of mode used.

2.4.4. Interventions targeting existing vehicle fleets

Italy reported modest success with vehicle scrappage schemes to remove the worst polluting vehicles and with local inspection and maintenance programs. These programs were initially significant but have become less so with the tightening of the national vehicle inspection system.

2.5. Non-motorised modes

2.5.1. Cycle networks and the pedestrian environment

The Netherlands continues to develop its dense and extensive network of cycle lanes and gives increasing priority to bicycles at road junctions. Under Norway's inter-ministerial programme for environmentally friendly urban development, strengthening the role of cycling as an important urban transport mode is considered an important task. Germany provides statistics on cycling, which it estimates accounts for 12% of all trips and averages 300 km per head of population per year. It foresees significant potential to increase these figures, noting that the figure is nearer 27% of all trips in the Netherlands and as much as 40% in some of that country's towns and cities. A national cycling promotion plan is under preparation to co-ordinate federal, state and local measures.

Finland reports interest in developing cycle lane networks and mentions in its review that the Ministry of Transport and Communications is preparing a national walking policy programme, one important aim of which is to improve the pedestrian environment. The review also emphasises that non-hindrance is one of the principles for transport planning. Italy reports success with the introduction of car free city centre zones in the 1980s. Enforcement has proved increasingly costly and difficult in some of the cities applying these schemes.

2.5.2. Enhancing the urban environment whilst investing in alternatives to the car

Experience reported by France and Switzerland highlights the importance of opportunities to redevelop and enhance whole streets when, for example, roads are closed to traffic, traffic calming measures are introduced or tramways are constructed. The benefits to residents and commerce of improving pavements, planting trees, cleaning buildings etc., to accompany transport investments or changes in the use of roads can be a vital factor in overcoming opposition to such changes and enhancing the attraction of similar initiatives for other areas of the city.

Notes

1. In France revenues from parking fines go to the central government and are earmarked for spending on public transport.
2. See procedings of the ECMT/ACEA/OICA Turin Conference on Smart CO_2 Reductions, *www.oecd.org*/CEM/*topics*/*env*/CO2*turin.htm*

3. Lessons for Policy Implementation

3.1. Decentralisation

The biggest success story to emerge from this collection of policy reviews is the positive results achieved from decentralising power and responsibility for urban transport and environment management, matching responsibilities with the scale of the problems to be tackled. Frequently a regional scale that reaches beyond the borders of the city, covering its outer suburbs and into its hinterland, is most appropriate. Most of the countries surveyed reported successes as a result of decentralisation although some recorded problems, either as a result of failing to transfer sufficient funds or finance raising powers to match responsibilities, or with problems for central government to influence policy in the new regional authorities or to ensure co-operation between different lower levels of government.

3.2. The important role of Central Government

3.2.1. *Providing a functional framework for sustainable transport for lower levels of government*

Several countries underline the importance of a coherent policy for sustainable mobility across all government levels. For that purpose, Norway has established a "co-operation forum" involving the six largest cities and 9 national ministries. In the Netherlands and Switzerland the small geographical scale allows for a specially intensive interaction between inter-city and urban transport. The Swiss Federal Government, backed by repeated popular votes, has reached a high degree of cohesion between its national policies and local policies for promoting public transport services and developing the network and for holding back additional road investments.

The Swiss review emphasises the importance of national government policies on fuel taxation and road use charges in creating the framework within which local policies towards sustainable development act. In a similar vein, the Czech Republic reports on a clear commitment from the national Government to the goals of stabilising transport impacts on the environment through measures including promotion of public transport, co-operation between the operators of different transport modes and progressive internalisation of external costs.

3.2.2. Influencing regional and local government policies

The interests of the majority of citizens represented by different levels of government can differ markedly. In many cities suburban residents have different transport policy priorities than city centre residents. Similarly the distributional impacts of major transport infrastructure projects can differ markedly between different administrative units of a city – for example depending on the location of stations in the case of a rail line. The taxation base for raising the revenues for investment frequently does not correspond to the distribution of the main beneficiaries of such projects. Without guidance from a large regional authority or from central government it may be very difficult to overcome such atomisation of interests between authorities at the small regional and local scales.

Stimulating the formation of new groupings of local government authorities has been important in a number of countries (Switzerland, France, UK) in matching the geographical scale of decision making bodies to urban transport networks and their hinterland. The forming of such groups is in some cases linked to eligibility for funding from central government. Effective co-ordination between local administrations has most often been achieved through provisions of planning law, for example requiring new layers of integrated regional planning. It works best when this is done as a modification to mainstream planning requirements rather than as an independent and parallel process. This view is supported by the partial failure of experiments with the ten main urban areas in Norway.

The United Kingdom's transport planning system is now centred on integrated assessments that require network effects of infrastructure projects to be taken into full account. This drives the formation of new groupings of authorities depending on the reach of the planning decision to be taken. Development of effective guidance manuals from central government on assessment from the perspective of sustainability for consistent policy making at the local level has been an important part of the process.

Planning relationships are very much the traditional approach to managing central and local government interfaces. The Netherlands, however, reports a new philosophy for institutional interactions. Negotiation will take over from planning guidance, with central, regional and local governments set the task of drawing up common strategies for sustainable transport as equal partners.

In Germany the law provides the framework for interaction between federal, regional and local governments, with requirements for consultation and the co-ordination of land-use and transport plans. Within this framework co-operation between municipal authorities and with the local authorities in the hinterland of major cities has developed well with the aim of ensuring rational patterns of urban development and the prevention of open spaces being built up where this can be avoided.

3.2.3. *Central government role in financing local public transport*

Central government roles in financing local public transport (rail, tram, bus, etc.) vary between countries from direct, to indirect, to none. Recent experience suggests re-routing financial support to a more local level is productive. The experience of France, Germany and Switzerland in regionalising rail expenditures is significant. Replacing central government transfers to national railways with transfers to regional government to purchase services from the regional divisions of the rail companies has generally resulted in improved services and additional investments in regional rail services.

Central government policy towards subsidising fares for urban rail and bus services can be critical. Cities that have been granted powers to raise their own revenues through specific local transport levies (*e.g.* Paris) have generally been able to keep fares low whilst improving services and attracting ridership, at least on rail, metro and tram services (results have often been slower to emerge on buses). There are plans for cities in the United Kingdom to be given similar powers through transport charges earmarked for expenditure on transport. Other city authorities rarely have the resources to subsidise fares, and central government intervention could have a major impact in breaking downward spirals of falling ridership, increasing deficits, rising fares and declining services, always providing that subsidies are judged to provide value for money in achieving sustainability goals.

3.3. Participation and new partnerships

3.3.1. *Consultation*

One of the most striking features of the Swiss review is the importance of consultation in developing and implementing policies successfully. Switzerland does have a strong tradition of popular referenda on government decisions and these have played an important role in sending urban transport plans back to the drawing board for further negotiation between parties with conflicting interests. Even more important is the role of consultation with a wide spectrum of interested parties and the public at large from the very early stages of problem identification, through the setting of goals, to proposing strategies and ultimately in monitoring the results of the policies adopted. This has made the difference in converting conflictual stalemate into constructive long term dialogue on resolving natural differences in apparent interests between residents and commerce, inner city and suburban residents and between municipal and regional governments.

France and the United Kingdom have long traditions of public inquiry into major infrastructure plans. In France the procedures have been widened to cover the new urban mobility plans, and improved to begin earlier in the planning process. Interesting use has been made of the internet to widen participation. Switzerland, however, shows a higher degree of sophistication reflected in the amount of qualified man-power employed in running carefully structured discussions with the public. Consultation is also seen as far more binding on decision makers than in other countries. Cost is a limiting factor, however, and consultation on the urban mobility plan for the Paris region costed EUR 1.8 million.

In Germany the law provides extensive rights of consultation for interest groups and individual members of the public. Public consultation and transparency of decision-making are also important national themes in the USA. TEA-21 and the Clean Air Act both encourage active public involvement throughout all stages of urban transport planning. In several urban areas there have been interesting developments with private and public partnerships taking the lead in public and business consultation, successfully influencing the transport planning process.[1]

3.3.2. Information, communication

Many countries report on the crucial role of information and communication in developing better transport policies. Poland reports on some inadequate communication of planners with the public and with policy makers. The Czech Republic perceives a great need for education in achieving sustainable mobility. Education is also a theme in the Netherlands with its *"Permanently safe"* programme for road safety. The French policy of "concertation" more generally aims at informing the public and key stakeholders on projects and their evaluation. Switzerland is characterised by its intensive public information campaigns over more than a decade in the frame of its Energy 2000 Programme.

3.3.3. Seeking new partners

It is increasingly recognised that a policy of sustainable transport requires more than government action. The need for behavioural change makes involvement of transport users, urban businesses and residents themselves essential.

In the USA, several States have seen the emergence of creative public-private partnerships to co-ordinate land use development and transportation over a long term horizon. Many communities are creating transport management associations whereby employers organise reductions in car travel by employees to and from work through providing public transport passes, ride-sharing programmes, flex-time and telecommute options.

In Poland some local governments have decided to use a "Canadian style" multi-stakeholder process to cope with complex transport problems. To this end the Warsaw Transportation Round Table was established in 2000.

Switzerland has developed various forms of mobility management that aims to increase the share of public transport by developing co-operative linkages between enterprises, transport operators and local governments. Some renowned large firms are especially active in re-examining environmental aspects in their transport policies, both for freight traffic and commuter traffic. Such private involvement is not only of direct relevance for sustainability in transport but also smoothes the political climate in that responsibilities are shared.

Following the 1992 UN Earth Summit, Germany has seen the formation of 21 Local Agenda groups in around 1650 towns and cities, which aim to develop strategies and actions for sustainable development through joint initiatives of local authorities, organised groups and non-organised citizens. Local business and industry is also extensively consulted by local authorities over land-use and transport policies.

Key to summary table below

The table below is intended to provide a quick reference check list of instruments highlighted in the self reviews as important parts of established policy, promising new initiatives or areas where particular problems of implementation have been encountered. By its nature it is subjective and non-exhaustive. It should not be used to try and rank countries in terms of success or failure.

Note

1. See proceedings of the ECMT/OECD Madrid workshop on overcoming institutional barriers to implementing sustainable urban travel policies.

Table 1. **Simplified Summary Table**

	CZ	FIN	F	D	H	I	NL	N	PL	P	RU	CH	UK	USA
Local and regional government capacities														
De-centralised infrastructure and public transport: planning									••					
De-centralised infrastructure and public transport: funding									✖					
Integration of regional and local policy making									✖					
Central government ability to affect local policies		✖									✖			
Integrated transport and environment policy														
Integrated policy making											✖			
Effective cost benefit analysis			✖								✖			
Effective environmental impact assessments														
Integration of transport and land use planning														
Integrated traffic/mobility and environment plans														✖
Guidance on integrated transport and land-use														
Planning targets for reducing sprawl														
Planning targets for reducing environmental impacts					••									
Zoning to limit out of town commercial centres									✖					

Table 1. **Simplified Summary Table** (*continued*)

	CZ	FIN	F	D	H	I	NL	N	PL	P	RU	CH	UK	USA
Public transport														
Competitive tendering for public transport with effective incentive structures for reducing costs		■	▨	■		▨	▨		▨			■		
Transfers provided to keep fares down to promote ridership as part of sustainable transport policy	■	■	■	■		■	■	■	✗		✗	■		■
Effective control of costs			■		▨	▨	▨	■			■	■	■	
Integrated public transport passes and simplified fares	■			■		■	■							
Traffic light bus priority and real time arrival information	■	▨				■	▨			▨				
Guided buses/dedicated bus lanes	▨						■							
Park and ride schemes	■	■	■				■			■		■		
Economic instruments and parking policy														
Parking charges/capacity management city-wide	▨	■			■	■	■	▨		■		■		
Variabilisation/differentiation of road user charges						■	■	■						
Congestion tolling/road pricing			••				■	■						▨
Freedom to transfer of revenues from tolls to other modes, with a test of efficient use of resources														
Traffic management														
Co-ordination of traffic lights to limit access						■						■		

Table 1. **Simplified Summary Table** (*continued*)

	CZ	FIN	F	D	H	I	NL	N	PL	P	RU	CH	UK	USA
Deployment of telematics														
Air quality, noise exposure and accidents														
Positive impact of emissions and fuel standards														
Fleet renewal/scrappage programs														
Vehicle inspection programs														
Noise abatement			✖											
Effective safety policy														
Non-motorised modes														
Car free zones in city centres														
Effective promotion of walking														
Effective promotion of cycling														
Consultation procedures														
Effective consultation with public and stakeholders and involvement in decision making														
Negotiating voluntary car and parking restraint measures with private/ commercial property owners														

Successful/advantageous instrument/structure

promising recent initiative

problematic/disadvantageous instrument/structure

initiative with potential downside

✖ ••

••

Notes:
•• France – although tolls on some interurban motorways vary with time of day/week in order to manage congestion, urban road pricing is not permitted under the law.
•• Hungary – comprehensive zoning exists in several cities but too many exceptions are currently made.

NATIONAL REVIEWS BY COUNTRY

Czech Republic

1. The Context

1.1. Trends in urban transport

There are eleven main urban areas in the Czech Republic (Table 2). These urban areas cover some 6 236 communes, accounting for just over half of the country's total population of 10.3 million inhabitants.

Up until 1997, the major trend in urban transport was a shift away from public transport to private cars. The central administration and municipal authorities have consistently tried to control urban car traffic by making public transport a viable alternative. However experience from other OECD countries has shown that even excellent public transport does not reduce private car use to sustainable

Table 2. **Main urban areas**

Urban area	City	Other major cities	Population (thousands)
Suburbs of Prague, Central Bohemia	Prague	Kladno	1 700
Suburbs of České Budějovice	České Budějovice		130
Suburbs of Plzeň	Plzeň		310
Suburbs of Karlovy Vary	Karlovy Vary	Cheb, Sokolov	240
Suburbs of Ústi and Labem and Most	Ústi nad Labem, Most	Děčín, Teplice, Chomutov	500
Suburbs of Liberec	Liberec	Jablonec nad Nisou	220
Suburbs of Hradec Králové and Pardubice	Hradec Králové, Pardubice	Chrudim	370
Suburbs of Brno	Brno	Blansko, Vyškov	660
Suburbs of Olomouc	Olomouc	Přerov, Prostějov	370
Suburbs of Zlín	Zlín	Otrokovice, Kroměříž, Uherské, Hradiště	270
Suburbs Ostrava	Ostrava	Havířov, Karviná, Nový Jičín, Třiec, Opava, Feýdek-Místek, ČeskýTěšín, OrlováBohumín	1 050

Source: ECMT.

Table 3.   **Trends in vehicle ownership in Prague and the country as a whole**
Cars/1 000 inhabitants

	1971	1981	1990	1996	1999
Prague	123	241	276	489	523
Czech Rep.	72	182	233	325	360

Source: ECMT.

Table 4.   **Trends in car use in Prague, 1971-1999**

	Total vehicles		Private vehicles		Private cars
	Million vehicle kilometres	Index 1990 = 100	Million vehicle kilometres	Index 1990 = 100	Percentage of total vehicle traffic
1971	5.061	69	3.543	65	70
1981	5.562	76	4.338	79	78
1990	7.293	100	5.848	100	80
1996	13.896	191	12.426	212	89
1999	15.979	219	14.503	248	91

Source: ECMT.

Table 5.   **Public transport in Prague, 1971-1999**

	Operating length (kilometres)				Average working day	
	Subway	Trams	Buses	Trolley buses	Passenger.km (million)	Passengers (thousand)
1971	–	138.0	332.0	9	30.0	1 745
1981	19.3	122.9	545.0	–	46.7	3 638
1990	38.5	130.5	607.3	–	57.6	4 186
1996	43.6	136.2	724.6	–	54.5	3 423
1999	49.8	136.4	797.5	–	56.1	3 343

Source: ECMT.

levels. The car fleet grew by 51.5% to 3 456 million vehicles between 1989 and 1997 (Table 3). This represents an average of 2.98 inhabitants per vehicle, although the figure is lower in urban areas.

Road infrastructure has not kept up with traffic growth, resulting in congestion. There is a real risk of serious traffic collapse in some areas if public transport use is not encouraged through improved services or economic measures, particularly if road infrastructure investments decline. The share of public transport fell in all cities in the early 1990s, while private car use increased (Tables 4 to 6). The split between

Table 6. **Urban transport trends, 1993-1999**

	Passenger kilometres (million)					Passengers (million)				
	Subway	Trams	Buses	Trolley buses	Total	Subway	Trams	Buses	Trolley buses	Total
1993					30 871					2 635
1994	6 318	10 209	11 865	2 534	30 926	531	833	963	236	2 563
1995	6 315	10 649	11 530	2 636	31 130	413	749	835	233	2 230
1996	6 349	10 841	11 492	2 893	31 575	415	736	826	239	2 216
1997	6 408	10 941	11 599	2 919	31 867	418	742	834	241	2 235
1998	6 508	10 855	11 078	2 782	31 223	407	756	767	245	2 175
1999	7 163	10 784	11 275	2 844	32 066	428	734	857	245	2 264

Source: ECMT.

Table 7.   **Public/private modal split for commuting in major cities, 1999**

	Public transport %	Private transport %
Prague	58	42
Brno	60	40
Ostrava	65	35
Plzeň	70	30

Source: ECMT.

the two modes in 1990 was 75% urban public transport to 25% private car use, rising to 90:10 at peak times (Table 7). The present 60:40 split is considered unfavourable.

1.2. Environmental issues

The main objective of environment and transport policies is to stabilise and gradually reduce the environmental impact of transport infrastructure and traffic through sustainable development programmes, the application of the polluter pays principle, as well as environmental protection and prevention.

Environmental impact assessments are conducted on transport infrastructure and strategic environmental assessment is applied at the planning stage to develop an environment friendly transport system, conserve energy and reduce air, noise, soil and water pollution from infrastructure. Other measures include:

- development of road, rail, water and air transport systems compatible with the international environmental impact and safety standards;

43

- research on and gradual introduction of economic instruments, including internalisation, to support environment friendly and economically viable transport systems;

- provision of infrastructure for non-motorised transport (cycling and walking);

- development of an intermodal and integrated approach to transport infrastructure planning, covering environmental, spatial, economic and social aspects;

- development and priority given to the use of public transport and integrated transport systems., as well more environmentally acceptable vehicles;

- improvement in the regulation and organisation of road transport, particularly with more efficient traffic control systems and the development of infrastructure and parking systems using road transport pricing integrating environmental costs.

1.3. Urban land use planning

Forecasts of demand for transport infrastructure are continuously adjusted and updated. Major projects involving transport infrastructure plans must be included in general urban land use plans. Such plans are small scale for regional purposes. Urban land use plans must include draft transport plans and detail transport infrastructure changes as well as measures for traffic management and regulation.

The key stage in transport planning is the draft proposal, which contains details of the proposed transport infrastructure and various options:

- land use zoning is provided by the Ministry for Local Development. The Ministry of Transport and Communications is responsible for contacting local organisations and regional governments;

- the draft proposal must be compatible with the land use plan and general transport policy, and options must be chosen at this stage;

- additional suggestions or comments from the transport sector must then be included and changes agreed by the appropriate bureau councils;

- changes and corrections are made according to the same protocol as the transport planning proposal.

Traffic planning follows the same protocol as land use planning, although significantly more attention is given to traffic analysis.

Land use planning for transport infrastructure must also include the rail network, which is particularly important for the reconstruction of the international transit corridor and the provision of land for high speed rail infrastructure.

1.4. Safety

Traffic accidents are the main cause of death for people under 40. Improving traffic safety has become one of the major priorities not only for transport policy, but for general policy in developed countries. The situation in the Czech Republic is worse than in most European countries. Until the mid-1980s road safety figures were comparable with the safest European countries, though accident figures have since increased. At the end of the 1980s, as in all western European countries, the increase in the accident rate remained lower than the increase in vehicle numbers. Since 1990 both the accident rate and mortality have exceeded the increase in vehicle numbers and performance (Tables 8 and 9).

Priority is being given to reducing the accident rate through:

- running campaigns to make road users aware of the permanent risk, including the promotion of public transport;

- targeting driving schools to improve training of new drivers;

- introducing an effective driver assessment points system, with possible suspension of licence for serious offences;

Table 8. **Road accidents in Prague**

	Number of accidents	Deaths	Serious injury	Light injury	Accident rate (accidents/ mill.veh.-km)
1971	8 496	123	567	4 046	5.1
1981	13 064	81	401	2 572	7.1
1990	18 024	91	369	2 806	7.5
1996	38 091	85	654	4 048	8.3
1999	44 192	74	540	3 558	8.4

Source: ECMT.

Table 9. **Road accidents in the Czech Republic**

	Accident with injury or death	Motorway accidents with injury or death	Total number of road deaths	Total number of road injuries
1993	25 147	282	1 524	32 277
1994	27 590	317	1 637	35 667
1995	28 746	343	1 588	36 967
1996	29 340	335	1 568	37 743
1997	28 376	369	1 597	36 608

Source: ECMT.

- making driving under the influence of recreational or medicinal drugs an offence and introducing checks;
- checking the performance of professional drivers;
- making mandatory for car owners to report any proven traffic violations involving their vehicle to the police, in the case of the driver being any other than the owner;
- harmonising regulations for the behaviour of drivers and pedestrians on crossings;
- finalising regulations for the behaviour of cyclists;
- making the use of headlights at all times, day and night compulsory;
- improving the professionalism of the police, notably by improving equipment.

The use of retaining systems for children is not yet a legal obligation. As transport infrastructure is a major factor influencing the behaviour of drivers, the following improvements are under way:

- modification of accident black spots;
- implementation of low cost measures to force motorists to obey the highway code, in particular speed limits;
- improved safety at crossroads and pedestrian crossings;
- individual provision for different modes of transport on roads;
- construction of by-passes around urban areas;
- establishment of calm zones in urban areas;
- large scale introduction of road traffic telematics;
- promotion of public transport.

Transport safety policy must be integrated into land use planning. This is not a single step procedure, but a set of successive steps, systematically researched and analysed to achieve the objectives.

2. Institutional Framework

2.1. *Institutional reform*

The Czech Republic was originally divided into 77 centrally governed districts, each subdivided into local municipalities. EU regional organisation has been adopted and fourteen new larger regions[1] created under political consensus. The new regions (classified by EUROSTAT NUTS 3) each comprise three to eight existing districts, under the 1997 Constitution Act and amendments to the 1993 Constitution. The size and borders of the new regions have been harmonised with population structure. Municipalities and regions have been reorganised leading to changes in land use planning which will in turn affect development.

Municipalities are classified according to their executive powers. Four district status urban areas (Prague, Brno, Ostrava and Plzeň) are known as statute cities and have exceptional powers. All 6 236 municipalities have minimum executive powers known as grade I commission, and 373 municipalities hold grade II commission. Further shifts in competence from district level result in the creation of 179 grade III commission municipalities in 2002. This increased competence should include the traffic inspectorate, although this decision awaits confirmation.

2.2. Institutional context

The new regions play an important role in the transport system. Central government is responsible for motorways and class I roads. The regions are responsible for all administrative aspects of class II and III roads, including systematic road maintenance. Local roads are under the responsibility of the municipalities. The railway infrastructure is divided into national networks administered by central government and regional networks administered by the regions. The regional railway network could be privatised or leased to private operators. This has already been done in some cases. Increasing the geographical area of competence (from district to region) increases the power of the managing authority, involving more operators and providing more potential for competition for local transport services, including the possibility of integrating different modes of transport and optimising connections. It also has the advantage of reducing inter-district conflicts.

In the past regional bus transport was funded from the state budget by district authorities and included a return transport service to schools, offices, courts and basic health care facilities. Central administration contribution to basic local railway transport was determined by the municipalities which also provided support to other territorial transport services, timetables being drawn up according to local requirements. National and regional railway transport was managed and supported by central administration while local councils provided basic transport services. Control of basic transport services (bus and railway) are now supported by the regions instead of the districts. The regional approach should smooth out the previous disparities in the provision of a basic transport system. Provision of other services remains unchanged.

2.3. National context

The Department of Land Use in the Ministry of Local Development provides land use planning methodologies but cannot influence local authority land use planning. The government manages the infrastructure of national railways, roads, motorways and the class I road network. Central government is competent to provide design, legislation, methodology and control.

47

2.4. Regional context

The regional transport system includes:

- marketing, to define travellers' requirements, including access to the transport market, the preparation and assessment of statistical data on transport needs, and real and projected demand;

- transport infrastructure, including the creation of a database of land communications, a description of terrestrial communications including tracks (public and private), stations and stops, mapping technical and construction parameters, information, facilities and accessibility;

- transport vehicles, including a description of the rolling stock and a definition of the requirements for individual categories;

- optimisation of transport technologies for the best modal split, and optimisation of connections and timetables;

- information technology for the provision of information for customers, transport operators, regional transport managers and governmental institutions;

- legislation to regulate transport and operating conditions, and fiscal support (accounts and data control);

- taxation, with a specific methodology for the calculation of transport expenses resulting from laws, notices and standards; pricing policy must be related to the obligation to provide a public service, demonstrable loss and adequate profit; the value of demonstrable loss (in regional bus transport) is set out in notice number 50/1998 and a similar notice is being prepared for regional railway transport.

2.5. Local context

Municipalities provide land use planning under building law. The municipalities manage local communications, supervise private tax services and investigate any loss in the continuity of the public transport service, including the penalty assessment process.

3. Policy Framework

3.1. Transport policy

The current transport policy was officially adopted by decree in 1998. This legislation was prepared in the context of the current transformation of the economy to meet EU entry requirements. For the first time environmental transport issues, which are very important given the current expansion of individual transport, were given a high profile. In particular, charges for regional public transport services must be carefully defined to achieve the internalisation of external costs as required by current and expected legislation. In this context, objective transport taxation must include cover all damages caused by transport, making it possible for all transport modes to compete more equally. Transport policy will evolve as the transport sector follows EU membership requirements.

The main objective is to bring private car use within acceptable environmental limits, hence the priority given to the development of public transport and modernisation of the infrastructure. The principle of sustainable development and the need to reduce and stabilise the environmental impact of transport requires complex policy measures including:

- support from central administration to make public passenger transport as attractive as possible, within the possibilities of the national budget;
- improving co-ordination among transport modes to maximise unification (integrated information systems, timetables, transport plans, etc.);
- co-ordination in infrastructure construction to eliminate critical congestion points;
- harmonisation of approaches to individual transport modes in governmental funding (intervention of public budgets);
- internalisation of external costs in private car use;
- implementation of restrictions on car use in cities, especially in Prague;
- solving the problem of "stationary transport" by providing park and ride facilities at the edge of cities with good connections to urban public transport.

3.2. Regional transport policies

Previous regional transport policy was carried out at district level and only involved the provision of bus services, with the disadvantage of small geographical area coverage (districts). Today, competence is transferred to the regions, which have the resources and means to solve regional transport service problems. The regions are also responsible for regional passenger railway transport. In large urban areas, municipalities have their own transport policy. National transport policy covers infrastructure provision for national and international transport.

3.3. Integration of land use and transport planning

The Ministry of Local Development and its regional and district bodies are responsible for land use planning. Legislation for municipal and regional land use planning came into force in 2000.

49

For local planning, large urban areas have their own regulations. Regional land use planning provides for regional passenger transport services. Planning will be extended to include environmental design for land use and open spaces on a regional scale. The administrations responsible for the 1976 Land Use Planning and Building Law and the 1998 Decree on Local Planning and Local Planning Documentation are the Ministry of Transport and Telecommunications, and the Department of Transport Policy, International Relations and the Environment. The Ministry of Transport and Telecommunications or its Transport Research Centre keep a central record of all local plans.

The outdated old system can no longer provide for current transport planning needs. Fundamental changes will be required after reorganisation of the civil service. In the future it is hoped that management of class II and III roads will be subject to competition, meaning that information and decision-making for this part of the network will not be centralised. For national railways, major roads, motorways, class I roads, major airports, inland waterways and multimodal transport issues planning responsibility will remain centralised.

3.4. Urban public transport

Financial support

Urban public transport is funded by municipalities. Table 10 gives the breakdown in funding for four cities in 1999.

The renewal of urban public transport rolling stock has been funded by the central administration budget since 1995. Other subsidies from the central administration budget include:

- 10% of the purchase cost for buses (40% for low floor vehicles);
- 30% of purchase cost for tram and trolley buses (up to 50% for low-floor vehicles);
- up to 30% for modernisation and reconstruction of tram and trolleybus infrastructure;
- subsidies for construction of the Prague underground.

Transport infrastructure measures

The following measures have been taken (particularly in Prague, gradually extending to other urban areas) to ensure quality and continuity of the public transport service:

- separate lanes for public transport;
- low traffic flows in streets used by trams;

- separate lanes for trams;
- car lanes and tram tracks separated by a concrete barrier;
- refuges by tram stops;
- traffic lights programmed to give preference to trams (absolute and conditional).

Table 10. **Funding for urban public transport, 1999**

	Prague	Brno	Ostrava	Plzeň
Population (thousands)	1 187	383	320	168
City budget (CZK million)	30 300	6 300	6 300	4 200
City transport budget (CZK million)	11 800	1 500	1 000	9
Urban public transport share (CZK million)	8 024	720	840	423
Urban public transport costs per inhabitant (CZK)	6 759	1 880	2 625	2 518

Source: ECMT.

3.5. Transport management and traffic calming measures

The following measures have been taken in urban areas to ensure the quality of city centres :

- opening pedestrian areas;
- developing parking policy;
- introducing parking charges to help reduce the number of cars in city centres;
- reducing the number of parking spaces, because land for parking areas is not available in city centres;
- designing the park and ride network to connect with urban public transport. The next stage will involve linking park and ride with suburban railway stations (outside city centres);
- establishing central offices for the control and regulation of urban road transport, to provide the best possible continuity of service and best choice for passengers;
- optimising the location of railway stations – this is mainly funded from municipality budgets.

3.6. Other measures for solving urban transport problems

In order to create a unified transport system (from the users point of view), efforts are being made to integrate all modes of transport with an integrated ticket system, improve traffic conditions, co-ordinate timetables, introduce unified information systems and provide terminals in urban and rural areas. This system is supported by contracts between individual carriers, the administration and municipalities. The integrated transport system is already highly developed in Prague and to a lesser extent in Ostrava and Zlin. It is in preparation for other major cities. Integration of the tram and railway system will reduce the number of changes in the track transport system and will also reduce travel time. This system is being set up in Liberec (completion date 2007). The integrated track-rail system is on the drawing board in Ostrava and Prague.

3.7. Success in the provision of a sustainable transport system

The success of all the measures which are completed or in progress depends on the fiscal income of individual urban areas. It is important to ensure a close relationship between individual departments of the administration and municipalities to ensure optimisation of infrastructure construction, maintenance and application of all the planned measures.

Note

1. The EU accession process involving structural funds created eight Associate regions, to which have been added one to three new regions. This division is statistical rather than institutional.

Finland

1. Context

Finland is the seventh largest European country. It is sparsely populated with just 5.1 million inhabitants. Population density is about 15 people per square kilometres. Long distances, geographical location and climate impose special requirements on transport.

1.1. *Public transport*

The main objectives of Finnish transport policy are public transport development and the promotion of non-motorised transport so as to reduce congestion and environmental pressures, and promote safety.

Public transport accounts for 20% of total passenger transport (Figure 1 and Table 11). Urban public transport represents about 80% of the total public transport market. The number of passengers using public transport has been relatively stable since the 1970s. However, the modal share of public transport has decreased while total passenger traffic (and particularly car traffic) has increased rapidly (Figures 2 and 3). The long term objective of the Ministry of Transport and Communications is to maintain the current share of public transport.

1.2. *Cycling*

There are about 3 315 000 bicycles in Finland (a 78% ownership rate). Cycling has an 11% share of all journeys and accounts for around 2% of the national personal transport volume, though there is considerable seasonal and geographic variation. For example, in Kerava and Oulu, cycling represents around 20% of passenger transport. Safety is always an important element in cycling policy.

Urban and regional structure

The main urban and regional trends are urban sprawl and concentration of population in few urban areas. A growing share of the population lives in urban areas: 55% in 1960 to more than 90% of the total population today. The figures for the four major urban areas presented in Table 12 include the centre and surrounding

Figure 1. **Distribution of passenger transport (passenger-kilometres)**

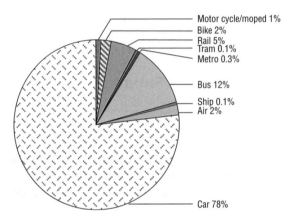

Motor cycle/moped 1%
Bike 2%
Rail 5%
Tram 0.1%
Metro 0.3%
Bus 12%
Ship 0.1%
Air 2%
Car 78%

Source: ECMT.

Table 11. **Urban public transport by mode**

	Bus	Tram	Metro	Urban train
Number of passengers/unit	40-130	100-180	140-400	140-310
Carriages/unit	1	1-3	1-10	1-10
Departures/time unit	60-120	60-120	20-40	10-30
Passenger capacity	2 400-8 000	4 000-15 000	10 000-40 000	8 000-35 000
Speed (km/h)	15-40	12-20	25-60	40-75
Stops or stations/km	200-600	100-500	500-2 000	800-5 000
Average trips length (km)	4-8	2	7	10

Source: ECMT.

Table 12. **Major urban areas**

Major urban areas	Population	Growth (%) 1980-95	Density of population inhabitants/km^2	Urban sprawl (%) 1980-95
Helsinki capital area	985 718	25.0	1 701	−3
Tampere	253 572	16.7	1 143	−13
Turku	229 513	13.0	1 017	−16
Oulu	145 271	32.3	836	−20

Source: ECMT.

Figure 2. **Distribution of public transport (passenger-kilometres)**

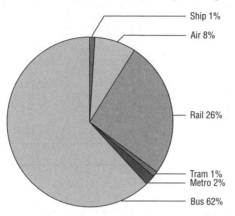

Ship 1%
Air 8%
Rail 26%
Tram 1%
Metro 2%
Bus 62%

Source: ECMT.

Figure 3. **Distribution of public transport (passenger numbers)**

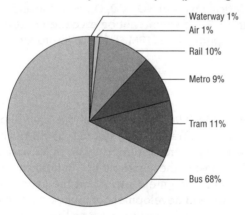

Waterway 1%
Air 1%
Rail 10%
Metro 9%
Tram 11%
Bus 68%

Source: ECMT.

communities. They are still growing rapidly with significant migration from sparsely populated areas accompanied by urban sprawl as new residential areas are built in new locations outside the city centres.

Urban air quality

Urban air quality has improved continually due to vehicle technology and fuel quality developments even though absolute transport volumes have grown. Results

55

Table 13. **Urban air quality in Helsinki**

	WHO threshold levels exceeded		Highest concentration (microgrammes/m³)		Average concentration (microgrammes/m³)	
	1995	2010	1995	2010	1995	2010
NO_2 (annual)	No	No	31	27	12	10
NO_2 (1 hour)	No	No	119	108	60	53
CO (8 hour)	No	No	3 mg	2 mg	1 030	961
Benzene (annual)	No	No	2	1	0.3	0.2
O_3 (8 hour)	No	No	–	–	–	–
PM_{10}	No	No	16	17	3	2

Source: ECMT.

of continuous air quality monitoring (SO_2, NO_2, CO, PM_{10}, TSP, O_3) in 40 urban areas indicate that air quality is good or satisfactory. However, in spring (March-April) emissions of small particulates ($PM_{2.5}$) often exceed target levels due to street sanding during the winter. Ozone levels remain within WHO threshold levels apart from a few days each year. Critical levels of NO_2, CO, O_3, benzene and particulate pollutants were not exceeded in 1995 and should not be exceeded in 2010 (Table 13). Despite increasing emissions of particulates (PM_{10}), future improvements in air quality are expected.

Noise

Research carried out in 1998 showed that about 560 000 people (10.9% of the population) suffer from road traffic noise (LAeq > 55 dBA) within urban areas. In addition to this, 65 000 people are disturbed by air traffic and about 35 000 people disturbed by rail traffic. Most of these people live in urban areas. Municipalities are required to prepare noise abatement plans and the agencies and companies in charge of the maintenance and development of transport infrastructure are required to implement noise abatement measures such as the use of acoustic barriers and porous asphalt, and appropriate flight routing. These measures have stabilised the number of people affected by noise, despite increasing traffic volumes.

Traffic safety

Transport safety (measured by the number of road traffic deaths) improved between 1990 and 1996. Since this date road deaths have been rising again (Figures 4 and 5). There is greater fluctuation in the trend for injuries. In 1999 road traffic accidents in urban areas accounted for about 24% of total number of traffic related deaths, and road accidents represented 53% of the total number of injured people in urban

Figure 4. **Road traffic accidents deaths 1980-1999**

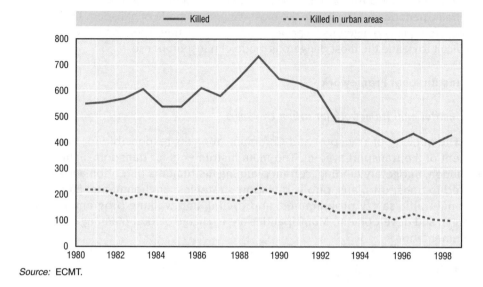

Source: ECMT.

Figure 5. **Road accident injuries 1980-99**

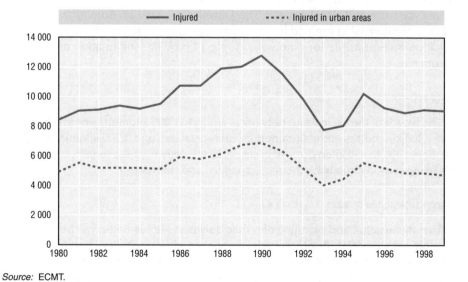

Source: ECMT.

areas. Of those who were killed and injured in road traffic, car drivers and passengers were the largest road user group. However, when the number of deaths is correlated with traffic performance, cycling is the most dangerous mode of transport. Driving and cycling are equally dangerous if considered in terms of time spent on the road, but it is difficult to define the most dangerous mode of transport per se.

2. Institutional Framework

2.1. Institutional framework for urban transport

The Ministry of Transport and Communications is responsible for the development of the transport system. The main instruments for transport planning are regulation, budgetary funding, certain planning instruments (intention agreements related to transport plans, public transport strategies, environmental guidelines, national traffic safety programmes, and cycling and walking programmes) and research and development. Municipalities are in charge of local planning and policy implementation.

Infrastructure

The road and rail networks are maintained by public funds. The Finnish Road Administration is responsible for the maintenance and construction of roads outside urban areas. Municipalities maintain the street network including cycle paths in urban areas. The Rail Administration is responsible for railways. Helsinki is the only urban area where there is a metro and tram network and the municipality is responsible for their maintenance and development. The Finnish Civil Aviation Administration operating as a commercial enterprise is responsible for airports and the National Board of Navigation is responsible for waterways. Table 14 provides information on transport infrastructure.

Cycling network

The length of the cycle route network is around 11 000 kilometres of which around about 7 300 kilometres are maintained by municipalities and 3 700 kilometres by the state. Some 400 to 450 kilometres of cycle paths are constructed annually, construction costs being shared equally by the municipalities and the state.

Transport system and services

The organisation and planning of public transport are regulated by the Passenger Transport Act (52/1994). Public transport consists of domestic rail services, trams, metros, buses and coaches, taxis, air traffic and ferry connections between Helsinki and the island of Suomenlinna. Urban public transport includes local rail traffic,

Table 14. **Transport infrastructure in Finland**

Network	Length (kilometres)
Public roads	77 969 km
– Motorways	
(including secondary motorways)	681 km
– Other highways	8 587 km
Urban streets	21 470 km
Cycle paths	11 000 km
Railways	5 886 km
Metro line	17 km
Tramways	76 km
Number of airports	22 airports (maintained by CAA)

Source: ECMT.

Table 15. **Capacity of urban public transport (1997)**

	Rail	Tram	Metro	Bus	Ferry	Total
Vehicles	142	105	42	4 875	2	5 166
Seats	23 397	3 900	5 460	230 651	330	263 738
All places	28 338	11 800	16 800	301 830	700	359 468

Source: ECMT.

Table 16. **Total capacity of public transport (1997)**

	Rail	Tram	Metro	Bus	Taxi	Air	Ferry	Total
Vehicles	863	105	42	6 928	9 676	27	2	17 643
Seats	58 003	3 900	5 460	327 432	48 699	2 174	330	445 998
All places	66 889	11 800	16 800	398 618	48 699	2 174	700	545 680

Source: ECMT.

trams and the metro in Helsinki, local bus transport and the ferry connection mentioned above. In urban areas taxis are part of public transport services. The total capacity of public transport and urban public transport in terms of vehicles, seats and total places is presented in Tables 15 and 16.

Organisation of public transport

The largest urban municipalities are in charge of organising urban public transport. Local transport enterprises in urban areas provide or purchase services

© ECMT 2003

from private bus companies. Urban public transport covers about 70% (400 million passengers per year) of the public transport market share.

Municipalities subsidise ticket prices. The attractiveness of public transport was increased by the introduction of advantageous regional monthly bus cards which are used in all major urban areas and have boosted the number of passengers by 15 to 20%.

Helsinki metropolitan area

The largest urban area is the Helsinki metropolitan area (Helsinki with the sur-rounding cities of Espoo, Vantaa and Kauniainen) with around 900 000 inhabitants. The municipalities are responsible for public transport in their respective areas, but the Helsinki Metropolitan Area Council is responsible for regional transport services that extend beyond the communal borders of the four cities in the capital area. The Helsinki Metropolitan Area Council has special powers to ensure co-operation with the metropolitan area municipalities.

The Helsinki City Transport company is responsible for public transport in the Helsinki urban area. Most of the bus lines are open to competition. Co-operation between the municipality and private bus companies means that the same tickets can be used on all buses, trains, trams and metros in Helsinki. There are 11 tram lines, 79 bus lines and one metro line. Public transport has 60% of the market share in Helsinki urban centre. The Helsinki Metropolitan Area Council purchases train transport that serves the capital area from the VR-Group Ltd (Finnish State Railways) and bus transport services through competitive tendering. Regional transport services are financed by ticket income (65%) and by contributions from the urban groupings (35%). The regional bus card system facilitates use of public transport services in the whole capital area. The share of public transport in the metropolitan area is at present about 42% and Helsinki Metropolitan Area Council intends to maintain the market share at this level in the future.

2.2. Institutional framework for land use planning

Responsibilities

The Ministry of the Environment is responsible for legislation and co-ordination of land use planning issues. However, the municipalities are responsible for zoning in their own area.

Instruments

In accordance with the Land Use and Housing Act (132/1999) the main instrument in land use policy is zoning:

- the regional zoning plan contains the zoning plan for major activities at regional level;
- the general zoning plan defined by the municipality contains the zoning plan for activities within all or part of the municipality;
- the city zoning plan defined by the municipality contains the zoning plan for all activities at local level.

Together all these zoning plans aim to create a safe, healthy, environmentally-friendly and socially well-functioning urban structure which should take into account the availability of public transport services and light transport.

The 1999 Land Use and Housing Act increased the decision making power of the municipalities. The general and city zoning maps which are approved by the municipalities do not need approval of the state. Only the regional zoning maps are subject to approval from the Ministry of the Environment. Ministry of the Environment regional environmental centres provide assistance to the municipal and regional administrations in the preparation of zoning plans. The aim is to promote environmentally sustainable development and urban planning on a more human scale.

Any complaints about municipal zoning plans are dealt with in the administrative courts and complaints about regional zoning plans are dealt with by the Ministry of the Environment.

2.3. Interaction between urban transport and land use planning

The zoning of residential areas, offices and services and the connecting transport network play an important role when planning and further developing urban structure. Land use and transport planning policies must be co-ordinated and integrated as well as other related measures, such as the promotion of public transport and non-motorised transport.

The availability of the public transport network and services is one of the main elements when zoning new areas for new purposes. Residential areas that require good public transport connections are zoned in those areas that can be reached by existing or feasible new public transport services.

The main urban areas in Finland (Helsinki metropolitan area, Tampere, Turku and Oulu) have been developed on the basis of the availability of public transport services. As population numbers and density of these areas are large, it is possible to maintain a high level of public services despite increasing passenger car traffic.

The major problems in all main urban areas are the peripheral suburban areas where the public service connections to the urban centres are poorest and the level of car use is the highest. Despite attempts to maintain a compact city structure, urban sprawl continues. Urban sprawl has generalised in recent decades following the strong trend to a decentralised, medium and low density life style with people choosing to live away from urban centres in green field suburban areas. This represents an increasing challenge for the co-ordination of transport and land use planning in the future. Co-operation between the authorities responsible for transport and land use planning must be improved and better planning oriented and research information for planning must be produced.

3. Policy Framework

3.1. Urban transport planning

Transport system plans

Since 1996, municipalities have implemented transport system plans, *i.e.* long-term strategic plans to develop an entire travel-related system. Transport system planning requires an assessment of the need to develop the transport network and services.

The development of a transport system requires extensive discussion of objectives for transport and land use. General guidelines and objectives must be formulated at the national level to shape the development path of a successful transport system, even though the practical planning and specific targets are set by the municipalities. The main target of transport system planning is to promote sustainable development which includes improvement of traffic safety and environmental protection. As such, the following national objectives have been set for transport system planning:

- land use planning should take into account the impact on traffic volumes, the choice of modes of transport, transport energy use, as well as any possible adverse environmental and health effects;
- community structures should be created and planned in such a way not to cause unnecessary travelling;
- the competitiveness and attractiveness of public transport should be improved;
- existing infrastructure should be exploited before building takes place;
- the required movement of passengers and goods should be minimised by using the most socially advantageous modes of transport and transport links;
- co-operation between different modes of transport and travel should be increased.

As transport system planning is very important for the local and often also regional and national development of the transport system, continuous and close communication between and within different interest groups is essential. The municipalities need to communicate with governmental agencies responsible for transport networks and management, local people and other interest groups, such as the business sector and environmental groups. Therefore, extensive approval and commitment to the plan is needed.

Transport system planning has been conducted for all 12 major urban areas. Transport system development requires continuity of the operations initiated during planning throughout the development process. Municipalities monitor the transport system plan and its implementation, including any impacts.

The Transport System Plan for the Helsinki Area was last updated in February 1999. This transport system plan extends to 2020 in three project phases:

- 1999-2004: projects include transport connections to the new Helsinki harbour, horizontal bus connection, Ruoholahti-Matinkylä metro line, Tikkurila-Kerava city rail link, Marja-rail link, ring road II : EUR 445 million;

- 2005-2010: projects include the Leppävaara-Espoo Centre and Tikkurila-Kerava city rail link, Ruoholahti-Matinkylä metro line, ring road II, Helsinki-Vantaa Airport road connection: EUR 564.27 million;

- 2011-2020: projects include the rail link to Helsinki-Vantaa Airport, Pisara rail link, enlargement of metro line: EUR 455.79 million.

Intention agreements for transport plan implementation

The intention agreements between the government, municipalities and regional councils provide an instrument for the implementation of transport system plans in urban areas. The municipalities are responsible for maintaining and developing the public transport system and transport infrastructure within urban areas. With the intention agreements the government provides funding for the implementation of such transport projects that are in accordance with the transport system plans. The intention agreements enable the government to guide the transport planning of municipalities which can autonomously decide on transport planning at local level. So far 15 intention agreements have been agreed between the government, municipalities and regional councils.

National public transport strategy

The Ministry of Transport and Communications is adopting a new national public transport strategy with the objective to show the directions in which the Ministry intends to develop public transport and to present the main implementation methods. The strategy aims to develop an efficient and high-quality public transport system that supports the general objectives of balanced regional development, environmental sustainability and traffic safety. It is aimed at maintaining the existing public transport market share and ensuring basic levels of service at the national level.

63

The main priorities of the national public transport strategy are:

- land use and transport network planning, which take into account the needs of public transport;
- the priority given to public transport and traffic safety when determining national transport infrastructure investments;
- participation of the government in specified urban public transport investment projects which are in accordance with transport system plans in these areas;
- increasing the co-operation between different modes of transport and the development of door-to-door travel links;
- the Ministry of Transport and Communications will create the preconditions to establish a national information system to provide passengers with door-to-door information on public transport services;
- improving the availability and quality of information on public transport services in travel centres;
- a commitment by the Ministry of Transport and Communications, regional councils and the municipalities to ensure balanced regional availability of public transport services even though individual companies will plan and provide these services;
- making public transport services easily available, easy to use and attractive to consumers, with the help of technical requirements, quality and service criteria, R&D, subjecting the services to public competition, defining service criteria and defining the transport system plan;
- exploiting information campaigns and user inquiries to support the development of public services.

The Ministry of Transport and Communications monitors the implementation of the strategy and achievement of its objectives.

Other measures promoting public transport in urban areas

Municipalities grant public transport subsidies to control fare prices. Urban municipalities provide advantageous monthly regional bus cards in all major urban areas. The government gives a 50% subsidy for bus fares in small urban agglomerations, but does not subsidise bus fares in big urban areas.

The Helsinki City Transport enterprise (HKL) has introduced some fare differentiation. In addition to normal differentiation of charges for different user groups (children and retired people) there is also a price differentiation between tickets bought in advance or from the driver, at the time of travel. The objective is to promote the smooth flow of public transport services. One-trip tram tickets are also cheaper than changeable tickets in other means of public transport.

The large urban areas have introduced allocated lanes reserved for public transport to ensure the smooth flow of public transport. In Helsinki there are plans to extend the environmentally-friendly tramway, underground and city rail network. Some 30 buses in Helsinki run on compressed natural gas (CNG) and the CNG fleet will be enlarged in the future.

Environmental Guidelines for the Transport Sector

The Ministry of Transport and Communications introduced the Environmental Guidelines for the Transport Sector in July 1999. These guidelines establish the basic tool for environmental management of transport policy and planning for 1999 to 2004. This programme sets operational policy targets in following areas:

- reducing greenhouse gas emissions;
- reducing traffic emissions;
- preventing soil and water pollution;
- reducing exposure to noise;
- taking environmental impacts into account in developing transport systems: land take and landscape;
- promoting ecological sustainability: biodiversity, waste problem and eco-efficiency.

All these policy targets also concern urban traffic. The programme shares responsibilities between the different units of the Ministry of Transport and Communications, agencies and institutions of the administrative sector, business enterprises and companies as well as other ministries and local administrations. The first follow-up report published in 2000 showed positive development in all sectors where targets are set.

National traffic safety plan

The government has adopted national traffic safety plans which set traffic safety targets for a five year period. The aim of the 2001 to 2005 plan is to reduce traffic accident deaths to less than 250 in 2005 (in 1999, there were 391 traffic accident deaths). The programme contains a specific action programme to improve traffic safety in urban areas through:

- active use of differentiated speed limits in urban areas;
- differentiated speed limits enforced with traffic calming structures (*e.g.* bumps) when necessary;
- careful planning of crossings between non-motorised and car traffic to reduce risk;

- looking into the feasibility of introducing of speed limit surveillance in the largest urban areas to support the surveillance carried out by police;

- improvement of the transport infrastructure of urban centre feed roads;

- checking speed limits in villages and urban areas;

- legislation concerning the use of reflectors;

- traffic information and campaigns to increase knowledge on traffic regulations and compliance.

The programme contains a wide variety of general measures to promote traffic safety, including:

- making drivers more aware of safety;

- reducing the effects of accidents;

- reducing traffic growth;

- increasing the use of new technologies;

- promoting the importance of traffic safety in all decision making.

Speed limits in urban areas

The general speed limit in urban areas is 50 km/h. However, many urban areas have introduced stricter 30 km/h or 40 km/h speed limits in certain streets to calm the traffic in residential areas or shopping streets. In residential areas, court-yard streets have been introduced, where walking on the road way is allowed; cars must adapt their driving accordingly.

Economic instruments

The main economic instruments are vehicle and fuel taxes. Fuel taxation contains a differentiation scheme. The diesel fuel prices are adjusted according to the sulphur content and petrol fuel prices are differentiated between the reformulated and non-reformulated fuels.

Vehicle taxation will be reformed by the government to encourage the purchase of low-consumption and energy saving cars. The government is also investigating withdrawal of the tax deduction for company cars and commuting which should promote public transport for commuting. To this effect, a recent study on the influence of fuel prices on traffic behaviour has been conducted by the Finnish Road Administration and Statistics Centre. The study showed that of the 1 700 people interviewed, some 50% had reduced their car use, particularly for short trips in urban areas for business, work, leisure and shopping due to high fuel prices. About 20% of those interviewed now use public transport occasionally at least and about 75% have combined various trips in order to reduce the total number of trips. This means that the number of trips has reduced more than the volume of passenger kilometres.

National cycling policy programme

In 1992, the Ministry of Transport and Communications introduced the first national cycling programme. The aim of this programme was to double the cycling performance and to halve the number of cycling accidents by 2000 compared with 1989. The programme included measures to develop the cycle path network, cycle routing and travel information, parking and safety. A Ministry report (1999) has indicated some improvement in transport safety, but no increase in cycling performance. The Ministry target is for the share of cycling trips to attain 25% by 2005. The aim is to pay more attention to land use planning in built-up areas and to improve the preconditions for the co-operation of public transport and cycling. Implementation of the 1999-2002 Development of Walking and Cycling Routes programme should accelerate the construction of pedestrians and cyclists routes. Another objective is to develop cycling as feeder traffic for public transport and integrate carriage of bicycles on public transport into the public transport travel chain.

Ministry of Transport and Communications committee for promoting non-motorised transport is responsible for promoting cycling and updating the cycling programme. The committee's draft cycling policy programme gives emphasis to the promotion of cycling and cycling safety in urban areas and aims to double the share of cycling by 2020.

City bicycles

In 2000, the city of Helsinki introduced 250 city bicycles. For a FIM 10 coin (EUR 1.68) deposit these bicycles are available to use around the urban centre, the coin is returned on return of the bicycle. The purchase of city bicycles has been sponsored by various companies. The city of Helsinki plans to double the amount of city bicycles in the forthcoming years.

National walking policy programme

The Ministry of Transport and Communications is preparing a programme to promote walking. The aim of this programme is for walking to be included on an equal basis to other modes in all policy making and planning decisions. The walking programme should present an action programme to promote walking as an environmentally-friendly and healthy mode of transport, with specific targets to improve safety and ease of access for walkers.

67

Car sharing

In March 2000 the first car sharing organisation started to operate in Helsinki. The City Car Club has 80 cars that are shared by the members who have registered as share-holders of the organisation.

Ease of access planning and vehicles

Ease of access has become a guideline in urban transport planning, for both the transport system and vehicles. Low-floor buses, trams and trains have been introduced, terminals and platforms are designed to allow unhindered and easy access for the disabled, mothers with children and pushchairs and elderly people.

Strategy towards Intelligent and Sustainable Transport

Towards Intelligent and Sustainable Transport is a long-term strategy prepared by the Ministry of Transport and Communications to plan future developments for a transport system to be achieved by the year 2025. The report sets out the targets and strategies to attain these objectives. It draws together the aims and objectives of the various sectoral policy programmes described above and integrates economic, ecological, social and cultural factors. The strategies encompass passenger traffic, freight traffic, transport infrastructure, international transport connections, the environment, traffic safety, regional development, transport economy and social justice. The report shares responsibilities between the Ministry of Transport and Communications and different partners to attain these targets.

The main objectives for passenger transport are much the same as defined in the national public transport strategy. The aim is to increase the share of bus and rail transport in inter-city traffic, to integrate walking and cycling more closely in transport system planning and to improve door-to-door travel linkage. The general objective for regional development is to increase the co-operation between land use and transport planning and to promote balanced regional development.

The strategies and objectives in favour of the environment and traffic safety are in line with those defined in the Environmental Guidelines, the transport sector programme on greenhouse gas emissions and the national traffic safety programme as well as other policy programmes.

3.2. Land use planning

The 1999 Land Use and Housing Act

The 1999 Land Use and Housing Act came into force on 1 January 2000. One of the leading principles of the legislation was to support sustainable development in land use planning and to take into consideration the environmental effects caused by land use planning. The previous legislation (1958) with some minor amendments had stipulated that zoning plans should include an accessible and efficient public and non-motorised transport system. In practical terms the new legislation has provided municipalities with better instruments for guiding the zoning of new supermarkets and shopping centres. Supermarkets and shopping centres above 2 000 square metres can no longer be built outside urban centres.

National targets for land use planning

Following the adoption of the Land Use and Housing Act, a report was presented to Parliament in May 2000 by the government with short and long term national targets for land use planning. The main challenges are migration and its effects on regional structure, urban sprawl, environmental quality, ensuring the preservation of cultural heritage, maintenance of biodiversity and reduction of transport demand with attendant reduction of greenhouse gas emissions. The report also contains a draft Council of State Decree setting national targets for land use planning, which should act as guidelines for municipalities and regional councils in land use planning of national importance. The targets are set for land use and urban structure, quality of the environment, cultural and natural heritage, use of the natural environment for recreational purposes, use of natural resources, transport, telecommunications and energy networks.

Strategic project on traffic and land use planning

A Finnish Road Administration summary report has collated information from approximately 115 research reports and publications. This literature survey provides an information base on the interaction between land use and traffic, to assist in promoting sustainable development and reduce transport demand.

Guide on measures for promoting public transport in land use planning

The Ministry of the Environment has produced a publication on measures for promoting public transport in land use planning. The aim of this guide is to emphasise the importance of effective land use planning as a basis for an efficient and financially viable public transport system. The guide gives the following general guidelines:

- integrated residential areas and new places of work must be located near existing or planned public transport connections;
- land use divisions must be dimensioned on a viable scale for public transport services;
- land use that generates a large volume of public transport trips must be concentrated in areas where public transport supply is good;

69

- high-density land uses must be located near stations and bus stops;
- new shopping centres or residential and employment areas must not be planned in isolation from the rest of urban structure;
- scattered settlements must be located near population centres with existing public transport connections;
- the public transport network must be planned so that routes are as direct as possible;
- integration between different modes of transport is a priority;
- transport terminals must be designed to facilitate transfer connections and accessibility for pedestrians and cyclists (including bicycle parking facilities and arrangements);
- parking spaces must be determined in relation to the level of car ownership and the level of public transport service and must be located within walking distance to public transport connections;
- connections for pedestrians and cyclists from surrounding areas to stations and bus stops must be as short, smooth and safe as possible.

Measures proposed in the context of the National Climate Change Programme

The National Climate Change Programme should be finalised by spring 2001. Sector programmes from both the Ministry of Transport and Communications and the Ministry of the Environment emphasise the importance of urban and regional structure in developing measures to reduce the volume of transport and thereby greenhouse gas emissions. The Ministry of the Environment draft programme concludes that if the trends of increasing urban sprawl and population migration from peripheral areas to a few urban regions continue at the current rate, greenhouse gas emissions will increase by 31% in line with consumption caused by traffic increase and new housing. Urgent action is needed to meet the Kyoto requirements. The draft programme suggests measures to support compact urban and regional structure in land use and transport planning, zoning and housing policies, fiscal policy, integration between these policies, co-operation between the municipalities and distribution of information.

In addition to measures aimed at maintaining the density of urban city structure and balanced regional structure the transport sector programme also emphasises:

- developing vehicle taxation is a priority to take fuel consumption better into account;
- training in eco-driving techniques;
- promotion of non-motorised traffic;

- public transport and energy-saving agreements between transport operators and the administration.

The Ministry of Transport and Communications considers that application of these measures should bring greenhouse gas emissions down to 1990 levels by 2010.

3.3. Integration of transport and land use planning and other policies

Research and development work is the main instrument for producing policy packages that promote sustainable transport. The Ministry of Transport and Communications, the Ministry of the Environment and other agencies and offices, transport enterprises and companies have established a research programme designed to produce information to facilitate implementation of integrated and sustainable policies and planning (the LYYLI-programme). Some of the most recent studies conducted for this programme include:

- interaction between transport and land use in the Helsinki Metropolitan area: the study provides information on land use and transport policy impacts in the region of the capital;

- modelling of urban sprawl and fragmentation: the study aims to simulate an environmentally advantageous transport system and urban structure and to develop methods for evaluating urban sprawl and fragmentation.

- long-term impacts of fuel price changes and withdrawal of tax reduction based on commuting costs: the study shows that fuel price is an efficient measure to control transport behaviour in urban areas where there is an available sufficient public transport supply. Higher travel costs for passenger car traffic should decrease the rate of people using their own cars. However, in the countryside and other sparsely populated areas where no other modes of transport are available, transport demand is rather inelastic to any changes in price level;

- changes in urban structure and transport demand by year 2020: the study analyses future changes in the urban structure and transport demand in Finnish cities with a view to providing various planning scenarios: 1) Virtual Society in which the largest urban areas continue to grow and peripheral areas become uninhabited; 2) Experienced Society with growth in urban areas, urban sprawl and increasing transport demand; and 3) Eco-Society with low migration and transport demand;

- car sharing in the Helsinki Metropolitan Area: the study evaluates the feasibility of car sharing models in the Helsinki metropolitan area and provides a business plan for organising car sharing in the region. This study was used when car sharing was launched in Helsinki in March 2000;

- impacts of information technology on transport and the environment: the study provides information on the impact of information technology activities (such as e-commerce, tele-banking, tele-education), on transport demand and the environment, the main focus being road traffic and passenger cars. The report recommends controlled introduction and use of IT services if aimed at reducing transport demand. However, use of IT services does not implicitly reduce transport demand as distance working can increase commuting distances;

- travel behaviour as a function of changes in lifestyle parameters: the study provides three different land use, transport system and service structure scenarios evaluating the changes in travel behaviour as a function of the location of housing, workplace, services and changes in transport system. The study shows that land use should be based on public transport corridors in order to promote urban integration and to reduce urban fragmentation. Shopping centres and workplaces should be located near railway stations to improve public transport accessibility. New housing areas should be within easy reach of railway stations.

4.   Evaluation and Conclusions

The main positive trends regarding urban transport are:

- continuing improvements in air quality in urban areas mainly due to advances in vehicle technology and fuel specifications;

- positive developments in traffic safety in urban areas even though this development has stagnated since 1996.

The main unsustainable trends are:

- transport growth, especially in passenger car traffic;

- urban sprawl and population migration to a small number of urban areas.

Urban municipalities have significant autonomy for transport and land use planning and are responsible for local planning transport infrastructure and land use, as well as for maintaining public transport services in their area. The government is mainly responsible for transport infrastructure outside urban areas and for providing guidance and funding for transport infrastructure of national importance. The government also finances public transport in small urban areas. The government ratifies the regional land use plans which transfer national and regional land use goals to the local level. Even though the division of work between the government and municipalities is clear, the main disadvantage is that the government has very few measures to influence urban transport and land use planning. The main instruments are regulation, some funding, policy programmes to provide general guidelines and principles, and research and development.

With new regulations (especially the Land Use and Housing Act) and a number of policy programmes, the government aims to reverse the unsustainable trends of urban sprawl and increased transport demand, and thereby reduce greenhouse gas emissions and noise, and improve urban air quality and traffic safety.

Promotion of sustainable and balanced development is an important principle and general objective in transport and land use planning, both at the national and local level. However, the interactive complexity of transport, land use, regional and other policies as well as individual consumer choices have so far continued urban sprawl and fragmentation. It is a priority to produce information and raise awareness to help people understand the complexity of these processes and so encourage more sustainable behaviour.

Research and development work is in progress (the Lyyli-programme) to promote better integration of transport and land use policies and planning. This research has contributed to producing and implementing new strategies and guidelines. Applying all the available information on integrating transport and land use planning is a real challenge. The municipalities and their transport and land use planners will have to find practical solutions to meet these challenges.

It is very positive that there is increasing awareness at local level of the potential cost of urban sprawl and population migration, as this awareness has affected local land use and transport planning. In addition to the increasing autonomy of municipalities in land use and transport planning, the government and communities have found new approaches to co-operate in transport planning, such as intention agreements for the implementation of transport system plans.

Recent surveys indicate that citizen awareness is also increasing. The population as a whole is concerned about environmental issues and supports public transport services in the communities. However, there still seems to be some contradiction between the values and critical choices that each individual has to make in his or her daily life about whether to use public transport or a private car. Active information and promotion campaigns have been organised to address this problem, supported by efficient policy measures such as economic instruments, the promotion of public transport and non-motorised transport and the prevention of urban sprawl.

References

Car sharing in the Helsinki Metropolitan Area (in Finnish), Series of Lyyli-Research Programme No. 13, Helsinki 2000.

Changes in urban form and transport demand in Finnish cities by year 2020 (in Finnish), Series of Lyyli-Research Programme 19, Helsinki 2000.

City without car? Finnish Road Administration Publications 51/1996, Helsinki 1996 (available only in Finnish).

Environmental Guidelines for the Transport Sector, Ministry of Transport and Communications, Helsinki 1999 (available also in English).

Follow-up report on the environmental guidelines 1999-2000, Ministry of Transport and Communications, Helsinki 2000 (available only in Finnish).

Follow-up report on Cycling Policy Programme for 1997-98, Publications of the Ministry of Transport and Communications B4/99, Helsinki 1999 (available only in Finnish).

Helsinki Metropolitan Area Transportation System Plan 1998, Helsinki Metropolitan Area Publications A 1999:2, Helsinki 1999 (available only in Finnish).

Impacts of tele-presence on transport and the environment (in Finnish), Series of Lyyli-Research Programme, No. 21, Helsinki 2000.

Interaction between transport and land use in the Helsinki Metropolitan area (in Finnish), Series of Lyyli-Research Programme No. 1, Helsinki 1999.

Long-term impacts of fuel price changes and removal of tax reduction based on commuting costs (in Finnish), Series of Lyyli-Research Programme No. 11, Helsinki 2000.

Modelling of urban sprawl and fragmentation (in Finnish), Series of Lyyli-Research Programme 9, Helsinki 2000.

National cycling programme, Publications of the Ministry of Transport and Communications 20/1993, Helsinki 1993 (available only in Finnish).

National Public Transport Strategy (draft) available only in Finnish.

National Traffic Safety Programme 2001-2005, Ministry of Transport and Communications, Helsinki 2000.

Passenger transport survey 1998-1999 (in Finnish), Publications of the Ministry of Transport and Communications 43/1999, 1999 Helsinki.

Public Transport in Finland, Ministry of Transport and Communications, Brochure in English.

Public Transport in Finnish Land Use Planning, Guide 3/1995, The Ministry of the Environment 1995, Helsinki. Brochure available in English.

Public Transport Performance Statistics 1997, Publications of the Ministry of Transport and Communications B 7/99, Helsinki 1999 (available also in English).

Road Traffic Accidents 1999, Statistics Finland and Central Organisation for Traffic Safety in Finland, 2000/13, Helsinki 2000 (available also in English).

The travel behavioural effects of changes in transport system and location of housing, working places and services (in Finnish), Series of Lyyli-Research Programme 10, Helsinki 2000.

Traffic and Land Use, Finnish Road Administration internal publications 44/1998, Helsinki 1998.

Transport and Communications Statistical Yearbook for Finland, Statistics Finland 1998/15, Helsinki 1998 (available also in English).

Transportation system plan, Finnish Road Administration, Helsinki 1996 (available also in English).

The Auto Oil II Programme, Communication of the European Commission, October 2000.

The Effects of the Transportation System upon Air Quality, Helsinki Metropolitan Area Publications B 1997/11, Helsinki 1997.

Towards intelligent and sustainable transport. Draft strategy report (will be available also in English).

France

1. Context

1.1. *Key trends in urban mobility*

Household mobility surveys conducted since 1976 (sometimes two or more over a ten year interval in the same urban area), have shown changes in mobility and trends in urban areas due to modifications in the organisation of transport. All forms of mobility stagnated in the 1980s and began to increase again in the 1990s, when both the number of trips and average distance covered increased. Despite investment in public transport, car numbers have also increased, partly encouraged by infrastructure investment. Grenoble is a rare exception: between 1985 and 1992, the city put a tramway into service along with a policy supporting cycling.

The market share for public transport is conditioned by the size and density of the urban area, the quality of the services offered and the type of urbanisation. Market share indicators are characterised by density of urbanisation combined with policies to develop alternative modes to the car (public transport, walking and cycling), with additional variability according to the urban area (urban centres, inner suburbs and the peripheral urban zone).

The household mobility surveys highlight other trends:

- growth in the number of people with driving licences, particularly women and the elderly, and an increase in car ownership;

- an increase in the distances covered due to a shift from slow non-motorised modes (cycling, walking) to faster (car, public transport), and performance improvements in motorised modes;

- slightly higher total male mobility, though the difference between male and female mobility is decreasing; mobility increases with the level of education;

- variation in mobility according to trip purpose: commuting and school runs mobility fell then stabilised, shopping and leisure travel increased. The most rapid increase is for passengers, particularly children being taken to

76

school or college. The rate of car use has tripled in twenty years, mostly to the detriment of walking.

1.2. Ile-de-France (Paris region)

The Ile-de-France is unique due to the size of its urban area and the quality of the public transport service in the densest zone. The market share of the various modes is very different. Due to the extent of the Paris region, there are significant differences in mobility within the urban area. The demand for travel follows demography and therefore urban sprawl. The population is stable in the inner city area of Paris, growing slightly in the inner suburbs and more strongly in outer suburbs (Figure 6).

Figure 6.   **Population growth in the Paris region, 1975-2015**

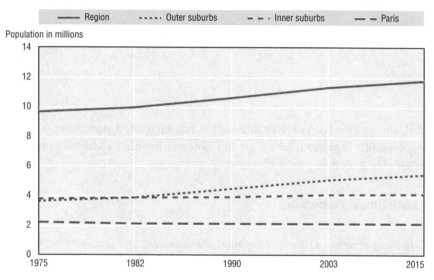

Source: ECMT.

Rates of car ownership vary from one to eight in Paris and the outer suburbs (Figure 7). This difference can be partly accounted for by smaller average sized households in Paris (many students and elderly people), but the type of urbanisation and quality of the different modes of travel offered are more important factors.

Over the past twenty years, the population of the Ile de France has increased by 12%, car travel has increased by 69%, but public transport has only grown by 15%. The growth in car traffic is particularly high in sprawling outer suburbs.

Figure 7. **Rate of car ownership in Ile-de-France households, 1976-1997**

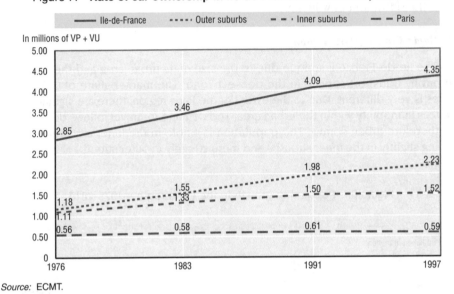

Source: ECMT.

Overall, the number of vehicles kilometres has increased significantly more than regional wealth represented by gross domestic product (GDP) (Figure 8). This unsustainable growth must be changed.

2.   Institutional Framework

2.1. *Planning of urban areas: development, environment and transport responsibilities*

The role of the central administration: decentralisation and inter-municipality

France has a tradition of centralisation. Nearly 20% of its 60 million inhabitants lives in the Paris area and produces one third of GDP. In addition to the central administration, there are three local institutional levels: urban areas, one hundred départements and 22 regions created in 1962 and with elected assemblies since 1992. Unlike many countries, these three levels of local administration do not have legislative powers. Laws passed in 1982 began the decentralisation of power to local levels, giving them autonomous powers and allocated resources for each level. Decentralisation has developed inter-municipal co-operation.

Figure 8. **Increase in traffic in Paris region (1975-2000) compared with GDP**

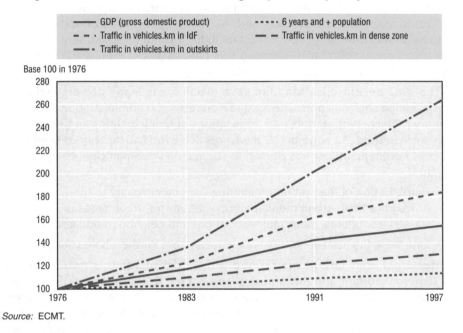

Source: ECMT.

A scatter of urban areas

France has 36 000 geographically scattered urban areas. Urban infrastructure has grown slowly over time, with an abrupt acceleration in the last half century. A number of large urban areas have evolved: the Paris area, three urban areas of approximately one million inhabitants (Lyon, Lille, Marseille) and six urban areas of more than 500 000 inhabitants (Toulouse, Bordeaux, Nantes, Strasbourg, Nice and Grenoble). The municipalities running these urban areas are responsible for urban planning, transport management and local public services (social housing, water, drainage, gas, electricity, waste management and sporting and cultural activities). In some municipalities the organisation of public transport has been delegated to inter-municipal co-operation structures. Half of the budget for urban areas comes from local tax contributions (EUR 70 billion compared with the government budget of EUR 215 billion) which are locally decided and collected, the other half comes from central administration.

Reinforcement and simplification of inter-municipal co-operation

Intermunicipal co-operation dates back to the end of the nineteenth century, originally for rural rather than urban problems. The population of urban areas expanded after the Second World War and the creation of urban districts in the 1960s enabled inter- urban co-ordination. The large urban areas remained reluctant to associate into districts and in 1966 the government imposed urban municipal association status on Bordeaux, Lille, Lyon and Strasbourg. Only five other urban areas voluntarily adopted this type of association. Paris remained under the authority of the central administration.

The 1982 decentralisation laws gave urban areas many powers including urban planning and transport. The 1992 law on territorial administration promoted voluntary project co-operation, and associations of municipalities and neighbour-hoods were formed. As none of the measures achieved satisfactory co-operation, the 1999 Chevenement Law was passed to strengthen inter-municipal co-operation, through:

- simplification of the system by limiting inter municipality to three categories (instead of five): urban municipal associations for urban areas of more than 500 000 inhabitants, municipal associations and neighbourhood associations;
- improving financial solidarity (single tax system for the whole country).

Municipal associations are formed with a central administration grant of EUR 36 per inhabitant and this status enables them to contract directly with the government. Inter-municipality has favoured stronger and more effective decentralisation and in 2001 there were 90 municipal associations grouping together more than eleven million inhabitants. Eighty-two per cent of the large urban areas (with the exception of the Paris region) have been inter-municipalised including nearly all of the metropolitan and overseas regions.

Paris has slightly less than 10 million inhabitants, however the management entity of the area remains the Ile-de-France region (11.3 million inhabitants) with an elected assembly and autonomous powers. Some 80% of the Ile-de-France region is still rural and is organised into eight départements and 1 281 neighbourhoods. The central administration has a much bigger role in the Ile-de-France than in other urban areas, as each territorial community exercises its own powers. In particular, the central administration is responsible for the 2000 Urban development plan (PDU[1]) which replaced the 1994 Development plan.

2.2. Public transport context

Transport tax

The 1971 Paris region transport tax (VT)[2] was progressively extended to the provinces for urban areas of up to 10 000 inhabitants. The transport tax is an additional tax, based on the wage bill, paid by companies and central administration services with more than 9 employees situated within the urban transport zone (PTU[3]). All revenues are used to subsidise public transport. This has been a significant factor in the development of public transport since the 1970s. Transport tax revenue totals almost EUR 2 billion in the Ile-de-France and EUR 1.4 billion in the provinces.

Delegated management of the urban public transport system

With the exception of the Ile-de-France, public transport is managed by urban areas (31%), intermunicipal structures (30%), transport only associations (26%) or other associations (13%). The majority of urban areas (93%) delegate the management of their transport network to an operator. The remaining 7% have direct management (public authority). The delegated management contract is drafted as a public service or delegation of a public contract depending on the level of risk which the municipality wishes to assume. Three transport groups share the biggest urban transport networks (Ile-de-France). Most of the development in urban public transport is occurring on the outskirts of the urban areas but the real competition between the companies is on the international market. The major growth area for local companies and agencies are urban areas with less than 100 000 inhabitants.

The specific case of Ile-de-France

The 2000 Act for Urban Solidarity and Renewal (SRU[4]) associated the 1959 Paris Transport Association (central administration and the eight départements) and the Ile-de-France region. The association was renamed the Ile-de-France Transport Association (STIF[5]). The STIF delegates management contracts to two public transport companies (the Paris metropolitan transport network and the Ile-de-France urban rail network) and the OPTILE Association which manages the 104 private transport companies. 12 million journeys are made per day, with an operating budget of EUR 5.3 billion and an annual investment budget of EUR 1.2 billion. The Ile-de-France Transport Association decides on routes and timetables (transport plan), appoints operators and sets fares. Ile-de-France public transport is funded by :

- passenger fares: 38%;

- employers transport tax: 35%;

- public authorities: 27% of which 51% comes from the government, 18% from the region, 18% from Paris and 13% from the seven other departments.

Transport companies in the Ile-de-France benefit from the existing infrastructure.

2.3. *Future perspectives and interactions*

Administrative context of inter-municipality

The representatives of the 1999 local associations are the elected representatives of each of the initial urban areas. A major issue in encouraging inter-municipal co-operation is that of legitimacy. The danger is that integration of the intermunicipal powers increases the potential for power specialisation and structures tend towards general authority over the majority of the inter-municipal territory. This improves efficiency but distances the service from its users.

Mixed transport associations

The SRU law allows for the creation of mixed transport associations. These associations would enable the optimisation of travel policies in urban areas of more than 50 000 inhabitants by co-ordinating the three different organisational levels – regions, départements and transport management authorities. They should encourage development of peripheral urban transport and intermodality. Mixed transport associations could co-ordinate services and provide a passenger information system. They can levy an additional transport tax, within a ceiling set by law. The conditions are still to be established but might include the development of tramways in lower population density areas beyond the urban transport zone.

Ile-de-France

The inclusion of the region in the STIF means that infrastructure (government-region plan) and operating problems are now tackled by the partnership of government and region. The conditions of the partnership still remain to be determined, but government will be pre-eminent since the prefect is the STIF chairman.

Under the SRU law, the Ile-de-France Transport Association can recognise second level organising authorities (new urban area association, municipal association, district) which provide and fund local bus networks in the outer suburbs. After an urban development plan has been drafted, these authorities can ask the Ile-de-France Transport Association to allocate them regular road services within their area. The Ile-de-France Transport Association retains total control of fares. The details for the creation of these second level organising authorities are still to be determined.

Co-operation between associations

Decentralisation has meant that funding now comes from different sources, government grants and co-funding between different institutional levels. The 1992 Framework Act on Territorial Administration made it possible to specify the conditions of co-operation between territorial authorities. This co-operation can be implemented by contract or by the creation of a public organisation. Although too many contracts can lead to confusion, the approach has proved effective with the creation of urban contracts, county and urban area contracts and government-region plan contracts.

The contracts developed by mutual co-operation between the government and each of the regions outline a set of priorities for the period from 2000 to 2006. Sustainable development is one of these priorities, with promotion of an alternative type of long-term development with the creation of sustainable employment, going beyond the single objective of constructing infrastructure. Joint sustainable development projects for the region are also an innovation, whereby regions or urban areas can draw up a contract with the government, from the effective date of the government-region plan contract and up to 2003, for a regional sustainable development project. Urban travel plans which involve several institutional levels can be co-funded.

Public consultation : legislative and regulatory framework

Public inquiries were introduced by law in 1933 and extended by the 1983 Bouchardeau law which requires public inquiries to be more democratic. This has introduced new procedures including public participation in development decisions and guarantees for environmental protection.

Urban travel plans are covered by the Bouchardeau law which states that any project likely to impact the environment must be submitted to public inquiry. The purpose of the inquiries is to inform the public, and gather information on the assessments, options and counter-proposals of a project. The law makes it possible to organise public meetings and makes it an obligation to consult the urban areas which might be affected by the project. The 1995 Barnier law introduced public debate for big projects organised by *ad hoc* committees, prior to the public inquiry. The 1985 law set out the principle of consultation prior to any development operation, to inform the public on the preliminary studies for major projects. This consultation, which can be conducted by public meetings, exhibitions, posters, press information or a public register for comments, does not constitute a local referendum and developers are not bound by the results. The descending role of communication from issuer to receiver is still considered insufficient. Consultation is essential at the time of the preliminary discussions for *policy* development, whilst the public inquiry is a well established administrative dossier on a *project*.

Governance and co-operation : review and prospects

The public inquiry stage has been integrated into the management of large infrastructure and development projects in France for some time now. However, associations have criticised the procedure for not being sufficiently democratic. The objective of the next reform is to make the development process more democratic and transparent, reinforce community responsibility in the assessment of project utility and generally simplify and rationalise the whole procedure.

To develop the urban travel plan in the Ile-de-France, local communities, business and associations have participated to achieve practical implementation of the guidelines. This flexible partnership avoids the issue of geographic responsibility.

There are a number of inherent problems to this approach. Firstly, involvement of many parties is more democratic but can result in dilution of responsibility. Secondly very often only a restricted number of local inhabitants are involved, the objective is to widen the participation as much as possible. Finally, the procedures as they exist are very time consuming (up to 2 years) and expensive, the legal consultation fees are EUR 150 per Ile-de-France inhabitant. However, this is not excessive in comparison with the debate involving the Mediterranean TGV (EUR 1 500 per inhabitant of the urban areas passed through).

3. Policy Framework

3.1. Legislative framework

1982 Domestic Transport Framework Act (LOTI)

The general principles of this law assert the right to a public transport service, define the objectives of an all-inclusive transport policy and allow for the development of urban travel plans (PDU). The government and local communities develop and implement the policy by means of specifically prepared transport development plans. The different public authority levels (region for regional road and rail transport, département for inter-urban road transport, inter-municipal groups for urban transport) organise the public transport service and then delegate to operators. This law does not apply to the Ile-de-France.

1996 Law on Air Quality and Sustainable Energy Use

The objective of this law is for the right to breathe clean and safe air for all citizens. It defines air quality objectives, warning thresholds and limit values. It targets preventing, monitoring, reducing or eliminating atmospheric pollution in order to preserve air quality and in so doing saves and rationalises energy use. Various instruments exist to achieve these objectives:

- regional plans for air quality set the strategies for the prevention or reduction of air pollution (and its effects) to achieve air quality objectives, as well as air quality objectives specific to certain zones. These plans are developed by the region and are audited at the end of five years when they can be revised if necessary;

- atmospheric protection plans are compulsory for cities of more than 250 000 inhabitants to reduce the concentration of atmospheric pollutants within the zone below legal threshold limit values;

- urban travel plans define the principles for the organisation of passenger and goods transport, traffic management and parking in the urban transport zone. These plans are compulsory for urban areas of more than 100 000 inhabitants.

2000 *Urban Solidarity and Renewal Act* (SRU)

This act aims to :

- renovate urban policy by combining planning, housing and transport issues;

- harmonise urban policies by simplifying development procedures;

- promote a sustainable development travel policy through development of the urban travel plan, mixed associations promote co-operation between transport organising authorities;

- give regions a role in regional passenger railway services;

- make regions support municipal policy.

3.2. Urban travel plans (PDU)

Objectives and contents specified by law

Urban travel plans figure in the three major urban transport policy laws. Instituted by the 1982 LOTI, the 1996 Air Quality Law specified the content of urban travel plans and made them compulsory for urban areas of more than 100 000 inhabitants, the 2000 SRU Act reinforced their role.

The urban transport organising authority develops urban travel plans for an area corresponding to the urban transport zone. The government is the urban transport organising authority for the Ile-de-France region.

The urban travel plan defines the organisation principles for passenger and goods transport and traffic management and parking in the urban transport zone. The objective is to co-ordinate all modes of transport, in particular by appropriate allocation of roads and the promotion of less polluting and energy consuming modes. The aim is to sustainably optimise mobility, access and the protection of environment and health.

Urban travel plans must:

- improve the safety of all modes of travel;

- reduce passenger car traffic;

- develop public transport and other economic and environment friendly modes of transport particularly walking and cycling;

- develop and operate the main road network in the urban zone, to make its use more effective, in particular by providing for different modes of transport;

- organise parking on streets and underground;

- reduce the impact of freight transport on the environment;

- encourage companies to favour sustainable transport modes for their staff, in particular public transport and car-sharing;

- set up a pricing and integrated ticketing system.

Under the conditions of the 1983 Bouchardeau Law the urban travel plan is subject to public inquiry, is assessed after five years and can be revised if appropriate.

Experience with PDUs

The objective of most urban travel plans is to reduce car use by a better split of the different modes on roads in particular favouring specific site public transport projects (tramways) cycle routes and measures to reinforce the comfort and safety of pedestrians. In addition to road requalification in city centres, most urban travel plans include projects for new roads, particularly the creation or completion of bypasses around central zones. Inter-modality is also a priority, aiming to smooth the connections between modes. Parking projects include both the creation of park and ride at tramway stations and better management of facilities in the urban centre in favour of residents and visitors, without necessarily increasing supervision. Goods, a new theme in urban transport plans, are included in all documents; although lack of information is a problem, some very innovative action measures have been presented in some urban areas. Mobility plans for companies or communities are an emerging new concept in a number of urban areas. The plans include set objectives for noise and pollution but implementation details remain to be defined. Road safety is included in urban planning.

Urban travel plans have raised the awareness of elected representatives and the general public to the challenges of sustainable mobility, initiating discussion on all modes of transport and on the movement of both people and goods. For the first time, a comprehensive approach has been taken for mobility, linking all modes of transport, walking, cycling, road safety and environmental issues and including new uses of the private car with consideration for the future. The issue is not only about increasing the use of a mode of transport but envisaging the reduction or increase of its market share compared to other modes and improving urban quality and safety. The objective is to improve transport systems without necessarily increasing the services offered or creating new infrastructures. The priority is interaction between modes and harmonising travel and development policies.

Urban travel plans have enabled bridges to be built between different jobs and different authorities: elected representatives, transport organising authority departments, urban services (roads, urban planning…), representatives of local municipalities, public transport companies, parking managers. New powers within organising authorities have emerged (PDU project managers), central administration departments, urban planning agencies and design offices. The law on air quality has accelerated awareness of a necessary link between planning procedures for transport and environmental effects. Co-operation around urban travel plans has emerged as the key issue at the development phase.

Implementation of the plans is in progress and monitoring systems are being set up to enable evaluation of the plans in five years time.

Urban travel plan experience : Ile- de-France

The Ile-de-France urban travel plan was developed on the initiative of the government by the Paris Transport Association (now the STIF), the Regional Ile-de-France Council and the Paris Council. Task forces from other organisations also participated including public authorities, transport companies, professionals and associations. In 2000 the project was the object of the largest public inquiry ever to be conducted in France.

The five-year objectives for the Ile-de-France urban transport plan are :

- a 3% reduction in car traffic over the whole region, differentiated according to the different zones of the urban area, with a 5% reduction for travel within Paris and the departments of the inner suburbs, and between Paris and the other departments and a 2% reduction for internal travel within the outer suburbs and between the inner and outer suburbs;

- a 2% increase in the use of public transport;

- a 10% increase of the share for walking for school trips and for journeys of less than one kilometre;

- a doubling of bicycle journeys.

These guidelines were set at regional level and will be passed down to the local level through local and branch committees.

Influence of the SRU law

The SRU transforms two new strategies into instructions : namely overall improvements in safety for all modes of travel and the setting up of an integrated pricing and ticketing system, these are added to the six strategies set out in the air quality law. The SRU combined with reinforced inter municipal co-operation also contributes to ensuring that travel decisions are taken at the right level.

The efficiency of measures should be increased by the transformation from *transport* organising authority to travel organising authority. Up until now measures for urban travel plans have been limited by the fact that urban planning powers and decisions were taken separately, indeed parking and management of roads currently falls under the jurisdiction of individual urban municipalities. By involving the department and the region, the SRU law also allows the creation of mixed associations between several transport organising authorities to co-ordinate their services. This boosts intermodality over a greater area than that of the urban area itself including peripheral zones.

In the Ile-de-France the SRU law modifies the institutional context:

- the Paris Transport Association has become the Ile-de-France transport association (STIF) which now includes representation from the regional council;

- second level transport organising authorities can be created in the outer suburbs.

3.3. Urbanisation and travel

Legislative and regulatory framework

Neither the 1982 domestic transport framework act, nor the 1996 law on air quality and rational use of energy made any clear provision for urban areas on issues of urban structure, urbanisation and social relations. This resulted in extensive compartmentalisation in transport planning.

The air quality law states rather generally that urban planning documents which define the rights over land (zoning plans for the entire urban area, zone development plans for a district) should respect the guidelines of the municipal urban travel plan. The law also stipulates that the urban travel plan must be compatible with the urban planning development plan. The 2000 SRU act makes more specific provisions. For example it requires the existence of a public transport service as a precondition for the urbanisation of new sectors. Also car parking regulations can be reduced along routes heavily frequented by public transport. Urban planning plans become territorial coherence plans, they must be updated every ten years and submitted to a public inquiry (this was not previously the case). The plans express long term trends in urban planning, social balance and travel for the urban area.

As far as urban planning is concerned, local urbanisation plans set the general rules and exploit restrictions on land use to achieve sustainable development objectives. Local communities are responsible for developing urban planning documents: harmonised territorial plans are developed by a public organisation for inter-municipal co-operation, local urbanisation plans and zone development plans are developed by municipalities or municipal associations.

The development plan for the Ile-de-France is developed by the government. This difference is due to the region's size, capital city status, its economic weight and also its guarantee of regional coherence despite the split into different discrete urban areas. The current plan dates from 1995 and should now be revised on the initiative of the region in 2005.

The main regional plan in the Ile-de-France is divided into compatible local plans corresponding to groups of urban areas. A relatively complex system for harmonising regional level plans (urbanisation plan, urban travel plan) and local level plans (local territorial coherence plans, local urban travel plans) should enable integration of the two levels.

Recent changes in social demand

The lack of legal harmonisation between urban planning and travel policies is also a problem in practice. The split in urban planning responsibility means that it is increasingly difficult to provide for mobility by any mode other than the car in the urban sprawl which accompanies the creation of additional road infrastructures on the outskirts. However, recent developments should reverse this trend. For the past ten years, the development of tramway lines has recommenced in complement or as an alternative to the underground in the largest urban areas and in the Ile-de-France and as the main feature of the public transport network in average sized urban areas. The new tramway lines have provided an opportunity to redevelop roads and are accompanied by urban transformation in terms of property and land values. The close relationship between urbanisation and transport services has become very visible which further encourages policy in this direction. Tramways which are less costly and more visible than the underground become a significant structuring and development factor enabling recovery of the urban fabric.

Speed restrictions enforcing 30 km/h are another visible and popular measure in traffic calming zones, improving safety and noise levels in residential areas. Central districts benefit even more than peripheral housing estates, making the street an important component in the re-qualification of the urban fabric.

89

Issues and problems

The 1996 law on air quality and the 2000 law on urban renewal are too recent to gauge their long term effects and impact on urbanisation processes. In the absence of *ex ante* simulation tools, it will probably take years or even decades to assess the long term effects of urban policies. Although the trend is to reduce compartmentalisation, there are still areas of urban development where transport is a minor factor. The choice of location for social housing programmes is based more on land opportunities than the quality of the available transport service. Commercial urban planning is still awaiting instruments to enable the impact of organisation and distribution of businesses on transport demand to be taken into consideration.

Public decisions are not the only deciding factor in the construction of an urban area. The involvement of private individuals, land and property developers and the general public are also essential and their motivation is essential to take up the challenges of sustainable development. This problem can be seen in the low production of high density individual or semi-communal housing in France. The government introduced zero interest loans to stimulate the building industry, however, these loans do not have sustainable development conditions and conse-quently the grants have favoured low density peripheral housing estates. Much housing is built in the sprawling outskirts of urban areas where sites are cheap. However, developers do not take into account the consequences of distancing and dispersion on the travel budget of households nor on the capacity of the public transport service. Social housing and neighbourhood life are the hardest hit.

There are two areas which represent a challenge to the public authorities and land and property investors:

- the recovery of intermediary districts which include the inner suburbs between the centres and the peripheral districts, often crossed by transport infrastructures; fallow industrial areas and sectors which could be provided with a tramway service and where traffic noise levels currently make living conditions unattractive.

- peripheral urban zones where restructuration is needed to make the provision of a public transport service possible. This often involves difficult choices to be made between the multiple community initiatives.

3.4. Project funding: Government contributions

Government grants for public transport in the provinces

The government has been funding local urban transport organising authorities through public transport development contracts for some decades, contributing to network modernisation and to a significant number of tramway projects. The government has provided not only financial support, but also aid to decision making and technical expertise. Efficient urban public transport has become a popular issue through the willingness of local elected representatives and conclusive results from the first projects (Nantes and Grenoble tramways were put back into service at the beginning of the 1980s).

The government grant system is being updated to include the implementation of urban travel plans and specific site public transport projects. In specific site public transport projects, a distinction is made between underground (which can receive a 20% subsidy) and surface public transport projects (tramway, guided buses on protected sites) which can receive a 35% subsidy. The subsidies are granted for contracts defining the exact nature and level of costs which can be subsidised, with an upper limit of EUR 7.6 million for underground and EUR 3.8 million for surface specific site transport projects. Apart from these grants, the government is encouraging urban communities to conduct pre-operational and feasibility studies on themes such as: restructuring the public transport network, inter-urban links, exchange centres, request services for low demand zones or periods, bicycle safety plans and cycle routes, improvement of pedestrian routes and communication plans. To implement such actions government grants will concentrate on investments linked to the modernisation of transport network operations (vehicle localisation on the network), informing customers (real time information), customer comfort at stops, accessibility for reduced mobility passengers and terminuses. In particular ticketing assistance will be given so that the requirements for ticketing compatibility are met between the different urban, departmental and regional transport companies. All these grants will be subject to the existence of an approved urban travel plan which satisfies all legal requirements.

The government plans to significantly increase the level of financial assistance given to public transport in the provinces to EUR 152 million per year (half for specific site transport projects and half for the other actions of the urban travel plans).

Public transport funding in the Ile-de-France

The government is the main organiser and the main source of funding for public transport in the Ile-de-France. The travel plan contracts drawn up between the government and the region define the main investments. The contract for the current plan (2000 to 2006) has significantly reversed previous trends giving priority to public transport. Over the six year period, two thirds of programmed investment is for public transport infrastructure (EUR 3 350 million) and less than a third for road infrastructure (EUR 1 200 million), this represents EUR 305 and EUR 109 respectively per inhabitant of the region. The priority of public transport action will be to improve suburb to suburb connections to create a linked network around Paris.

3.5. Project assessment

The socio-economic assessment of transport projects reached a peak during the period when budgetary choices were being rationalised and during the advent of econometric methods. Despite the development of macro-economic tools for public policy assessment, transport policies are designed on the basis of transport infrastructure project assessment. Policy assessment is conducted for larger scale national analyses which examine the relationships between factors such as production and consumption, money and saving.

Legal context

Texts and recommendations on assessment are based on the 1982 LOTI which states that transport infrastructure projects costing more than EUR 83 million, must be subject to *ex ante* assessments and *ex post* assessments, one year, three years and five years after implementation. For projects costing less than EUR 83 million or for a transport policy consisting of a large number of small or medium sized projects, no socio-economic assessment is required by law.

Assessment based on micro economic theory

Project appraisal is calculated on the basis of the cost-benefit analysis, which only includes quantifiable monetary costs and benefits for passengers or the community. Pollution prevention costs are used to calculate pollution assessment ratios. Time saving is evaluated with a standard time value which is identical for all citizens. The ratios which are used suggest a very large contribution of time savings in the overall calculation. This, combined with a high discount rate (8%) makes the environmental factor negligible compared to the economic factor. The product indicator (rate of economic and environmental profitability) is thus very sensitive to the standard time value used.

Themes not taken into account

Discussions on phasing or seeking optimal implementation dates are not common. Analysis of the impact of infrastructure on the financial accounts of infrastructure operators or public facilities is often lacking. In classic socio-economic approaches, overall cost benefit analysis can mask important local costs or benefits. Projects should be more multimodal and better account should be taken of competitive and complementary elements between the different modes of transport in the assessment. Projects often concentrate on a single mode. The effects of employment and economic development are also often sidelined. It is easy to assess the impact of a project on direct jobs (construction site operation), but much more difficult to assess its impact on the economic development of corridor regions. The impact of freight transport in terms of traffic volumes and pollution is often lost in analysis. Passenger infrastructure projects are often also infrastructure projects for freight transport. The impact of new road infrastructure is often underestimated, and can be positive with better transport provision and negative with increased pollution. Scientific data on the health impact of transport is too inaccurate to characterise projects. The medium and long term effects of infrastructure on changes in the location of certain activities and on the resulting urban sprawl are not clear and insufficiently taken into account. Finally, the positive or negative impact of transport projects on privately owned or company property values, whether or not the property is located in the neighbourhood of a project, are not included in impact assessments.

Consequences

Firstly, cost-benefit analysis encourages a short term view and overvalues road projects since time is saved in the few years following implementation but less as saturation builds up in the urban area. Secondly, overvaluation of time savings supports projects which save more time for users, in particular radial road links. This leads to favouring projects which encourage urban sprawl. Although the spread of urbanisation can result in high rates of profitability for projects such as roads, there are many external costs which are not included in project assessment, including the direct costs of urbanisation and indirect social costs.

Future prospects

Progress should involve improving assessment tools and making implementation more transparent, particularly traffic simulations and definition of reference criteria. More factors should be included in assessments. For a more complete view of a project the most effective tools are probably multicriteria methods which combine quantitative and qualitative parameters (even if some of these are currently vague). Finally, these assessment methods should remain consistent with urban policy assessment and be integrated into public policy where upstream consultation is critically important.

3.6. Options

There are a number of other options in transport planning which are under discussion and have not yet or only partially been translated into direct action. These include:

- urban tolls to reduce traffic. There is no legal provision for such tolls. A full scale trial is under discussion;

93

- private ownership and funding of urban motorways. There are several private urban motorways in France (Prado-Carenage tunnel in Marseille, East West tangential in Lyon, A14 motorway and a planned section of the A86 West in Ile-de-France). However, experience has shown that it is difficult or even impossible to achieve strict financial equilibrium. There are no tolls on the motorway network in urban areas and therefore charging might be considered to restore financial equilibrium;

- local modulation of domestic tax on petroleum products, with income from such a tax being used as an additional resource to fund public transport. This idea has come from local communities but has so far been refused by the government;

- modification of the Highway Code. Currently fines are decided and collected by the government. For example, for parking offence fines the government receives the money which is then paid into a fund which contributes to financing public transport, particularly in the Ile-de-France. However, local communities cannot set fines to make them consistent with parking costs. France has one of the lowest ratios in Europe between fines and parking fees.

4. Conclusions

Faced with sustainable development issues, public authorities have sought to overcome past inadequacies by developing the legislative and regulatory framework. Transport, housing, urban planning and the environment have been linked to achieve consistency and participation of the population. Various developments are in progress to improve sustainable mobility:

- specific laws related to the objectives and methods of transport planning;

- the development of inter-municipal co-operation and devolution of a number of specific powers to local communities;

- the recently implemented urban travel plans, which are beginning to provide consistent and encouraging results;

- budgetary choices progressively re-oriented in favour of public transport and the re-development of existing highways;

- growing public support (as shown by surveys and debates) for sustainable mobility measures.

The results are all very recent and cannot yet be considered conclusive. There are still a number of negative factors to sustainable development:

- strong trends in daily mobility in favour of the car;

- urban sprawl of the last fifty years, which is unfavourable to public transport and local modes of transport;
- the uneven level of awareness of decision-makers, elected representatives and technicians to the challenges of sustainable development against the other challenges to their responsibilities or working methods;
- low participation of the public in democratic debate as a result of a poor match in the consultation process.

Discussions are under way to prepare detailed reforms which should overcome these problems. In particular, changes will involve decentralisation in funding powers and methods, a more efficient democratic consultation process and better planning methods.

Notes

1. PDU: *Plan de Développement Urbain*.
2. VT: *Versement transport* [transport tax].
3. PTU: *Plan de Transport Urbain*.
4. SRU: *Loi relative à la solidarité et au renouvellement urbain*.
5. STIF: *Syndicat des transports d'Ile-de-France*.

Germany

I.   Introduction

The objective of German transport policy is to ensure mobility. This objective can only be achieved by creating a framework for maximising economic activity whilst minimising traffic, in order to produce a truly efficient, environmentally friendly and socially acceptable transport system. This definition of sustainable mobility is the basis of transport policy decisions.

Transport policy aims to strengthen the transport system as a whole. A key factor in achieving this goal is improving the interplay between all components of the system. Each mode must be able to make the most of its specific strengths. This is the core of an integrated transport policy, supported by a package of regulatory and investment policies, and fiscal and technological measures. Sustainable mobility goals, along with economic, ecological and social considerations, point to a multiplicity of transport policy issues. For instance the strong link between settlement patterns and transport means that regional planning must be designed to reduce the need to travel and increase urban density.

Because of Germany's federal structure, responsibilities are divided between the federal government, the States and local authorities, in accordance with the principle of subsidiarity. As many government tasks as possible are performed at local authority level. One of the key areas of local government is physical planning. Every municipality has the right and obligation to plan urban development and land use within its boundaries.

After an overview of the situation and trends in transport and environment, this review illustrates integrated transport policy in Germany with a number of examples of projects and programmes. The selection is based on the realisation that only a large number of fine-tuned measures can lead to any real improvement in transport systems, in accordance with sustainable mobility goals.

2.   Present Situation and Trends

Mobility in Germany is characterised by the following trends (Table 17):

- a constant number of journeys;

Table 17.   **Selected indicators of mobility, 1976-2000**

	1976	2000
Number of journeys per inhabitant	3.1	3.8
Passenger car ownership	0.3	0.47
Journey time per day	68 minutes	83 minutes
Journey length	8.7 km	11 km

Source: KONTIV.

Table 18.   **Modal split in large cities**
Shares in %

Cities with over 500 000 inhabitants	Local public transport	Car	Walking	Cycling
All journeys	21	44	26	9
Commuting	26	56	12	6
Journeys to school, college, etc.	40	20	28	12
Shopping trips	18	35	40	7
Leisure trips	19	44	29	8

Source: Prognos AG (2001), *Die Bedeutung des öffentlichen Personenverkehrs in Deutschland*, Basle.

- a sharp rise in passenger car density;
- a sharp increase in travel time and the average length of journeys.

One of the main factors behind these trends is the significant increase in the distance between workplaces and residential areas as a result of continuing migration from city centres to the urban hinterland, and of the suburbanisation of workplaces. Consequently, there has been a steady growth in commuter flows and, above all, in commuting distances.

As shown in Table 18, private car traffic dominates in cities with a population of over 500 000. Passenger cars are used mainly for journeys to work and leisure trips. Local public transport accounts for just over one fifth of all journeys, mainly for school runs and commuting. In many large cities (*e.g.* Frankfurt/Main), buses, trams and light rail systems are used for almost as many journeys as passenger cars. In some cities (*e.g.* Freiburg, Leipzig, Stuttgart and Munich), residents travelling into the city centre travel more by public transport than by car. There is a remarkably high percentage of non-motorised transport (walking and cycling), accounting for over one third of all journeys.

Table 19 shows that the significance of local public transport depends strongly on the size of the city.

Table 19.   **Share of residents using local public transport**
in the course of one week

	Percentage of local public transport users
City with over 100 000 population (excluding residential areas on the outskirts)	52
City with over 100 000 population (including residential areas on the outskirts)	28
City of Munich	72
Munich Integrated Transport Association	56
Cologne, Nuremberg and Dresden	46

Source: Prognos AG (2001), Die Bedeutung des öffentlichen Personenverkehrs in Deutschland, Basle.

In general, the larger the city, the greater the percentage of public transport users (Figure 9). However, there are also medium-sized towns and cities that can reach the level of large cities (*e.g.* Weimar), indicating that transport behaviour can be influenced by urban and transport planning.

Figure 9.   **Average and range of percentage of residents using public transport**

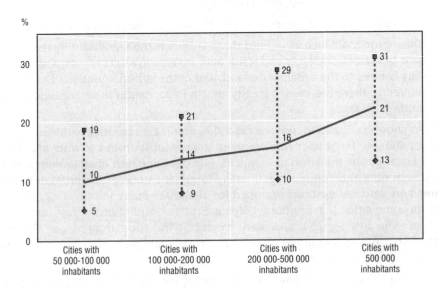

Source: Prognos AG (2001), *Die Bedeutung des öffentlichen Personenverkehrs in Deutschland,* Basle.

© ECMT 2003

Road traffic will continue to grow in the foreseeable future. The federal government's Transport Report 2000 states that between 1997 and 2015, passenger traffic will grow by 20% (passenger road traffic by 22%) and freight traffic by 64% (freight road traffic by 79%). The causes include the globalisation of markets, European integration, the expansion of trade with Eastern Europe, as well as changes in production and consumption patterns. The interaction between transport trends and settlement patterns (characterised by suburbanisation) is also contributing to traffic growth, along with lifestyles adapted to these trends (notably individualisation), as well as forms of leisure and tourism that involve long distance travel.

Efforts to reduce the transport emissions of carbon monoxide (CO), hydrocarbons (HC) and oxides of nitrogen (NO_x) have been very successful. Between 1991 and 1999, CO emissions were reduced by 53%, HC emissions by 60% and NO_x emissions by 28%, despite the growth in traffic. A further significant drop in these emissions is likely by 2010.

High levels of particulate (PM_{10}) emissions from road surface, tyre, brake pad and clutch lining abrasion and from swirl, continue to be a problem. In recent years, the only significant reduction has been in the mass of engine emissions, though not the number of particles in exhaust emissions, which is probably more environmentally relevant. Ultrafine particulates, although not predominant in terms of weight, are worrying for health reasons.

Transport energy consumption continues to pose a challenge. As a result of the growth in road transport, the share of transport in final energy consumption rose by 3.4 percentage points between 1991 and 1999. Carbon dioxide emissions from transport rose by 10% between 1991 and 1999, with an increase of 13% for road transport. Transport's share of total national CO_2 emissions rose from 17% to 21%.

One positive trend is that in 2001, gasoline consumption was 3.5% lower than in 2000 (when it dropped by 5%), while diesel consumption stagnated. On balance, the result is a reduction in CO_2 emissions. In addition, over four years, the number of newly registered vehicles with a standard fuel consumption of 6.5 litres/100 km has risen from 13.5% to almost 40% as a result of the greater share of diesel fuelled vehicles, improved propulsion technology and vehicle engineering, and weight reductions due to new materials.

Despite recent tangible technological improvements in noise emissions from transport, there is still a high level of noise pollution from road, rail and air transport. Any improvements are offset by the continuing growth in the volume of traffic. Almost two thirds of all Germans are annoyed by road traffic noise, around one quarter by rail traffic noise and one third by aircraft noise. Traffic noise has a range of effects: it hampers verbal communication, impairs rest and relaxation, disturbs sleep and leads to reduced performance. For just under 16% of the population, road traffic noise may even be a health risk.

Land used for settlement and transport currently covers around 12% of the total area of Germany. As a result of greater infrastructure requirements (transport and leisure facilities, housing) and demand for commercial building land, it is growing by about 430 km^2 annually. Land for housing, trade and services makes up most of this increase, along with green spaces, leisure and recreational facilities, whereas the growth in the amount of land used for transport purposes has slowed in recent years.

The steady increase in the amount of land used for settlement and transport purposes has many negative impacts. Important habitats for flora and fauna are lost, soils are degraded, the fragmentation and reduction in size of habitats reduces the diversity of species and biotopes, groundwater is more vulnerable to pollution and, because less precipitation percolates into the ground, it is more difficult for groundwater supplies to be replenished.

Between 1991 and 2000, the number injured in road accidents fell from 385 000 to 382 947, and the number of fatalities fell from 11 300 to 7 503. Given the sizeable increase in traffic, this good result can be credited to the road safety activities of the federal Government and the other partners involved. Nevertheless, accident figures are still too high, especially on roads, and this remains one of the main challenges facing transport policymakers.

3.   Overall Strategy for Environmentally Acceptable Urban Transport

Because traffic growth was for a long time taken for granted, public and private sectors concentrated on technological and organisational measures designed to limit its negative impact. Since the 1990s, however, more and more people have become convinced that the causes of transport demand and traffic growth also have to be addressed. The overall strategy to solve transport problems, which is also relevant at the local level, comprises the following components, which complement one another and should be implemented together:

- reducing the need to travel;
- shifting traffic to more environmentally friendly modes of transport;
- improving transport operations;
- introducing fiscal incentives and user charges;
- improving environmental protection;
- promoting new technologies and alternative fuels;
- enhancing road safety;
- carrying out mobility research.

3.1. *Reducing the need to travel*

Reducing the need to travel means containing the volume of traffic, or at least its increase. It involves tackling the causes of traffic, *i.e.* transport demand, by eliminating journeys altogether (*e.g.* empty trips for heavy goods vehicles) or shortening them. Dense and mixed-use urban patterns can help, and greater interaction of land use and transport policies can shorten journeys.

Innovative mobility services can also reduce traffic flows, especially road transport. This includes, for instance:

- making better use of existing road haulage capacity and reducing empty running, for instance by applying telematics for freight and fleet management and modern logistic concepts for commercial transport;

- company plans for reducing the volume of freight traffic, business trips and commuter travel;

- mobility management (comprehensive and accessible information on all mobility options);

- car pool and car sharing programmes.

Integration of regional and transport planning

Regional development and transport are linked. Towns and cities are the nodal points of transport networks. Transport links and accessibility are the most important locational factors. Modern industrial and service societies based on a high degree of division of labour are inconceivable without efficient transport. Traffic growth is the result of a growing division of labour between sites, where the best use has to be made of each site's suitability for housing, workplaces, shopping, education/training and leisure facilities. This is a precondition of increasing prosperity, but at the same time it means growing land and energy use. Greater travel speed and distances promote spatial separation of residential areas and places of work, of shopping centres and recreational areas. Land price differences, pollution, and the trend towards more individual lifestyles and smaller households are also driving forces behind this process and also result in new transport requirements and traffic flows.

Polycentric settlement patterns and compact cities

In Germany, there is a broad-based consensus between the federal government and the States on the objectives for regional development. The aim is a balanced, diverse and polycentric settlement pattern. The model at local authority level is the mixed use compact city, well developed city centres with settlement and development patterns that can easily be served by public transport.

101

Responsibilities of the federal government, the States and local authorities

In Germany, spatial planning reflects the federal structure. In a graduated system of responsibilities, the federal government only has a framework responsibility for regional planning, except for significant infrastructure planning, such as federal motorways and highways, the rail network and federal waterways, for which it has sole responsibility. The States translate the general concepts and principles of the federal Regional Planning Act into concrete regional programmes and plans. Subregional plans specify the contents of the regional plans for the individual regions of a State.

Translating general planning concepts and objectives into concrete land use plans is the responsibility of local authorities as part of their self-government and planning autonomy. Local spatial planning (development planning) is subdivided into a land use plan (preparatory development plan) for the entire municipality and local plans (binding development plans) for single, delimited construction areas. The principles and rules governing development planning have been standardised. The federal Building Code stipulates that local development planning must be adapted to the objectives of regional planning at federal and State level and subregional planning. Municipalities also have a say at the level immediately above them, *i.e.* subregional planning.

Through cross-sectoral, cross-cutting overall planning, each local authority reconciles the multiplicity of private and public interests. Overall spatial planning is complemented by a number of sectoral spatial plans dealing with sectoral problems and tasks, for instance, local transport planning and environmental protection.

The 1993 Guidelines for Regional Planning drawn up jointly by the federal government and the States call for the road traffic pressure in urban areas and corridors to be relieved by shifting to railways. They state that in urban areas with dense traffic, priority should be given to transport modes with large mass transit capabilities (buses, trams and light rail). The amended 1998 Regional Planning Act states that by allocating and mixing land uses such as residential areas, workplaces, and shopping and recreational facilities, land use should be shaped to reduce traffic, though all areas should remain accessible.

New forms of co-operation, public participation and Local Agenda 21

New forms of co-operation known as public-private partnerships are appearing because local authority plans are ineffective without feedback from the private sector. Interest groups and individual members of the public have many opportunities, backed up by law, to participate in local planning. To ensure that their interests are given more attention, citizens frequently form action groups. This leads to wider public discussion, forces municipalities to become more citizen-oriented and review project implementation approaches.

New and longer term forms of co-operation between local authorities and citizens have been introduced since the 1992 UN Earth Summit. The councils of around 1 650 German urban areas have adopted local sustainable development programmes formulated according to Local Agenda 21. Institutions, local organisations and citizens discuss for instance land use, climate change, energy, mobility, sustainable consumption, local development co-operation, and sustainable regional trade and industry.

Co-operation between cities and their urban hinterland

Urban areas can help contain or control migration from city centres to the urban hinterland. Co-operation across local authority boundaries makes it possible to pursue common land reserve policies and develop settlement centres. Closer co-operation between city centres and urban hinterland communities is required for designating trading estates and residential areas, providing local public transport, and planning and operating public utilities. Regional State and sub-regional planning can help strengthen medium-sized urban centres in the hinterland of large cities which have good public transport links.

In many areas, urban redevelopment is now given priority over development of greenfield sites. Numerous examples of renewal of city centres, infill development, conversion of derelict industrial sites, re-use of former military sites for civil purposes and denser new housing illustrate the potential inherent in such redevelopment.

Mixed use development

To re-establish the mixed use development customary in the past to shorten journeys, reduce traffic problems and enhance social integration, three tasks are necessary:

- preserving remaining mixed use developments;

- providing new functions (employment, services, leisure facilities) to single use areas such as large housing estates;

- applying the concept of mixed use development to new projects.

103

The Bremen-Hollerland settlement: an example of car-free housing

By designing a residential area without the usual parking spaces per housing unit (0.8 to 1), it is possible to do without 140 to 180 parking spaces in a development with 210 housing units and 30 spaces for vehicles belonging to visitors, disabled people and car-sharing schemes. This is equivalent to an area of around 5 000 m². Though space could also be saved by constructing an underground car park, a monthly rent of at least EUR 100 would have to be charged, showing that conventional underground car parks are cross-subsidised by the rent charged for housing. In Bremen, construction costs are reduced by 6 to 8% and the same building density uses less land.

Pilot Project: Stringent Environmental Standards in Local Public Transport Competition

This pilot project launched by the federal Ministry of the Environment is designed to demonstrate that competition for local public transport services and environmental standards are economically compatible. It is directed at authorities responsible for public transport who wish to include environmental standards in calls for tenders for local public transport services, and at local public transport operators who, in the run-up to competition, wish to apply stringent environmental standards. It promotes the procurement of a minimum of five and a maximum of fifty new standard buses meeting exhaust emission and noise standards that are as stringent as possible. Only the best concepts (including contents and organisational structure) receive investment assistance. Organisational, economic and legal advice are provided as the concepts are implemented. An overview and appraisal of all the concepts submitted, plus the results, are published.

3.2. Shifting to more environmentally friendly modes of transport

Local public transport

Every day, 26 million passengers use local public transport in Germany, avoiding around 18.5 million car journeys. However, the quality of local public transport can and should improve. For this reason, the federal Government is calling for the State and municipal authorities responsible for planning and organising local public transport as well as transport operators to provide products and services that are more customer-centred.

Operators should provide innovative products and services to extend their market and attract new groups of customers, notably through fleet modernisation (low-floor vehicles, air-conditioned buses, trams and light rail vehicles, lightweight and low-cost rolling stock for local and regional passenger rail services). In addition, measures that speed up traffic (*e.g.* traffic signals that give priority to public transport) should be implemented systematically. There is further scope for improvement, notably by improving links between transport modes (*e.g.* integrated regular-interval timetable), providing comprehensive customer information (*e.g.* real-time intermodal passenger information), creating a compatible, customer-centred fare system, and guaranteeing safety, security and cleanliness. Increasing competition in local public transport can improve service. The opportunities presented by competition, such as improvements in efficiency and quality, can also be used to enhance environmental protection.

Local and regional passenger rail services

Since regionalisation in 1996, the provision and funding of local and regional passenger rail services has been a responsibility of the States. The public transport authorities designated by the local public transport State law agree with railway undertakings on the services to be provided, their quality and pricing, while transport operators decide other practical matters for service provision. Since regionalisation, the co-ordination and quality of transport services have improved significantly in terms of the rolling stock, and the frequency and regularity of services.

One of the major objectives of railway reform was to introduce competition to improve efficiency. Competition puts pressure on the costs of rail service providers and, in doing so, increases the economic efficiency of local public transport. Non-discriminatory access to the rail network for all railway undertakings has created the legal basis for competition on the railways.

Local Authority Transport Infrastructure Financing Act

One of the major tasks of the State is to provide a modern and efficient transport infrastructure. In this context, local public transport is one of the most important tools for integrating urban development and mobility. Within the framework of the Local Authority Transport Infrastructure Financing Act, the federal Government grants the States investment support to improve municipal transport. This means that specific investment assistance is provided on a uniform basis throughout the country. It is used not only for fleets, but also infrastructure

105|

Karlsruhe: an example of an attractive light rail system

The light rail system links Karlsruhe city centre and its urban hinterland, using Deutsche Bahn AG tracks, creating a through-service on which passengers do not have change. A large number of additional stops have been created in the hinterland communities, meaning the system also provides transport within the community. Since 1980, the network has expanded from 75 to 135 kilometres and the number of passengers has grown significantly. In 2001, as a result of index-linking, the States received regionalisation funds totalling around EUR 7.7 billion from the federal Government's fuel duty revenue. The funds were allocated to new transport services – especially local and regional passenger rail services – and for investment to improve the quality of local public transport services

---

(*e.g.* construction and upgrading of transport infrastructure, stops, and park and ride facilities).

Of the funds made available by the federal Government (EUR 1.64 billion), 80% are allocated to the federal States using a fixed formula. Individual States decide how the funds are spent on the basis of local priorities. The assistance covers up to 75% of eligible costs. Some 20% of the funds are reserved for a special programme designed by the federal Ministry of Transport, Building and Housing on the basis of proposals and consultations from the States and updated annually. Funds from this programme can be used to provide financial assistance to railway infrastructure used for local public transport in and around urban areas, covering up to 60% of eligible costs of over EUR 50 million providing the rest is covered by States and local authorities.

Promoting non-motorised transport

Measures to encourage cycling and walking are a key factor in improving urban quality of life. Cycling and walking are the most efficient and environmentally friendly ways of covering short distances. It is up to those responsible "on the ground" to adopt appropriate strategies in the field of urban and regional development to create favourable conditions for non-motorised transport. Examples of good practice include self-contained and safe cycle track networks, traffic calming schemes and pedestrian precincts.

In Germany, cycling accounts for around 12% of all trips, with an annual average of around 300 kilometres per inhabitant, though these figures could increase, as shown in neighbouring countries. In the Netherlands, for instance, cycling accounts for around 27% of all trips, and as much as 40% in some urban areas. In Germany, the aim is to significantly increase the number of cycling trips over the next ten years to relieve congestion in city centres, improve the quality of life and promote cycling as an enjoyable and healthy means of travel. In addition, the bicycle industry and trade, which consists predominantly of small and medium-sized enterprises, contributes significantly to growth and employment. Last but not least, good cycling facilities will help to make Germany more attractive as a tourist destination and promote less developed but beautiful regions. A first national cycling plan is being developed to pool and co-ordinate federal, State and local measures.

Fiscal incentives

The federal government has changed the system of tax refunds for journeys to work. Since January 2001, the mileage-based flat rate has been replaced by a distance-based flat rate which is the same for all means of transport. This has put an end to the preferential treatment enjoyed by car users and has provided an incentive for them to switch to other means of transport.

Linking the different modes of transport

One of the major elements of an integrated transport policy is the linking of modes of transport. For passenger transport, it can help to improve the division of labour and enhance efficiency. If sustainable mobility is to be achieved, rivals have to become allies who make the most of the advantages inherent in their systems. Linking focuses on two elements:

- intermodality, i.e. optimising transport interfaces;
- inter-operability, i.e. harmonising operating conditions of individual modes (e.g. between different rail systems in Europe or between different integrated transport associations that provide local public transport services).

Integrated journey chains in passenger transport are designed to optimise the means of transport in terms of cost and performance. In local public transport, linking modes of transport means, among other things, that residents on the periphery of conurbations can switch to public transport. The principal way of achieving this is by providing park and ride facilities at local public transport stops. What is also important is the connection of local public transport and mainline rail services, and cycling facilities and local public transport/mainline rail services (boarding bicycles on trains, rapid transit systems and buses; bicycle parking at stations and local public transport hubs). In innovative pilot projects, park and ride facilities are combined with modern information systems that provide motorists with information about the arrival and departure times of public transport services while the motorists are still on the road, thereby increasing the incentive to switch to public transport.

Telematic applications

Telematics have so far focused on road transport. On federal motorways, traffic control systems help reduce accidents and congestion. Since the autumn of 1997, automated real-time traffic information has been broadcast nation-wide – as in almost all other European countries – by means of the digital Traffic Message Channel. Individual traffic information and route guidance are common in passenger cars. Dynamic car park guidance systems are standard in almost all large cities.

In local public transport, too, there are many instances where transport telematics are widely used. Almost all major transport operators have long been using computerised operational control systems in local public transport. In many regions, electronic local public transport user information systems are in opera-tion. The DELFI project (a country-wide electronic timetable information system), sponsored by the federal Ministry of Transport, Building and Housing, provides information for journeys beyond the borders of the various integrated transport associations and combines information on local, regional and long-distance ser-vices. The scope for facilitating journey chains (*e.g.* intermodal electronic seat res-ervation systems and electronic ticketing) has by no means been exhausted. Another example is introducing smart card ticketing in local public transport. In addition to business management aspects, telematic applications in local public transport are therefore part of a comprehensive marketing strategy designed to improve customer service.

A recent study conducted by Prognos AG on behalf of the federal Ministry of Transport, Building and Housing provided impressive evidence of just how important information and communications are compared with the hardware (infrastructure and rolling stock). The research project centred on the potential effectiveness of transport telematics in improving the use of transport infrastruc-ture. In a favourable scenario – assuming appropriate co-ordination for the deployment of transport telematics to achieve standardisation and interface optimisation – local public transport passenger growth rates can reach 10% as a result of motorists switching to public transport, and peak journey times could be reduced by 6% using vehicle-activated traffic signals with optimised control algorithms. These findings underline the importance of telematics in solving urban mobility problems.

3.3. Improving transport operations

Shifting existing traffic plays a major role in sustainable urban mobility, as does the improvement and optimisation of transport operations, for instance by traffic calming measures. Selective measures, such as the pedestrianisation of city centres, were supplemented in the 1980s by extensive traffic calming programmes.

Buxtehude: an example of extensive traffic calming

The concept is based essentially on the area-wide introduction of a 30 km/hr speed limit, supplemented by a small number of traffic control and structural measures arranged so their sequence and interaction cause motorists to drive more smoothly and slowly. Noise and air pollution have been significantly reduced. The extensive traffic calming scheme has resulted in environmental and quality of life improvements, promoting a sense of local identity. The traffic-calmed areas have become much more attractive than the other areas of the town. Walking and cycling have become easier. On the whole, this concept has resulted in a change in the way in which transport is used. Residents are making more local journeys and have rediscovered their neighbourhood.

Spaces reserved for cars are converted into vehicle-restricted areas and reclaimed for pedestrians, cyclists or local public transport, enhancing the attractiveness of residential areas and reducing traffic. The structural redesign of roads is often combined with speed reduction, creating 30 km/hr or walking speed zones. Such concepts improve local quality of life and also encourage the most environmentally friendly means of transport (walking and cycling).

Traffic calming measures are closely linked to regulations to control and limit traffic. These include comprehensive and area-wide parking space concepts allowing goods vehicles to enter for loading and delivery, while giving priority to residents and reducing traffic from customers and commuters, by limiting and charging for parking.

3.4. Fiscal incentives and user charges

Fuel duties including environmental tax

As a result of the 1999 ecological tax reform, excise duty on fuel is rising by EUR 0.03 per litre each year until 2003, providing an incentive to purchase fuel-efficient vehicles and drive economically. At the same time, the environmental tax introduced selective tax reductions and exemptions. For instance, the fuel duty on liquefied natural gas for motor vehicles has been cut substantially until 2009 and the environmental tax on fuels for public transport has been halved. The tax increase is designed to provide an economic incentive for energy conservation. The revenue is used to reduce pension insurance contributions, unlike previous fuel duty increases which did not compensate by reducing labour taxes or social contributions.

109|

Tax incentive to encourage the use of low and ultra low sulphur fuels

In November 2001 the fuel duty on gasoline and diesel with a sulphur content over 50 ppm was raised by three pfennigs per litre. A second stage on 1 January 2003 imposes the same surcharge on fuel containing more than 10 ppm of sulphur. The use of ultra low sulphur fuel will result in an immediate reduction in emissions from all vehicles, because the vehicles do not have be converted and the effectiveness of catalytic converters and exhaust systems is enhanced and their life extended. In addition, it will facilitate the use of energy conservation technologies which can result in a reduction in fuel consumption of around 20% in the case of gasoline-engined cars, making a major contribution towards reducing CO_2 emissions from road vehicles.

Motor vehicle tax

Since 1986, and to an even greater degree since 1997, motor vehicle tax for passenger cars has been determined not only by engine size but also by pollutant emissions (carbon monoxide, oxides of nitrogen, hydrocarbons and particulate mass) and carbon dioxide (since 1997).

Low-emission vehicles (complying with the EURO 3 emission standard for new vehicles registered after 1 January 2001 and, from 2006, EURO 4) are taxed at a lower rate. Vehicles with higher emissions (more polluting than EURO 1) are taxed at a higher rate. This is designed to provide a fiscal incentive for the manufacture and purchase of less polluting passenger cars and encourage motorists to convert emission-intensive cars or take them off the road. Over 88% of passenger cars first registered in July 2000 already met the EURO 3 standards, and over 42% of these met the EURO 4 standards.

Infrastructure user charges

The federal Government intends to replace the EU-wide system of time-related motorway user charges for heavy goods vehicles that has existed since 1 January 1995 by a new system for levying distance-related motorway user charges (with an emissions-based component), starting in 2003. This system of road charging for heavy goods vehicles is more in line with the user pays principle and is designed to shift traffic to rail and water transport. The charges will be collected automatically, without disrupting the motorway traffic. For occasional motorway users, especially those from other countries, a booking system will be established alongside the automatic system, to pay the charges using conventional means of payment without having to install in-vehicle equipment.

3.5. Improving environmental protection

Technical optimisation for reducing pollutant emissions

In recent years, air pollution from transport has been considerably reduced, primarily through the gradual tightening of the EU-wide emission standards. Over the next ten years, there will be a further significant improvement in traffic-related emissions as cleaner vehicles become more numerous in the vehicle fleet, despite mileage increases.

While emission standards have largely solved emission problems associated with gasoline fuelled cars, there is still a need for action in the case of diesel cars. Despite sophisticated fuel injection technology and low consumption values, high emissions of nitrogen oxide and particulates remain a problem. An even tighter emission standard (EURO 5) is required for diesel fuelled passenger cars and light goods vehicles, to lower the emission levels to the levels of gasoline fuelled vehicles. This will involve the use of effective exhaust after-treatment systems, such as DeNO$_x$ catalytic converters to reduce oxides of nitrogen, and particulate traps to remove ultra-fine particulates. Considerable efforts will also be needed to reduce particulate emissions from abrasion and swirl.

Reducing greenhouse gas emissions

Action to tackle climate change is one of the key issues of environmental policy throughout the world. For this reason, industrialised nations, meeting at Kyoto in 1997, agreed to reduce greenhouse gases by at least 5% below 1990 levels, with this commitment to be achieved between 2008 and 2012. Building on this general agreement, the EU pledged to reduce emissions of greenhouse gases by at least 8% over the same period. Taking into account different national circumstances, the federal Government agreed to reduce its greenhouse gas emissions by 21%, meaning that Germany alone will be responsible for three quarters of all cuts in the EU.

The federal government has set itself the objective of reducing CO$_2$ emissions by 25% below 1990 levels by 2005. Between 1990 and 1999, a 15% reduction was achieved, despite an 11% rise in traffic between 1990 and 1998 because of mileage growth. Transport currently accounts for around one fifth of CO$_2$ emissions. In its Climate Change Programme, the federal government states that the transport sector will have to deliver additional CO$_2$ reductions amounting to 15 to 20 million tonnes. The federal Ministry of Transport, Building and Housing is drawing up a programme of action for achieving this objective, focusing notably on technological innovations and transport choices and driving behaviour of the public. The scope for reducing CO$_2$ emissions if motorists drive in an energy-conscious and environment-friendly way is estimated at 15% at least. This change can also significantly reduce pollutant emissions and traffic noise, and enhance road safety.

If CO_2 emission reduction targets from transport is to be achieved, fuel econ-omy must improve The federal Government expects European car manufacturers (through their association, ACEA) to meet their 1998 voluntary target to reduce average CO_2 emissions from new passenger cars sold in the EU to 140 g/km by 2008. In 1996, EU environment ministers laid down a more ambitious target, stating that the average value should be reduced to 120 g/km by 2010 at the latest. European car manufacturers should take this target as their benchmark when they review their voluntary agreement in 2003.

Improving noise mitigation measures

Germany already has very stringent immission limit values compared with other European countries regarding traffic noise levels for new and upgraded road and railway infrastructure. The federal Government will continue unabated with its efforts to reduce traffic noise.

One of the priorities is reducing night time noise. New regulations are being prepared and in the meantime, a programme of measures for noise abatement on existing railway lines is being applied immediately. The Act on Protection against Aircraft Noise is being amended, notably to tighten noise limit values and introduce night-time abatement zones.

3.6. Promoting new technologies and alternative fuels

Clean fuels and alternative propulsion systems

Conventional propulsion systems based on fossil fuels will continue to domi-nate road transport, especially private transport. Advanced engines, exhaust emission control systems and improved fuels will further reduce pollutant and CO_2 emissions. However, a significant increase in the number of natural gas pow-ered vehicles is likely in the short to medium term, which can contribute to lower-ing air pollution and noise, especially in city centres. Moreover, this increase can prepare for a hydrogen economy. A range of measures encourage the take-up of natural gas powered vehicles (including a reduction in tax on natural gas and liq-uefied gasoline gas used for motor vehicles until 2009). So far, the incentives have mainly targeted local public transport and commercial vehicle owners. In the future, the aim is to focus on private vehicle users. The federal Government is also supporting the natural gas vehicle publicity campaign, launched in February 2000 and sponsored by the gas industry and some car manufacturers.

Pilot projects for the introduction of natural gas as a fuel

Between 1997 and 2001, the federal Ministry for the Environment, Nature Conservation and Nuclear Safety promoted the use of gas powered vehicles in pilot regions. The additional costs involved in the purchase or conversion of almost 3 300 vehicles were funded on a pro rata basis. The publicity around the project encouraged motorists from other locations to switch to natural gas. Demand accelerated the growth of the network of filling stations and improved the range of vehicles available.

In October 2000, the pilot project entitled One Thousand Environmental Taxis in Berlin (TUT) was launched by the State of Berlin and the gas industry. With the proviso that stringent emission standards are met and fuel-saving low-noise tyres are used, financial assistance is granted for the purchase and operation of natural gas powered taxis and driving school vehicles. The gas industry is rapidly expanding the network of filling stations in Berlin. The TUT project is designed to demonstrate that the experience gained in the pilot regions can be transferred elsewhere.

The Transport Energy Strategy (TES)

The TES is a joint initiative launched by the federal Ministry of Transport, Building and Housing, the car manufacturers BMW, DaimlerChrysler, MAN, General Motors Europe (Opel) and VW, and the energy suppliers Shell, ARAL, BP and RWE for the market introduction of alternative fuels. The ministry regards the TES as one of the most important initiatives in the transport sector. From a technological perspective, it is an innovative and forward-looking project. At the same time, it can deliver a major reduction in emissions and energy use from road vehicles, thereby helping to meet Kyoto climate change targets.

A similar initiative, the findings of which are used by the TES, was launched in the United States since 1993: the Partnership for a New Generation of Vehicles programme, which aims to manufacture by 2004 a prototype of a medium car that can be produced at a competitive cost and with triple the fuel efficiency of today's cars. The programme also aims to produce biofuels at the same cost as imported oil.

In the TES, automotive and energy supply industries, with the federal Government acting as a facilitator, have agreed on hydrogen as an alternative fuel that is suitable from a technological, economic and ecological point of view, having the following characteristics:

- it is as independent from gasoline as possible;
- it can be produced from renewable raw materials;

113|

- it reduces the emission of pollutants and CO_2 throughout the energy chain;
- it can be used for a wide range of propulsion systems (*e.g.* internal combustion engines, electric motors, fuel cells and hybrid drives).

Building on this, a joint strategy for the nation-wide market introduction is being developed, supported by the 2002 Clean Energy Partnership Berlin project, which is part of the federal government's national sustainability strategy.

Magnetic levitation

Magnetic levitation is a rapid, efficient and environmentally friendly means of transport up to 300 km/hr in densely populated areas. Compared with passenger cars, magnetic levitation systems reduce journey times, the risk of accidents, energy consumption, exhaust emissions and land use. Compared with air transport, it also has the advantage that city centres can be reached more quickly and could replace short-haul flights altogether. Demand is growing in Germany and other countries for rapid, efficient and environmentally acceptable transport from airports to city centres and for coping with the rising volume of traffic in high-growth agglomerations and between major urban areas.

The feasibility studies for the link between Munich Airport and the main station and for the Metrorapid project in North Rhine-Westphalia (Düsseldorf-Dortmund) are being completed so that the planning process can start by 2003.

3.7. Enhancing traffic safety

Enhancing traffic safety is and will continue to be one of the major tasks of an integrated transport policy. In a transport system that is becoming increasingly complex, accident risks have to be removed and potential safety risks have to be identified at an early stage. In all modes of transport the responsibility of users, transport operators and vehicle manufacturers has to be strengthened.

3.8. Mobility research

The purpose of mobility research conducted in Germany is to support integrated transport policy. Key areas include those outlined below.

A *better understanding of mobility and transport*

This involves studying the dynamics and routines in user behaviour, and the intermodal linking of passenger transport, with special focus on user needs. It also involves identifying factors influencing the use of bicycles in everyday transport, as well as for leisure.

Urban mobility

In Frankfurt/Main, Cologne, Munich, Stuttgart and Dresden, new ways of controlling traffic and connecting different modes of transport using telematics are being tested, with the aim of making urban mobility more sustainable. The research focuses on ideas for making better use of existing transport capacity and limited traffic space.

Mobility and transport

This framework programme is designed to assist not just transport policymakers but also the transport industry in solving increasingly complex transport problems. Innovative transport technologies and new types of transport concepts which are compatible with the objective of sustainable development can also develop for new fields of growth for industry and the service sector, and create highly skilled jobs.

Local Agenda 21: sustainable mobility in towns, cities and regions

The aim of the federal Environmental Agency's project is to develop and test quantified quality targets and indicators, as well as strategies and measures for sustainable mobility. The scope of the project ranges from proposals for improving the statutory parameters of sustainable mobility (draft local authority transport planning act) to implementing examples of good practice for environmentally sound transport (e.g. the pilot walking and cycling project).

3.9. International co-operation

By adopting the European Spatial Development Perspective (ESDP) in Potsdam in 1999, the Member States of the European Union and the European Commission have agreed on common aims for the development of the territory of the European Union. The ESDP lists policy options for sustainable and regionally balanced development. Reducing negative impacts in regions with high volumes of traffic is to be achieved by, among other things, strengthening environmentally acceptable means of transport using tools adapted to local circumstances. For this reason, the ESDP stresses co-operation between national, regional and local transport policies and considers efficient links between the transport networks to be indispensable.

Germany is actively involved in the international debate on how to develop solutions to the problems of megacities. In 2000, the Global Conference on the Urban Future (URBAN 21) was held in Berlin, an event that attracted much international attention. Another major contribution is Germany's participation in the Cities Alliance to promote sustainable urban development (under the auspices of the World Bank and HABITAT programme).

115|

4.   Conclusion

Transport policy faces considerable challenges. In recent years, traffic growth has been mainly on the roads and in the air, for both passenger and freight transport, while rail and waterway transport have not maintained their share of the growing volume of traffic. The federal Government has decided to pursue integrated regional planning, urban development and transport policy, focusing on the causes and effects of the continuing growth in traffic. This is based on the realisation that the current transport problems cannot be solved simply by constructing transport infrastructure, not only because of public funding constraints but also because of land shortages in a densely populated country such as Germany. Nevertheless, investment in infrastructure – and thus federal transport infrastructure planning, in particular – is of paramount importance. However, measures upstream of transport policy which facilitate mobility but also reduce the volume of traffic are increasingly necessary.

The federal Ministry of Transport, Building and Housing will conduct a broad dialogue at all levels on the future of mobility. Associations and organisations representing shippers, the transport industry and transport operators, associations and companies from the automotive industry, the transport and environmental technology sectors, transport users' organisations, environmental associations and organisations, the churches, trade unions and professional associations are invited to participate.

The aim of our dialogue on the future of mobility is twofold. First, it is to create awareness, acceptance and, as far as possible, consensus for an integrated transport policy. Second, the federal Government wishes to establish at an early stage the interests of the social groups, identify potential conflicts and discuss possible solutions with the parties involved. The numerous and diverse enquiries and suggestions concerning transport policy are proof of the great interest shown by our society in questions of mobility.

Italy*

1. The Context

1.1. Geographical and socio-economic characteristics

Italy consists of a long narrow peninsula and two main islands – Sardinia and Sicily. The peninsula is bordered by the Alps and the large plain of the Po Valley in the north and by the Adriatic, Tyrrhenian and Ionian seas on the eastern, western and southern coasts. The country is mainly mountainous or hilly, and only about 20% is flat land. Most of this is located in the Po Valley, known as the north region. Some 45% of Italy's 57 million inhabitants live in this urbanised area which averages 214 inhabitants/km². Slightly less than 20% of the population lives in the centre (190 inhabitants/km²) and the remaining 35% in the south (170 inhabitants/km²).

Italy has one of the lowest birth rates in Europe and a correspondingly ageing population. In the 1990s, only the south had a net natural population increase. In the north and the centre the net balance between births and deaths is negative, though it is compensated by higher immigration. The ratio of elderly people (over 65) to children (under 15) has increased from 62 in 1981 to 122 in 1998. Average family size is also slowly but continuously falling. In 1961, the average Italian household had 3.63 members; 30.2% of families had one or two members and 27% had five members or more. In 1997, the average size was 2.69; 48% of households had with one or two members, while those with five or more members had fallen to 7.7%. This trend has affected the whole country but has been more pronounced in the north.

National wealth has grown considerably since the 1950s. In 1998, average GDP per capita exceeded US$20 000. In 1997 nearly 100% of families owned a car and a television, 63% a video-recorder and 36% a mobile phone (a share which rapidly increased to 60% two year later). However the distribution of wealth is uneven, as average per capita GDP in northern regions is approximately double that in the Mezzogiorno. Unemployment is also very different in the three macro regions: slightly

---

* Report written by Michele Fontana, Department of Public Economics, Institute of Energy Economics, Bocconi University and Andrea Zatti, Istituto Universitario di Studi Superiori, University of Pavia.

more than 6% in the north (with some provinces now close to full employment), it increases to 21.9% in the southern regions, peaking at 30% in the poorest provinces.

The country was affected by the global economic depression of the early 1990s, amplified and prolonged by a serious political crisis from 1992 due to the Tangentopoli corruption scandal. The economy has recovered from this deep recession, with detectable signs of recovery from the end of 1996, to the current phase of expansion. However the system inherited a huge public debt from previous decades, severely constraining current and future economic policies, notably the balance between public expenditure and tax revenue.

1.2. Main characteristics of the transport system

Italy has experienced a considerable increase in both passenger and freight mobility volumes over the past decades. This growth continued despite the economic slowdown of the first half of the 1990s: between 1990 and 1998 total passenger and freight mobility in passenger-kilometres (p-km) and tonne-kilometres (t-km) increased by 19.3% and 11% respectively.

Road transport has the largest market share for both passenger and freight transport. The share of private cars increased continuously and steadily to the beginning of the 1990s, when it stabilised to around three quarters of the total p-km volume. The share of rail transport is low: in 1998 it barely reached 6%. The two other most relevant transport modes are buses (slightly more than 7%) and powered two wheelers (PTW) (9%) (Figure 10). The share of road passenger transport for cars, powered two wheelers and buses, exceeds 90%.

Since the early 1980s, internal freight transport has been dominated by the road with a stable share of more than 70% of the overall annual t-km volume, representing a

Figure 10.   **Modal split for passenger transport, 1998**

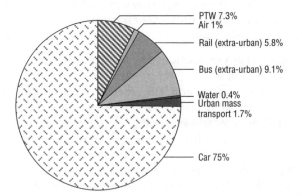

Source: ECMT.

© ECMT 2003

Figure 11. **Modal split of the Italian freight transport volume – 1998**

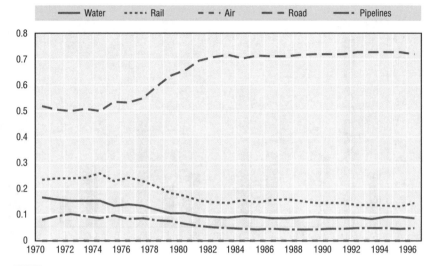

Source: ECMT.

constant corresponding annual increase in the absolute value of t-km transported. This share may be below the real value, since it only includes trips over 50 kilometres and therefore does not take into account most urban freight transport. It is considerably above the Western European average (which is less than 50%). Italy's trucking industry is very fragmented, characterised by a large number of small firms running a few older, polluting trucks. Sea navigation and rail are the other two most relevant modes, accounting for 15% and 10% of the annual volume respectively (Figure 11). Although sea transport has been showing signs of increasing its share, particularly in some southern ports such as Gioia Tauro, the rail system which lost more than half its market share during the 1970s has not managed to regain any significant proportion of the market.

The main feature of transport infrastructure in recent years has been a shortage of supply, which has affected most transport modes and tasks, although to different extents. Road intensity appears low compared to the other Western European countries, both in terms of infrastructure length per head and per square kilometre (Figures 12 and 13). Only motorway supply is slightly above the EU average (Figure 14). Road supply is even poorer when compared against the number of registered vehicles. Italy has one of the highest ratios of vehicles per road kilometre in the whole EU (Figure 15). However, this reflects not only a relatively low supply of roads, but also an extremely high motorization index, the second highest in Europe after Luxembourg. Surprisingly, the density of all kind of roads except motorways is

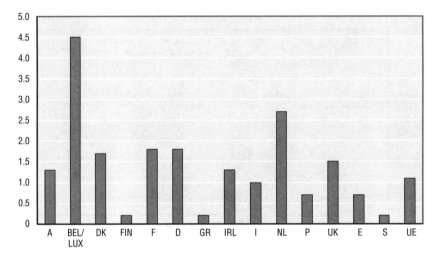

Figure 12. **Road length (kilometres) per square kilometre**

Source: ECMT.

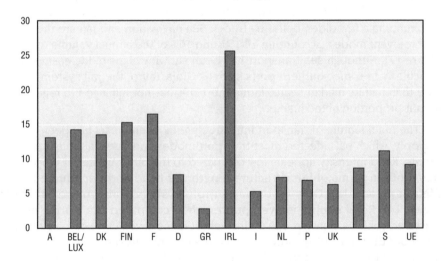

Figure 13. **Road length (kilometres) per 1 000 inhabitants**

Source: ECMT.

© ECMT 2003

Figure 14. **Motorway length (kilometres) per square kilometre in EU member countries**

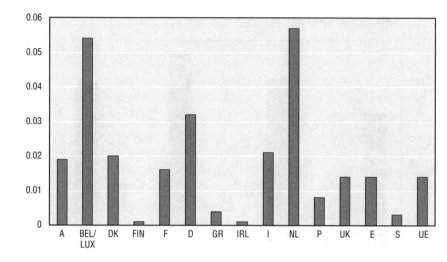

Source: ECMT.

Figure 15. **Number of vehicles in use per street kilometre**

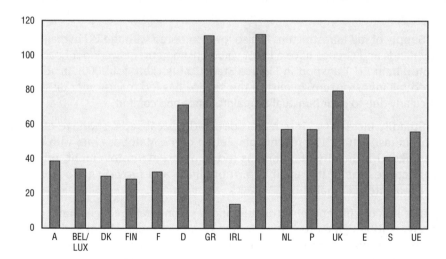

Source: ECMT.

|121|

Figure 16. **Road length per 1 000 inhabitants in north, centre and south of Italy**

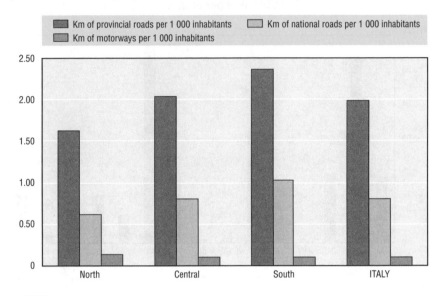

- ■ Km of provincial roads per 1 000 inhabitants
- ■ Km of motorways per 1 000 inhabitants
- ☐ Km of national roads per 1 000 inhabitants

Source: ECMT.

higher in the southern regions (Figures 16 and 17) than in the north, where population density, motorization index and economic activity are substantially higher.

Supply of rail infrastructure is also low compared with the EU average: only the Netherlands and Greece have a lower value of kilometre network per head (Table 20, adapted from EU Transport in Figures Statistical Pocketbook 2000). In addition to a limited rail infrastructure, quality of the service has led to customer dissatisfaction, particularly due to poor punctuality, maintenance and comfort.

Steadily increasing air transport demand has caused a shortage of adequate airport infrastructure. The recent completion of the Malpensa hub with its rail and road links with the city of Milan has led to a partial improvement, relieving the severe congestion of the small airport of Linate and providing the North of Italy with a real international hub.

The lack of efficient infrastructure and resulting traffic congestion (considering the remarkably high motorization index) seem the most critical and urgent problems of the Italian transport system, hindering economic growth and generating considerable social costs. Apart from specific cases of local congestion, the regions that are most affected by the shortage are those in the Po Valley where in the last two years economic acceleration has boosted transport demand.

Figure 17. **Road length per square kilometre in north, centre and south of Italy**

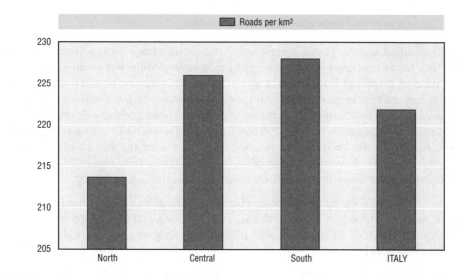

Source: ECMT.

Table 20. **Length of rail network per million inhabitants – 1998**

B	334.3
DK	421.1
D	464.9
EL	238.3
E	312.2
F	539.5
IRL	515.9
I	278.5
L	685.0
NL	178.8
A	696.6
P	279.4
FIN	1 128.2
S	1 253.4
UK	285.0
EU	409.8

Source: ECMT.

2. Key Trends in Urban Travel

2.1. Urban trends and socio-economic characteristics

The Italian state is young compared to most other large West European Countries. For many centuries it remained split into several different small states, each with its own government, currency and capital. This composite historical background has led to a large number of important urban areas, each with its own identity, a very different history and different cultural characteristics. Some 18 urban areas have a population of over 200 000 inhabitants. Nine of them are located in the north (in the Po Valley), two in the centre and seven in the south. Of these 18 urban areas, six have more than 500 000 inhabitants. Only three (Milan, Rome and Naples) have more than 1 million inhabitants in the urban centre.

In spite of the many geographic, climatic, cultural and even linguistic differences, most of the urban areas in the three macro-regions described share some characteristics which have direct and indirect consequences on urban transport and its sustainability:

- the heart of Italian urban areas is usually characterised by a large historic centre that has developed slowly over the centuries, is almost unchanged and represents a valuable cultural heritage and tourist attraction. It has narrow irregular streets, a legacy of Roman or medieval past, making it totally unsuited for intense motorised traffic and easily severely congested;

- like most Mediterranean towns (Table 21), Italian urban areas are compact and population density in the centres tends to be high compared with city centres of northern Europe, with values usually around 7 000 to 8 000 people per square kilometre, peaking over 20 000 inhabitants in residential neighbourhoods.

Urban areas in Italy have experienced the global trend of slow but continuous migration of inner city residents out to the first, second and even third "ring" of outer villages. This trend which has been occurring for about fifteen years seems to have stabilised in some large urban areas (*e.g.* Milan, Genova). This movement has involved young families with children, who cannot afford large flats in city centres and therefore migrate looking for cheaper and greener areas. Inhabitants more reluctant to abandon the central areas includes single adults, couples without children, and elderly people attached to their home and neighbourhood. The consequence of this trend (once again more pronounced in the northern regions) has been a decrease in the number of residents in city centres and an increase of average age, even beyond the national pattern. Despite this trend, the historical centres of all urban areas have generally remained extraordinarily lively, housing the head offices of the most important economic and bureaucratic activities and

Table 21. **Population, car ownership and air quality values in EU urban areas**
Highlighted minimum and maximum values

	Population density (inhab./km²) (1996 or 1997)	Average annual population change (%) (1981-96)	Average household size (1996 or 1997)	Residents over 65 (%)	Cars per 1 000 inhabitants (1996 or 1997)	Days/year of O_3 8-hour average over 120 $\mu g/m^3$
Berlin	3 879	–	1.9	13.7	351	–
Munich	4 257	0.15	1.8	15.1	552	24
Frankfurt	2 626	0.27	1.8	16.0	451	12
Vienna	3 895	0.37	2.1	18.8	364	–
Copenhagen	5 850	–0.23	1.8	15.3	143	0
Brussels	5 890	–0.29	2.1	19.8	463	23
Marseilles	7 271	–1.04	2.5	17.7	385	–
Lyon	8 678	0.23	2.2	16.4	563	–
Bordeaux	4 263	0.36	2.0	17.5	444	–
Madrid	4 722	–0.62	2.9	17.9	464	2
Barcelona	15 225	–0.93	2.6	20.7	414	0
Athens	22 728	–1.28	2.7	16.3	–	54
Thessalonika	22 870	–0.58	2.8	12.6	–	34
Rome	2 180	–0.09	2.5	17.1	658	–
Milan	7 377	–1.10	2.1	20.9	634	–
Turin	7 065	–1.22	2.2	19.7	615	43
Naples	8 854	–0.96	2.8	17.2	630	–
Palermo	4 847	0.37	2.9	13.2	548	13
Amsterdam	4 518	0.05	1.8	13.2	276	–
Lisbon	7 912	–1.79	2.7	18.8	–	–
Glasgow	3 515	–1.19	2.3	17.9	213	0
Edinburgh	1 726	0.05	2.3	17.7	341	2
Birmingham	3.810	0.16	2.5	16.8	–	10

Source: ECMT.

the most prestigious and luxurious shops. They represent a continuous attraction for tourists and for the leisure activities of residents.

2.2. Main urban mobility patterns

The main characteristics of Italian urban areas and major patterns in population dynamics influence mobility patterns. First the volume of daily trips between the city centre and the outer areas has increased continuously in the last decades as in most Western countries. At the same time, the number of trips with origin and destination within the city centre has often decreased in absolute terms, particularly in northern urban centres. This can be explained by the reduction and ageing of the population in city centres. However, this reduction has been more than compensated by the rise in commuting trips between inner and outer areas.

Table 22. **Urban public and private transport volumes (billion p-km) and percentage shares**

	Local public transport	Private transport
1988	17.36	136.57
	(11.3%)	(88.7%)
1989	16.31	152.07
	(9.7%)	(90.3%)
1990	16.18	164.01
	(9.0%)	(91.0%)
1991	16.62	188.1
	(8.1%)	(91.9%)
1992	16.01	202.83
	(7.3%)	(92.7%)
1993	16.15	198.15
	(7.5%)	(92.5%)
1994	15.96	209.06
	(7.1%)	(9.,9%)
1995	15.94	207.71
	(7.1%)	(92.9%)

Source: ECMT.

In addition, there has also been a continuous and substantial increase in mobility volume with both origin and destination outside urban centres, in the outskirts.

In the last few decades urban sprawl has resulted in a considerable rise in mobility originating in outer areas, irrespective of destination. As public transport cannot intrinsically capture this kind of mobility, this trend has resulted in a continuous loss of market share, with a gain for private motorised vehicles (Table 22). Urban public transport tends to offer most services in the urban centres where factors such as the ageing population and its correspondingly lower mobility demand has further contributed to a decrease in both share and absolute volumes of urban public transport measured in p-km.

In many cases this general trend has been reinforced by a poor supply of urban public transport services, both in terms of quantity and quality. Bus lines have been worst affected and to a lesser extent tramways. However, urban public transport has increased its annual p-km volume for metro lines and local railways services (Figure 18), which have proved to be more competitive than buses.

In parallel with urban public transport trends, the private motorization index in urban areas has grown more than the national average, in particular in northern and central towns. The main urban areas have a motorization rate of 600 cars per 1 000 inhabitants and sometimes even higher (Figure 19). Although the motorization

Figure 18. **Urban public transport volumes by mode (1988 to 1996)**

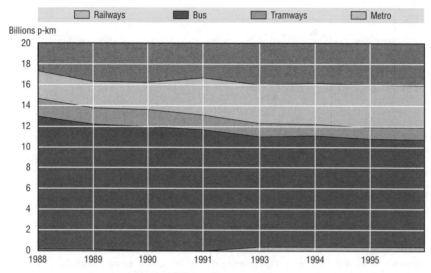

1. Data adapted from CNT; 1992 data is not available.

Figure 19. **Motorization index and per capita income in selected Italian provinces**

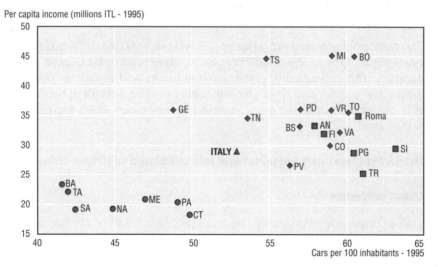

1. Round green circles, green squares and green diamonds refer to southern, central and northern provinces respectively. The green triangle shows the national average. Data sources include ANFIA, 1998 and Istituto Tagliacarne, 2000.
Source: ECMT.

Figure 20. **Average car fleet growth rate and motorization index by Province**

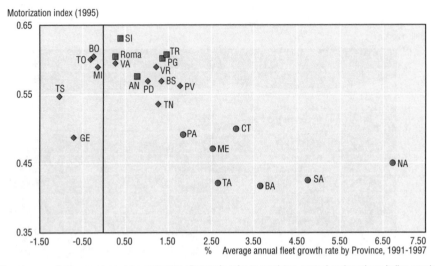

1. Round green circles, green squares and green diamonds refer to southern, central and northern Italian provinces respectively. Data adapted from ANFIA, *Automobile in cifre*, years 1994-2000.
Source: ECMT.

rate is higher in the wealthier regions, it is growing more rapidly in the poorer areas of the south (Figure 20).

The number of powered two wheelers (PTWs) per 1 000 inhabitants (Figure 21) is also much higher than in any other European country (except for Greece where it is comparable). This reflects different travelling habits and consumer preferences, and maybe the warmer and drier climate. It may also be a result of the high levels of traffic congestion in urban areas, where in many cases PTWs are quicker and easier than cars.

3. Urban Problems and Sustainability Issues Related to Urban Transport

3.1. Urban congestion

Traffic congestion is probably the main problem for all urban areas. The progressive, inexorable increase in mobility, in parallel with the continuous shift towards private motorised transport in compact, narrow and usually ancient urban areas makes the problem extremely serious. Most affected are the historic centres, which still attract a large number of daily trips for work, business, shopping, administration, leisure, freight transport (goods distribution to shops) and tourist

Figure 21.   **PTWs per 1 000 inhabitants in north, centre and south regions**

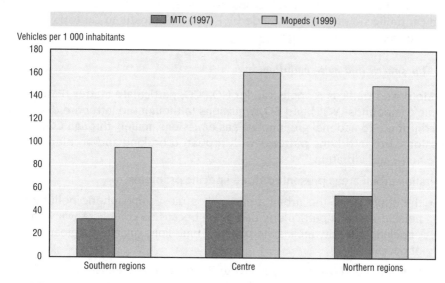

Source: ECMT.

trips. However, in the last decade congestion has also spread to most areas immediately adjacent to the centres and increasingly to the outskirts, where mobility is growing fast.

In addition to slowing traffic flow, congestion causes time losses for users and losses of productivity/competitiveness for the whole urban (or regional) system. Inner areas become completely congested due to a general and severe lack of space. In compact, ancient and densely populated urban areas, a car ownership rate of 500 to 600 registered cars per 1 000 inhabitants, plus the cars which commute and park in the inner area every day, inevitably lead to a vast amount of illegal parking, frequent occupation of pavements by cars and motorbikes, restriction of the usable space in the streets and traffic blockages. Extensive illegal parking also renders pedestrian mobility difficult, if not impossible, for weaker residents such as handicapped people, the elderly and small children. Illegally parked vehicles have become a real (and implicitly tolerated) physical barrier to normal mobility for these people. The further negative aspect of congestion is the additional environmental burden, particularly in terms of increased atmospheric emissions. In the urban context, difficult traffic conditions mean a slower driving cycle and, for most pollutants, higher average emission factors.

129|

A final point is that the high share of passenger transport by PTWs (10 to 15%) makes daily traffic particularly vulnerable to atmospheric conditions. On rainy days when car traffic slows, the trips made by PTWs shift mostly to car trips, causing a sudden increase in traffic congestion.

3.2. *Atmospheric and noise pollution*

Motorised traffic is responsible for NO_x, CO, particulate matter (PM), volatile organic compounds (VOC) and SO_x emissions (although the latter are decreasing) and contribute to national greenhouse gas emissions, mainly through CO_2 and CH_4 emissions. Urban driving patterns with repeated braking and acceleration also cause noise and vibration.

Italian urban areas presented three specific problems:

- the structure of the urban areas makes most atmospheric pollutants and noise emissions particularly damaging because a compact town with a high population density means the polluting emissions can affect a greater number of people;

- as warmer and drier climates favour the evaporative emissions of VOCs and the photochemical reaction that generates ozone, these pollutants (both potentially dangerous to human health) represent a particular threat for Italian (and all southern European) urban areas;

- the large number of PTWs registered and used in urban areas causes a high level of VOC running emissions (in addition to the evaporative emissions), particularly since a significant proportion of PTWs in use (especially mopeds first registered before 1992 or before 1999) have high VOC emission factors.

In addition, the highly urbanised Po Valley has particularly unfavourable climatic conditions, with low wind speed and frequency, and a low average height of the mixing layer, which prevent the dispersion of atmospheric emissions and result in high air pollutant concentrations.

Stricter policies on emissions from new vehicles in the last three decades have contributed to the reduction of air pollution. The most recent estimates suggest that total transport NO_x and CO emissions have been reduced since 1992, in spite of increasing vehicle numbers and the growth in mobility volumes. Transport VOC emissions have also been reduced since 1995, though to a much lesser extent. A decrease has also been observed in some pollutant concentrations (CO, total suspended particulates and NO_x) in urban areas, but it is still difficult to draw definite quantitative conclusions on these trends, due to lack of consistent data over time.

Despite these first signs of atmospheric pollution reduction, in most urban areas, peak concentrations of ozone, PM and CO and some organic compounds (*e.g.* benzene) occur too frequently and are above legal limits, and average daily and annual concentrations still represent a risk for the health of urban residents.

3.3. *Greenhouse gas emissions*

The compact structure of urban areas may offer certain advantages, as fuel consumption and CO_2 emissions are limited. There is a widely accepted empirical rule whereby the higher the urban population density the lower per capita fuel consumption for urban transport. However, in order to fulfil Kyoto requirements, the dynamics of CO_2 emissions must be considered and as the trend for CO_2 emissions from urban transport is steadily increasing, clearly some kind of intervention is needed to limit emissions.

3.4. *Urban transport safety*

In recent years the number of casualties from road accidents has been considerably reduced. Despite this improvement, safety still remains a major problem, particularly in urban areas where about 75% of accidents occur (71% of total injuries and 44% of total casualties). Pedestrians, bicycles and PTWs are particularly at risk. An investigation conducted on the accidents which occurred from 1989 to1990 in two Italian regions (Marche and Liguria) found that of the 11 298 road victims treated in hospital emergency departments:

- 9.8% were pedestrians;
- 7.0% were cyclists;
- 20.5% moped drivers;
- 12.7% motorcycle drivers;
- 50% car drivers.

Only 40% of moped drivers and 90% of motorcycle drivers were wearing a helmet when the accident occurred. Even more striking is that only 18.5% of car drivers had their safety belt fastened. This data suggests that much still remains to be done to further prevent and reduce casualties and injuries from road accidents.

4. Institutional Framework

The transport decision-making and policy implementation process is structured at four different administrative levels: central government, regions, provinces and at the most local level, the municipalities. Many institutional changes have been made since the beginning of the 1990s and are still in progress. Two main driving forces have underpinned these changes: a general trend towards decentralisation of competence, with power devolved to the three lower administrative levels, and an increasing need for reduced and/or more efficient public

131|

expenditure, under the pressure of huge public debt that has to be reduced and will have to be controlled in the future.

4.1. *Role of the central administration*

In the context of these two trends, the central administration primarily takes on a steering role for both transport planning and environmental regulation. The government prepares the General Transport Plan (PGT) which sets out the main objectives of transport policies at all administrative levels and gives general guidelines for the preparation of local plans. Central government has the legislative power to set minimum standards for public transport services and local environmental quality, apply new EU directives and provide general economic and industrial regulation for the transport sector. In addition, central government has direct control over the management, maintenance and improvement of the principal transport services and the infrastructure of the national transport network, and guarantees inter-regional and international communication. Over the past decade, the overall financial contribution of public bodies to the transport sector has been decreasing and this trend may continue with current reforms. The public share of total expenditure in the whole sector declined from 14.5% in 1990 to about 10% in 1997 due to cost cuts and privatisation of some public utilities. Although central government still contributes most in the share of public spending, this proportion has slowly decreased from 63% in 1990 and to 58% in 1997. Several ministries are involved with public expenditure, though in different ways. Formally, the main contributor is the Treasury, providing 75% of the funds in1997. In the same year the Ministry of Transport provided 18%. Other significant contributions came from the Ministry of Internal Affairs (3%) and the Ministry of Public Works (2.5%) which plays an important funding role in urban areas. In practice, the Treasury often acts as a mere executor of funding decisions taken by parliament (on the total amount of resources for specific transport issues) and by the Ministry of Transport (for detailed allocation of these funds within the tasks designated by parliament).

Recently the Ministry of the Environment has also financed some initiatives to support cleaner transport. Though smaller than the amount given by the other Ministries, this contribution is significant as it demonstrates a commitment to play an active and positive role beyond the usual setting of environmental standards and environmental impact assessments for projects.

4.2. *Role of the municipalities*

In the last ten years the priority has been to decentralise both the decision-making processes and financial responsibilities in the transport sector, giving more power to the regions, the provinces and the municipalities wherever transport issues are predominantly local as in urban public transport. After central government, municipalities and provinces have become the public bodies funding the highest share of transport expenditure. In 1997 they supplied 23.5% of total public contribution and this proportion is still rising. At the same time, local bodies are increasingly expected to produce coherent and integrated transport plans, particularly at the urban level. Since 1992, the new Street Code requires all municipalities with more than 30 000 inhabitants to prepare an Urban Traffic Plan (PUT) addressing the most urgent mobility-related problems of the urban area. The PUT was conceived as a short-term tool (it has to be renewed every two years) to tackle urban mobility issues in the framework of available infrastructures. The preparation and implementation of the PUT is financed by the municipalities together with the competent region. The competence does not include financing new infrastructures which until very recently had to be funded directly from the central government through special laws addressing single issues such as parking and new rail infrastructure. Although the PUT only provides a limited range of planning policy interventions it is the first important step towards creating a consistent municipal planning framework. It requires municipalities to give regular thought to urban traffic problems, communicate their plans to the citizens, and introduce an *ex post* assessment of the goals achieved.

The 2000 PGT introduced the Urban Mobility Plan (PUM), a longer-term planning instrument. The PUM has to be prepared by municipalities with more than 100 000 inhabitants (or groups of interconnected municipalities, or provinces, according to the local situation). It covers a ten year period and can provide more structural solutions, with changes in the infrastructure supply. In addition, the approved PUM receives financial support from central government. Each urban area thus has the opportunity to propose and fund an integrated and coherent set of interventions, whilst ensuring that central government can assess and steer local plans according to the most recent PGT general guidelines. The role of the regions is mainly to give more general regional guidelines through the Regional Transport Plan (PRT) and to co-ordinate and harmonise the various plans proposed locally by the main urban areas of the region. The regions also have direct responsibility for managing the railway system. Their share in funding public transport infrastructure and services has also considerably increased over the last decade.

4.3. The ongoing reform of urban public transport services

The ongoing reform of local public transport management is an important example of the trend for decentralisation, matched with efforts to introduce more competition and efficiency in the provision of transport services. A 1997 law amended in 1999 introduced the following main principles:

133|

- local governments – regions, provinces and municipalities – are fully responsible (within the guidelines given by national laws) for planning and regulating urban public transport services in their jurisdictions;

- management of urban public transport companies and local transport planning and regulation must be completely separate. Local transport planning and regulation must be dealt with by local administration – possibly with the help of a newly-created local transport authority, whereas transport company management must be under independent control stipulating a specific contract with the competent administration;

- urban public transport services have to be assigned to independent companies through competitive tendering. All the local public transport utilities have to become limited liability companies, with a requirement to achieve a 35% cost recovery in transport service management.

The 1999 reforming law has still to be applied by most of the local administrations. For instance, at the beginning of 2001 only 48% of the public transport utilities had achieved their transformation into limited liability companies and only 42% of local administrations had drawn up contracts with the providers of urban public transport services.

4.4. *Vertical and horizontal interaction among different administrative levels and government bodies*

Close and co-ordinated interaction between different government bodies of the same administrative level is extremely important to address urban sustainability issues. The diversity of issues involved, such as environmental matters, land use, transport and energy policies and socio-economic problems, requires the competence of many different institutions. A good signal of the intention ministries to work more closely was the co-operation of Ministries of Transport, of the Environment and of Public Works to prepare the GTP. However, such co-operation is in its infancy and more can be done to achieve really integrated long-term transport planning. The financial competence to fund transport sector interventions, particularly at urban level, is still shared among different Ministries. This fragmentation will be reduced as recent legislation will reduce the total number of Ministries from 18 to 12. In particular, the Ministry of Public Works will be merged with the Ministry of Transport, eliminating a source of administrative complexity.

Co-operation among different departments at lower government levels depending on local initiatives still seems poor. Initiatives such as urban mobility plans are improving vertical interaction among different administrative levels and the related interaction between municipalities and provinces (who have to submit the urban mobility plan to central government) and upper levels of government (which assess and possibly fund the plans). However, although "downward" interaction between the central government and local bodies is becoming more straightforward and better structured, it is less clear how local bodies can influence the general objectives of central planning.

5. Sustainable Urban Transport Policies

Greater urban traffic congestion and pollution have obliged all administrative levels and in particular local governments, to adopt and try different policies. There have been proposals for action in urban areas since the beginning of the 1980s. The main actions proposed and/or applied to tackle urban transport sustainability issues can be divided into two main groups:

- action taken at national or more local level to improve environmental and safety performance of vehicle fleets, whether public or private;

- a broader set of policies which bring together measures to control and influence urban mobility patterns, given the state of the fleet technology.

5.1. Policies to improve vehicle fleets

Since 1997, the central government and some local administrations have applied vehicle scrappage incentives and inspection and maintenance (I&M) policies to accelerate the introduction of newer, cleaner vehicles and the removal (or repair) of the older, polluting ones. From January 1997 the government awarded a bonus of US$900 to US$1 200 for each vehicle scrapped, depending on the size (engine displacement) of the replacement car bought. The incentive was conditional on a new car being bought and on car manufacturers/dealers reducing the car's price by an amount equal to the bonus. The programme expired in September 1997 and was extended for four months with a fixed bonus of US$900 for all car sizes, under the same conditions as the first programme. In 1997, about 1 148 000 cars (about 4% of the fleet) were retired under the scheme. In 1998 a second scheme was introduced offering a scrappage incentive of US$600 or US$900, provided that the new replacement model had an average fuel consumption (whether diesel or gasoline) between 9 and 7 litres per 100 kilometres or less than 7 litres, respectively. From October 1997 bonuses were also given if the new replacement model purchased was fuelled with LPG, methane or electricity. A scrappage programme for motorcycles was also introduced in 1998 and renewed in 1999. It has been found that older PTWs (motorcycles and particularly mopeds) are responsible for a large share of atmospheric pollution. In response, some local administrations, often cofunded by the Ministry of the Environment, implemented their own local PTW scrappage schemes. In particular, the municipalities of Rome and Naples have given substantial incentives to scrap older motorbikes and replace them with newer technologies, offering electric two wheelers at competitive prices.

135|

Unfortunately, the schemes did not increase the sales of electric vehicles, as most consumers preferred more traditional engines.

As well as these economic incentives, with the 1998 Decree on sustainable mobility, the Ministry of the Environment requires all local administrations to gradually replace (public) fleets of vehicles with a maximum gross weight below 3.5 tonnes, with cleaner technologies, specifically LPG, methane or electricity fuelled cars. The decree states that 50% of the local public car fleets must be replaced by the end of 2005. However the decree includes no sanctions for administrations that do not fulfil this obligation. This legislation has to be interpreted more as a way to introduce innovative policy tools and set long-term government objectives than a real, strict requirement. In addition to policies to accelerate fleet renewal, since the second half of the 1990s, most local administrations, usually at province level, have introduced local I&M programmes (called "blue dot", "yellow dot", "green dot"... depending on the urban area) for the car fleet in use. These inspections aim to check and reduce atmospheric emissions from cars. They must usually be made once a year, or even once every six months for older non catalytic vehicles in some urban areas. The inspections are additional to the biennial compulsory Ministry of Transport inspections. These local I&M programs probably made a significant contribution to local emission reductions in the first years after their introduction. At that time, the Ministry of Transport inspections only had to be made once every 10 years. With the increasing frequency of MoT inspections, local I&M programs, which are similar to those organised by the Ministry, have become redundant.

5.2. Policies to improve urban mobility

Local measures have been necessary since early 1980s to protect ancient buildings and attractive historical centres from car traffic and congestion. Perhaps the most interesting and strongest attempt in this respect is the introduction of car-free areas.

In 1984, most of the largest urban areas (*e.g.* Turin, Milan, Bologna) held a referendum to ask citizens if they agreed to close the city centres to car traffic. Results indicated a solid consensus for car traffic limitations. From there began a series of long-term ongoing attempts to limit car traffic in the historical areas, usually based on a system of permits to circulate by car in the centre. The permits were given free of charge to a limited number of people who needed them for work or health reasons (*e.g.* impaired mobility). Unfortunately two considerable practical problems soon emerged which hindered the effectiveness of the measure. Firstly, it was too difficult to check and sanction illegal entrance to the car-free areas. This task mobilised too many traffic policemen and was *de facto* unfeasible. Secondly, it was very difficult to find a rational and definite cut off point between those who really needed their car for work/health reasons and those who did not. The problem was delegated to a new office which dealt with permit issue in the municipalities. These offices represent an increasing and substantial burden in terms of time and money for the local administrations and have not been able to handle the problem, as in most cases the number of permits issued is increasing every year.

Since the beginning of the 1990s, two different directions have been taken to try and solve the problem. First, central government has introduced the possibility for local administrations to hire auxiliary staff at short notice to control illegal parking and access to car-free areas. Secondly, it has completed a long and complex institutional process to allow the use of electronic control for car access in urban centres and a corresponding system of cordon pricing. Laws to regulate the use of these electronic devices were approved in 1999. Since then, some towns (*e.g.* Rome, Florence and Genova) have developed their own electronic gate systems, although to date their use has been postponed (in Bologna, since 1995). These technological systems need both a technical validation and authorisation for their actual use in specific towns, the completion of which can take several months, if not years. There is some concern about claims and legal appeals against fines which could be given through these systems and the policy measure may still have to go through a long legal battle. However, at least the law has been finally approved, and it gives a definite and concrete framework for the use of this tool.

GALILEO, a EU satellite system being developed will enable accurate positioning services under civilian control. This might have several important traffic management applications including the implementation of more complex urban road pricing systems.

It has become clear that other pricing instruments such as parking fees, could be very useful, if not indispensable to influence and limit car traffic in addition to the use of car free zones in inner urban areas. After a slow start in implementing this policy tool compared with many northern European urban areas, Italy has rapidly caught up, particularly in historic city centres. At the beginning of 2000, more than 80% of municipalities had applied parking fees all over their historical centres. In the largest urban areas, implementation of this policy is being extended to areas adjacent to inner centres. A few urban areas have also proposed to introduce annual parking charges for residents – who up to date have been exempted from these payments in most urban areas. This proposal has encountered strong opposition and has been implemented only in a very few cases (*e.g.* Padua, Pavia).

A third main group of measures addressing urban mobility concerns action undertaken to improve and support local public transport. In addition to urban public transport reform, the wide spectrum of local action affecting the quality and quantity of urban public transport supply and the public/private urban modal split makes any comprehensive generalisation difficult. Firstly, there are many new urban public transport infrastructure developments in progress in the main urban areas, in particular for rail (metro, tramways and railways) and to a lesser extent, the construction of new park and ride facilities in the outskirts of urban areas to support public transport for access to the inner urban area. Secondly, many small, but important measures are being undertaken to improve the quality and the attractiveness of existing urban public transport lines: for instance a wider use of intelligent technologies that interact with the customers (real time information at urban public transport stops, development of a centralised system for traffic-lights with priority for public transport, etc.); an extension of the lanes dedicated to urban public transport and the development of new attempts to capture mobility demand with innovative transport services (*e.g.* "bus-on-demand"). Finally, the simplification of public transport fares in larger urban areas, together with the integration of these fares across different modes (*e.g.* urban public transport with railways) and sites (urban with extra-urban public transport services) is also under way in most of the larger cities.

Urban public transport volumes appear to be increasing in some large urban areas, after many years of continuous decline. Although this is an encouraging, it may be only due to the general improvement in the economy and the consequent increase in mobility. It is still too early to see significant results of the changes mentioned above in terms of urban public transport volumes and shares of urban mobility. Nevertheless, the high number of changes under way encourage a more optimistic view for future developments.

6.   Conclusions

It is difficult to summarise and assess the "state of the art" of sustainable urban travel policies in Italy: the country offers quite a complex panorama, with considerable differences among the three macro-regions (north, centre and south) and also among urban areas within each region. Moreover, at the moment the policy and regulatory framework is continuously changing: many institutional changes are under way at both local and national level.

Nevertheless, some general points are valid for the whole country. The urban structure of Italian cities – compact, very densely populated and with large historic neighbourhoods where traffic is difficult – together with a high urban motorization rate (up to 600 cars per 1 000 inhabitants in the northern and central regions) make urban congestion and its negative consequences particularly severe. Urban congestion itself leads to higher polluting emissions from motorised transport. Finally, the high population density is likely to cause a greater health impact per emission unit released by transport. Quite substantial and consistent efforts have been undertaken in the last 10 to 15 years to improve this situation.

Many measures have concentrated on the introduction of various kinds of technological improvements. The central and some local governments have implemented vehicle scrappage schemes and enhanced I&M programs trying to accelerate fleet renewal and eliminate dirtier vehicles (cars, motorcycles, buses). These actions have met with some – modest – success. Several local governments have also recently supported the introduction of new technologies for traffic management: e.g. centralised traffic light systems, real-time information on urban public transport, electronic gates to control car access to urban centres. Finally, the country has put forward the development of a new European satellite system, GALILEO, that could have several applications in the field of transport management and could address pollution and safety problems.

While there have been partial improvements in (atmospheric) pollution in the last decade, with a reduction in the overall emissions of some pollutants (e.g. CO, SO_x, and to a lesser extent NO_x) congestion has not improved at all. It is perceived as the most critical problem by urban residents.

In trying to tackle congestion problems, various attempts to limit car traffic in urban areas have been made, starting with pedestrian areas (in some towns during the 1970s) and daily traffic bans and circulation with alternate plate numbers (during the early 1980s), to the implementation of car-free zones and extensions of pedestrian areas, mainly in historical urban centres. Italy is also relatively ahead in Europe with road pricing experiments – on motorways – and cordon pricing attempts (though still not applied, cordon pricing systems have been set up and are now ready in Bologna and Rome). Although congestion problems have not been solved, extensive and useful know-how has been accumulated.

In recent years considerable efforts have been made to invest in urban public transport (especially rail) infrastructure and improve the efficiency and quality of services through the institutional reform of urban public transport services. The objective is to reduce public spending in urban public transport management while at the same time making public transport services more competitive and attractive for users. The reform – approved in 1997 and amended in 1999 – introduces the concepts of privatisation of urban public transport companies and liberalisation of the services (through competitive tendering), and imposes a minimum level of cost recovery. This represents a fundamental innovation for the whole system. It is however too early to judge what the results these changes have brought.

Besides this positive experience and these innovative changes, some policy tools have been developed belatedly and slowly. Systematic planning of urban transport management and infrastructure development was only introduced during the 1990s – later than some other European country. The preparation of an urban traffic plan only became mandatory in 1992 and the first urban traffic plans completed in 1994. Urban traffic plans are limited in their scope, as they are short-term plans based on existing infrastructure. Longer-term systematic planning for urban transport (the urban mobility plan) was introduced in 2000, along with urban traffic plans.

The horizontal co-ordination between different sectors of the administration needs to be developed further, both at local level and at the level of the central government. As stated in the urban traffic plan, sustainable urban transport competence is share by the Ministry of Transport, the Ministry of Public Works and the Ministry of the Environment. A law has been recently approved that will merge the competence of the Ministry of Public Works and the Ministry of Transport in this area, although concrete implementation may take some time.

References

ANAV, Federtrasporti, Federtrasporto, Fenit (2000), TPL 2000 – *Monitoraggio dello sviluppo del trasporto pubblico locale*, No. 1 – Maggio 2000.

ANCMA (2000) Internet site www.ancma.it/, Milan.

ANFIA (1992 to 2000), *L'automobile in cifre*, Torino.

ANPA (1999), *Émissioni in atmosfera e qualità dell'aria*, Roma.

ANPA (2000), *Le emissioni in atmosfera da trasporto stradale*, Roma.

ECMT (1999), *Cleaner Cars: Fleet Renewal and Scrappage Schemes, Guide of Good Practices*, European Conference of Ministers of Transport, Paris.

European Commission (2000), EU *Transport in Figures – Statistical Pocketbook*, 2000, Luxembourg.

Federtrasporto – Centro Studi, Bollettino economico sul settore dei trasporti (1999), *Efficienza e Sussidiarietà: il Trasporto Locale dopo la Riforma*. N. 8, March 1999.

Federtrasporto – Centro Studi (2000), *Città e Trasporto – politiche per la mobilità sostenibile*, Roma.

ISTAT (2000), *L'Italia in cifre*, Roma.

Fontana, M. (1999), *Car-free Areas and Pedestrianisation for Traffic Management: the Experience of Five Italian Towns*, Paper presented at the OECD/ECMT Conference: Managing car use for sustainable urban travel, 1-2 December 1999, Dublin (Internet site: www.oecd.org/cem/UrbTrav/).

Ministero dei Trasporti e della Navigazione – Direzione Generale Programmazione, Organizzazione e Coordinamento (1998), *Conto nazionale dei Trasporti* 1998. Roma.

Ministero dei Trasporti e della Navigazione – Direzione Generale Programmazione, Organizzazione e Coordinamento (1999), *Conto nazionale dei Trasporti* 1999. Roma.

Ministero dei Trasporti e della Navigazione, Ministero dei Lavori Pubblici, Ministero dell'Ambiente (2000), *Nuovo Piano Generale dei Trasporti e della Logistica*, Roma.

Taggi *et al.* (1997), *Le politiche della sicurezza: coordinamento, comunicazione e partecipazione*, paper presented at the 55th Conferenza del Traffico e della Circolazione, Stresa.

Taggi *et al.* (1997), Dall'epidemiologia degli incidenti stradali alla valutazione dell'efficacia delle misure preventive, paper presented at the 55th Conferenza del Traffico e della Circolazione, Stresa.

Norway

Introduction

1.1. General policy considerations

This self review concentrates on urban travel policy and local environmental problems. However it is important to bear in mind that environmental problems associated with transport can be global or regional as well as local. The main strategy for addressing global and regional environmental problems in Norway is the use of cross-sectoral instruments such as taxes. Regulatory measures are also used, in particular emission standards. Developing an efficient environmental policy in the area of transport is complex and requires a coherent approach. The complexity partly reflects the variety of environmental problems associated with transport and the fact that transport is only one of many sectors contributing to these problems. Furthermore, environmental policy must be reconciled with other transport policy considerations.

Transport, in particular road transport, is a major source of local environmental problems. The use of instruments directly targeting transport is more appropriate for such local problems than strategies addressing global and regional challenges. Many instruments are particularly appropriate for dealing with urban transport. Co-ordinating land use and transport planning is also important.

1.2. Trends in urban transport

The central area of eastern Norway (around Oslo) is the most densely populated, accounting for about 40 to 45% of the total population. In this area, population has increased by 11% in the last ten years. About 65% of the Norwegian population lives in this area, or in the other three largest cities of the country (Bergen, Trondheim and Stavanger).

There are large variations between cities in the share of passenger transport modes (Table 23 and Figure 22). The implementation of a wide range of measures to strengthen public transport in some major cities, along with favourable pricing since 1990, have increased the use of public transport in some areas. For instance

Table 23.   **Distribution of journeys on transport mode in different areas, as a percentage of total journeys**

	Oslo			Bergen, Trondheim, Stavanger			Next 6 largest cities			Country as a whole		
	1985	1992	1998	1985	1992	1998	1985	1992	1998	1985	1992	1998
Walking/cycling	31	30	28	31	26	27	27	25	25	31	28	25
Car (driver and passenger)	54	55	57	58	64	62	62	68	67	59	64	66
Public transport	15	15	15	12	10	10	11	7	8	10	8	9

Source: TØI, Reports 418/1999 and 307/95.

Oslo saw a 20% increase in the number of journeys made by tramway, bus and underground between 1992 and 1996. However, passenger car transport is the dominant mode, except for some cities where public transport holds the strongest position during rush hours. Public transport has been losing market shares to private cars since the beginning of the 1980s. Between 1992 and 1999, road traffic increased by 17% in Norway, 18% in Oslo and 31% in the surrounding county Akershus.

Figure 22.   **Journeys per capita by public transport, Oslo, Bergen, Trondheim, Tromsø and Kristiansand**

1986 = 100

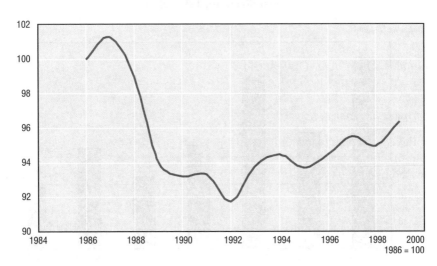

1986 = 100

Source: Carlquist, 2000.

1.3. *Environmental trends in major cities*

Environmental problems from transport in large urban areas relate to local air pollution and noise exposure, as well as land use, the visual environment and barriers in the urban landscape. Road transport is a major source of local air pollution and noise. Air, rail and harbour traffic primarily contribute to noise exposure.

Technological improvements are expected to reduce considerably several of these problems. Developments are slow in relation to noise exposure and growing traffic outweighs some technological improvements. The Government intends to strengthen efforts to reduce noise problems to meet the national objective to reduce noise nuisance by 25% of 1991 levels by 2001, when a new target will be set for 2005. Source oriented measures are essential in reaching these targets.

Most of the year air quality in the largest cities is generally good. However, there are periods when pollutant concentration is moderate or high, typically when the weather is cold and dry. The new EU directive on urban air quality will be implemented through national limit values for local air quality in the Pollution Control Act. In addition, the Government has set stricter non-binding objectives. Local air pollution from transport is mainly caused by particulate matter (PM_{10}), nitrogen dioxide (NO_2) and benzene. Figures 23 and 24 present data on particulate matter in Trondheim and Oslo.

Figure 23. **Particulate matter: number of days in Trondheim with concentrations over 50 $\mu g/m^3$, 1993-2000**

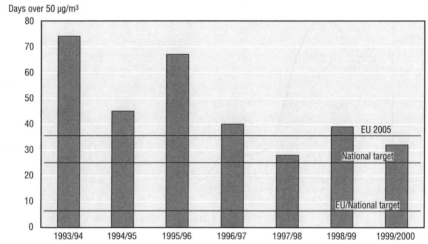

Days over 50 $\mu g/m^3$

Source: ECMT.

Figure 24.   **Particulate matter: number of days in Oslo with concentrations over 50 μg/m^3 on three monitoring stations in Oslo (the first is a background station, the other two are near the road stations)**

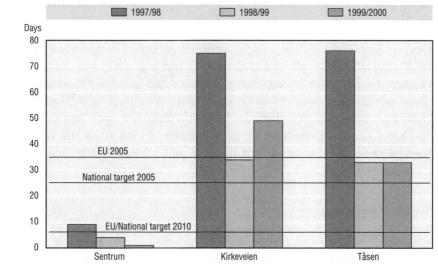

Source: ECMT.

1.4. Trends in land use

Urban population growth puts pressure on both residential and recreational areas. Housing spreads out in dormitory towns and residential areas, industry and businesses tend to move from central areas to satellite areas and along highways where parking facilities are often better than in city centres. All these factors make the private car more attractive than public transport for work related journeys and illustrate the need for a targeted land use strategy.

Although three out of four people in Norway live in urban settlements, only the four largest cities have more than 100 000 inhabitants (an urban settlement having at least 200 residents with houses less than 50 metres apart). On 1 January 1999, the population of Oslo, which stretches over 266 km² in 11 municipalities and 3 counties, was 764 000. Population density was 2 900 inhabitants per square kilometre, compared with about 2 400 in Bergen, 2 300 in Stavanger/Sandnes and 2 400 in Trondheim. The average for all urban settlements was 1 585 inhabitants per km² . Population density varies considerably within urban settlements. In the urban settlement of Oslo, the population was the densest in the area within

145|

the City of Oslo, with 3 800 inhabitants per km^2. In the parts of urban Oslo belonging to other municipalities, the population density ranged from 2 600 to 1 500 inhabitants per km^2. Both population density and percentage of built-up land tend to fall with the size of the settlement, although this pattern is not consistent because of large variations in land use.

Despite significant differences between cities, urban sprawl was most widespread during the 1970s, slowed in the 1980s and especially the 1990s. People increasingly prefer more concentrated housing and business development is also showing signs of concentration, though data is limited. In the largest cities road transport occupies 25% of available land. Public transport requires far less land and more concentrated urban development could make transport more efficient by reducing the need for transport and making better use of public transport systems.

1.5. Trends in traffic safety

Figures of police reported road traffic accidents and persons injured or killed between 1995 and 2000 are shown in Table 24. National road traffic safety policy was submitted to the Parliament on 29 September 2000, as part of the National Transport Plan 2002-2011, along with the Ministry of Transport and Communications' strategy, Road Traffic Safety 2002-2011. In both documents the long-term goal of no road fatalities or serious casualties is the basis for the government's work towards safer roads. Major measures include more safety audits of existing and new roads, and lower speed limits on dangerous roads. Since 15 March 2000 the use of hand-held mobile telephones whilst driving is forbidden. On 1 January 2001 the legal blood alcohol content was reduced from 0.5 to 0.2 per thousand. Other regulations are expected, including the implementation of a driving licenses point penalty system.

Table 24. **Road traffic accidents, killed and injured 1995-2000**

	1995	1996	1997	1998	1999	2000
Accidents	8 625	8 779	8 765	8 864	8 361	8 258
Killed	305	255	303	352	304	339
Injured	11 756	12 025	11 823	12 120	11 460	11 339

Source: Statistics Norway.

2.   Institutional Framework

There are three different levels of public administration in Norway: the national level, the 19 counties and about 430 municipalities.

2.1. *Institutional framework for urban transport*

National, regional and local authorities

The national government has overall responsibility for transport policy, providing a framework for local authorities and the private sector, setting regulations, and building national roads and railways. It is also responsible for national land use and transport planning systems. The counties are responsible for county roads and for managing public transport other than railways. Municipalities are responsible for local land use planning, parking regulation and municipal roads.

The Public Roads Administration, which is an agency of the Ministry of Transport and Communications, is responsible for planning, construction and maintenance of national and county highways. It is also responsible for financing the operation of national highway ferry links. Another subordinate agency, the Norwegian National Rail Administration, is responsible for railway infrastructure operation, maintenance and investment. It is also responsible for rail traffic control, track capacity allocation among railway companies as well as the collection of infrastructure charges from railway operators.

Public transport

At county level, the country council is responsible for the operation of public transport, purchasing services from public transport companies. This arrangement has several implications for urban transport. One consequence is that there is no formal or organisational distinction between public transport in urban and rural areas. Consequently, public transport in rural areas and urban areas compete for financial resources. Furthermore, this leaves the municipal authorities without formal responsibility for public transport, though they are responsible for local land use. Another aspect of this organisation is that the central government does not have formal responsibility for local public transport (except for overall financial allocation and the legal framework), whereas it does for national roads and railways, which are important parts of the transport system in several cities. National transport authorities are responsible for national roads and all railways (except metro-systems). This division of responsibility prevents any single level of government from developing a comprehensive strategy for urban transport and, ultimately, taking responsibility for unsatisfactory situations.

The case of Oslo is unique. The Oslo city council has the same status as a county council and therefore administers public transport within Oslo. However,

147|

the metropolitan area of Oslo consists of two counties (Oslo and its surrounding county Akershus), both of which have their own public transport administration purchasing services from independent or private transport companies. In addition, local rail transport within the Oslo area is managed by the National Railway Company, with direct financial support from the Ministry of Transport and Communications. Several reports have concluded this institutional arrangement could be hampering co-ordinated management of public transport in the metropolitan area of Oslo. However, extensive co-operation among the three administrative entities has for instance resulted in a joint fare system.

There have been some important changes in the institutional framework for public transport during the last 20 years. In 1981 responsibility for allocating subsidies to local bus routes and ferries was transferred from the central administration to the counties. Subsidies to transport companies were made on the basis of the companies' deficits until 1983. Thereafter, contracts defining the grants were established between individual companies and counties. After 1986 transfers from the national administration to counties were no longer earmarked so that counties could allocate resources to transport or other services, as required. Subsidies were based on a norm, *i.e.* costs based on experience. In 1987 the counties were allowed to determine public transport fares. The use of quality contracts as an alternative to competitive bidding is a recent development in public transport management. The idea of quality contracts is to develop quality-dependent subsidy contracts subject to conditions and subsidy arrangements which, based on commercial objectives (profit maximisation), can socially optimise the service provided. In 1991 the Transport Act was amended to allow bidding for subsidised public transport licences.

Government subsidies to public transport in many Norwegian urban areas have steadily diminished, falling by NOK 1.2 billion between 1986 and 1997 (in 1997 prices), a 42% fall in constant prices. In some areas, the reduction was considerably larger and several companies in the largest urban areas now operate without any subsidies at all.

2.2. Land use: The Planning and Building Act

The government and the Parliament define national objectives, while municipal and county authorities develop local plans. The most important land-use policy tool is the Planning and Building Act. Its planning provisions are the responsibility of the Ministry of Environment, who ensures that decisions made at national level are applied in county and municipal planning. The Ministry of Environment also drafts national guidelines for approval by the King in Council.

The Planning and Building Act requires each county to prepare county plans indicating the main features of land use and investment. The plans are provide

Figure 25. **Trends in subsidies for the five main urban areas**

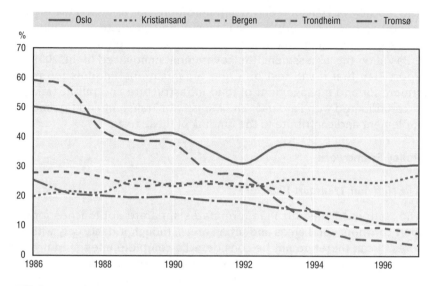

Source: TØI, Report 418/1999.

guidelines for municipal planning, though they are not legally binding or connected to transport investment budgets. Each municipality is required to prepare a
Municipal Master Plan covering the short and long term. The land use part of the
plan is legally binding. The tasks of the Planning and Building Act Committee established in 1998 include evaluating possible changes to the act and its regulations,
notably with respect to sustainable urban development.

2.3. Institutional co-ordination

Committee on Distribution of Tasks between Authority Levels

The present organisation of responsibilities can lead to sub-optimal situations, in transport as in other areas. The debate on the regional distribution of
responsibility lead to the establishment of a government appointed committee to
assess co-ordination and organisation between the three levels of government
across all sectors. The committee recently presented its conclusions which have
been subject to extensive public hearings. The Government forwarded a White
Paper to the parliament on this topic in 2001.

149|

New organisational models in urban areas

The Ministry of Transport and Communications has assessed the organisation of transport authorities in urban areas, considering alternatives in different types of urban areas allocating different responsibilities to the three levels of government. Based on this assessment, the government announced in the 2001 National Transport Plan that it will test different organisational models to ensure that investment for and management of road infrastructure and public transport are better co-ordinated with land use. The Ministry of Transport and Communications will implement and contribute to the funding of these tests.

3. Policy Framework

3.1. The National Transport Plan

The National Transport Plan formulates separate approaches for national transport corridors, rural areas and urban areas, though it deals only with national measures. It can therefore not be considered a complete integrated urban transport policy. However, the Ministry of Transport and Communications asked regional transport authorities to analyse the transport challenges facing the four largest urban areas over the period covered by the plan (2002 to 2011).

3.2. Integration of land use and transport planning

Several initiatives have been taken in recent years to develop more integrated urban transport plans.

National Policy Guidelines for Co-ordinated Land Use and Transport Planning

Developing more strategically oriented urban land use and transport plans that include environmental aspects requires an integrated approach to infrastructure investment and transport systems operation, as well as demand side instruments such as congestion pricing and parking restrictions.

A set of National Policy Guidelines for Co-ordinated Land Use and Transport Planning were adopted in 1993 to improve co-ordination between land use and transport planning in and across municipalities, sectors and institutional levels. The guidelines consist of three elements:

- national objectives of importance for land use and transport planning;
- practical guidelines on integrating land use and transport planning with a long-term sustainable perspective;
- guidelines for co-ordination between relevant agencies and the allocation of responsibility for implementation.

The guidelines are considered an important tool to limit urban traffic, land use and environmental problems and increase the share of public transport. They are being revised to differentiate between urban and rural areas and add guidelines for parking capacity and pricing policies.

National policy on the temporary ban on the construction of shopping centres outside city centres

Shopping malls outside urban agglomerations are believed to stimulate car transport and weaken urban centres, and are therefore contrary to national sustainable urban development objectives. Their construction was banned in 1999 for five years, during which time regional plans for the siting of shopping facilities are to be developed to avoid urban sprawl.

The Strategic Land-use and Transportation Planning Programme

The Ministry of Transport and Communications and the Ministry of Environment have carried out a joint project on experience with and potential for more strategic regional land use and transport planning. Some of the most important elements in the methodology are:

- a strategic view, clarifying the most critical issues to achieve the objectives of the National Guidelines for Land-use and Transport Planning;

- heavy emphasis on early planning phases, involving all relevant parties;

- a more comprehensive use of measures across sectors and authority levels;

- using the plan as basis for an agreement between the parties involved.

The TP10 project

In the late 1980s, the ten largest urban areas were encouraged to complete strategic transport plans, co-ordinating different levels of authority and sectoral interests, integrating environmental considerations and addressing land-use and transport issues as a whole. The experience from these plans was mixed, due to:

- lack of political involvement and support;

- weak links with normal planning carried out in the framework of the Planning and Building Act;

- inefficient and fragmented organisation and funding of public transport;

- weak co-ordination of municipal and regional land-use planning and national transport planning;

- too strong a focus on particular infrastructure projects;

- inadequate attention to the consequences of increases in transport demand.

151

However, the experience acquired through these plans is of substantial value, because it showed that more work on strategic and integrated urban transport plans was needed.

ABC *planning guidelines*

The Ministry of Transport and Communications and the Ministry of Environment are considering ways of applying Dutch ABC principles to Norwegian planning. These principles aim at reducing the need for transport and increasing the share of public transport through siting policy and the development of public transport.

Co-operation forum for city development

A forum consisting of the six largest cities and nine ministries has been established to co-ordinate efforts towards sustainable city development. It takes a broad approach to addressing the environmental challenges facing these cities and is notably expected to implement the recommendations of the seven-year Environmental City Programme finalised in 2000. It is also expected to clarify the need for co-ordinated action.

Development of instruments for urban densification

A large co-operation project on the development of instruments for urban densification has involved three Ministries and six municipalities. Experience from previous national and international studies, as well as 15 pilot studies, was used as a basis for developing economic, administrative and legal instruments, and identifying external conditions for urban densification.

3.3. Promotion of public transport

Overview

The need to strengthen the competitiveness of urban public transport is the main challenge for improving the sustainability of urban transport. Public transport must be attractive in terms of accessibility, capacity, travel time, punctuality, comfort and service, despite investment and operating costs. A lack of appropriate tools and methods for cost-benefit analysis across transport modes complicates resource allocation.

Counties have the main responsibility for local public transport. Central authorities provide financial support through lump-sum allocations which cover health, education, transport and county roads. The allocations are not earmarked. Public transport has for some years been a priority in budget programmes. The

Ministry of Transport and Communications has responsibility for railways, which is a priority area for funding. Subsidies total approximately NOK 900 million for rail and NOK 2 900 million for local bus transport. The largest cities account for NOK 400 to 700 million for rail and NOK 700 to 1 000 million for local bus transport.

The Ministry of Transport and Communications Public Roads Administration provides counties with the opportunity of using its knowledge of transport planning and development, though co-operation between the central government and local authorities can be further improved. The development of cost-benefit methodologies for public transport is a key activity of the Public Roads Administration, in close co-operation with local authorities. A set of figures including the most important costs has been developed and agreed, a cost-benefit methodology has been established and a textbook will be published so that the information can be brought to the attention of local and national planners.

Alternative use of national budgets and road toll revenues The parliament has decided that budgets for national roads and revenues from road tolls can be used for developing other parts of the transport system such as railways, local and county roads, parking, terminals and shelters. Alternative use of these sums has been limited, except in the Oslo area.

Separate subsidies for public transport infrastructure in the four largest urban areas

Since 1991 the Ministry of Transport and Communications has given separate grants for the development of public transport infrastructure in the four largest city areas (Oslo, Bergen, Trondheim and Stavanger) where improved public transport is particularly important for sustainable development. Experience from this arrangement points to improved co-ordination of public transport systems, primarily because financial resources can be allocated freely between administrative levels.

Packages of measures in Oslo

The Oslo-package 1 is an overall plan for road infrastructure investment between 1990 and 2007, covering 50 road projects. It is financed by the national budget (45%) and by revenues from the toll ring (55%). Some 20% of the funds are used for public transport infrastructure. Funding totals approximately NOK 28 billion (1999 prices).

The next step, Oslo-package 2, involves the development of public transport infrastructure in the larger Oslo area, including surrounding municipalities, in co-operation with local and national authorities. It includes the extension of the rail and subway system. Its funding (NOK 11 billion) should be provided by the toll ring, increases in public transport income, and national and local authorities. There

153|

are similar packages of measures in other urban areas, for instance the Bergen and Stavanger areas.

3.4. Minimising car use in urban areas

Parking policy

Parking policy is essential to reduce congestion and environmental problems especially in the largest cities as part of integrated land use and transport. Public roads and parking are regulated by the Planning and Building Act, notably with respect to the number of parking places in new buildings. There is a need to shift from the traditional policy of requiring minimum parking capacity to limiting parking in development projects. It is also necessary to co-ordinate parking policies within city areas. Local regulation is constrained by the fact that in many city centres most car parks are private. There is considerable scope for more active parking policies to reduce congestion and environmental damage. The Planning Act Committee is addressing this issue and should report by 2003.

Traffic management and calming measures: congestion pricing

At the end of 2000 the government forwarded a proposal to the Parliament concerning the legal framework to introduce congestion pricing. The main purpose of a congestion pricing system is to regulate traffic (primarily in larger cities), reduce congestion and improve the local environment. Charges should therefore be set according to the externalities created by road traffic and vary according to the time and place. Local authorities will not be allowed to use congestion pricing and tolls on the same route at the same time.

Congestion pricing will be mainly a local measure aimed at reducing local problems. Generally local authorities have the best knowledge of local conditions and are in the best position to assess congestion pricing in connection with other measures. They should play an important role in the decision process, though there might be some important exceptions. For instance environmental regulations can mean that the State, as the owner of the national roads, is responsible for applying expensive measures in cases where congestion pricing would be more cost effective and could therefore be the initiator of congestion pricing.

To encourage local authorities to implement congestion pricing, the Ministry is convinced that it is vital that revenues from congestion pricing are collected at local and regional level. Therefore the draft proposal states that net revenues will be distributed between the local, regional and national level, and always earmarked for local transport, including for instance public transport, traffic safety, environment and infrastructure. Such earmarking will be important to achieve public acceptance of congestion pricing and the revenue will make it easier to carry through local transport plans when congestion pricing is one of several measures. To avoid congestion pricing turning into general taxation, the Ministry has assumed that local authorities do not reduce their ordinary expenditure on transport as a result of income from congestion pricing.

In each case where congestion pricing is relevant, a broad assessment will be required before any decision is taken. Alternative and additional measures must be assessed together with effects on traffic and environment. The specific design of local system proposed must be described, including price levels, distribution of revenue and other questions. Both costs and benefits have to be analysed.

Experience in Norway and other countries shows that the introduction of congestion pricing might be a long and slow process. The positive experience with tolls, combined with the growing need to improve public transport and environment, will probably make it easier to accept congestion pricing as a natural next step. Properly used, congestion pricing is likely to be effective. Its principle was approved in the parliament three years ago. The next step will be approval of the legal framework, with local assessments and debates in the larger urban areas.

The question of congestion pricing is more political than technological. The political debate should focus on general questions concerning how to obtain a more effective and environmentally friendly transport structure, and the role of congestion pricing in this respect.

Toll rings

Toll rings have been in use in Norway since late 1980s. Their purpose is to finance infrastructure and charges are linked to investment costs. However the system can also be designed for traffic regulation (time-differentiated pricing). Local initiative and support is essential for establishing toll-rings and using time-differentiated pricing. The experience with toll rings in general is very good.

Technical development has brought more advanced methods for electronic payment. For instance in Trondheim payment is time-differentiated, so that prices are higher at rush hours in the mornings. There is no payment from 6 p.m. to 6 a.m., and at weekends. In Bergen driving is free between 10 p.m. and 6 a.m., and at weekends.

3.5. The Cleaner City Air project

The Cleaner City Air project was launched in 1998 by the Ministry of Transport and Communications as part of its efforts to reduce local air pollution from road transport. It involves central and local authorities and includes coherent air pollution monitoring and warning systems for the largest cities. It considers short and long term measures:

155|

- lower speed limits during days when the level of PM_{10} is expected to be high;
- a ban on studded tires during days when the level of PM_{10} is expected to be high;
- traffic bans based on registration numbers during days when the level of NO_2 is expected to be high;
- a ban on cars registered before 1989 (when the catalyst was introduced) when the level of NO_2 is expected to be high.

Only the first measure, reduced speed limits, has been adopted in one city (Oslo).

3.6. Studded tires

The use of studded tires in winter has an adverse effect on environment and health due to PM_{10} emissions. In the 1998-2007 Road and Transport Plan, car users are given the opportunity to switch to unstudded tires. The plan estimates that the share of cars with unstudded tires in the four largest cities (Oslo, Bergen, Trondheim and Stavanger) must be about 80% in 2002 to meet the limit values set in the Pollution Control Act for noise and particulates. In the winter of 1999/2000 local authorities in Oslo imposed a charge of NOK 1 000 per winter or NOK 25 per day on studded tyres. The municipality of Oslo also offers a grant of NOK 250 per studded tyre delivered when buying new unstudded tires.

Poland

1. The Context

Over 60% of Poland's 38 million inhabitants live in urban areas. The largest are the capital Warsaw (1.7 million inhabitants), the Upper Silesian Agglomeration (GOP) centred on Katowice, (2.2 million inhabitants) and the Tri-City Agglomeration of Gdansk, Gdynia and Sopot, each with about one million inhabitants. Lodz, Krakow, Wroclaw and Poznan each have between 500 000 and one million inhabitants. Average urban densities are medium (2 000 to 3 000 inhabitants per square kilometre). In most large cities there is a striking contrast between dense, multi-purpose historic centres and the post-war developments on the periphery, with single-purpose housing estates or industrial areas. Central areas have retained their dominance as locations of jobs and services, mixed with residential areas.

The roles of central and local authorities and the legal framework for urban public transport were totally changed at the beginning of the first transition period in 1989. Responsibility for urban roads and the transport sector was shifted from the central to the local government. In particular, the central administration stopped funding urban public transport (except the Warsaw metro project and part of the Poznan Fast Tram project) and now contributes very little to urban roads. Suburban railways have also been affected.

Rapid motorization (the fleet grew by over 30% between 1990 and 1995) and rising personal income have caused a modal shift from public transport to cars, reinforced by changes in the ratio between car operating costs and public transport fares. The pressure to reduce subsidies to public transport due to local public budget shortages led to sharp fare increases. In 1995, the average net salary could afford 2.5 times more gasoline than six years before, but one third the number of single ride tickets. Public transport cost recovery increased by 60% to 70% of operating costs, but the quality of service and infrastructure (tracks, power supply) deteriorated and fleet renewal slowed. Consequently, use of urban public transport declined from 9.1 billion trips in 1986 to 7.2 billion in 1990 and 5.5 billion in 1994. The modal split between the car and public transport, changed from 10/90 in the late 1970s to 30/70 in the mid-1990s. Suburban railways which used to be significant in serving urban areas such as Warsaw, Upper Silesia and the Tri-City agglomeration, also declined.

Substantial reductions were achieved in urban transport deficit by increasing ticket prices and improving managerial efficiency, but also by reducing expenditure for repairs, modernisation and development. Under-investment was alarming and widespread, and well developed tramway systems in many areas suffered from neglected infrastructure and ageing fleets. Development of road networks had practically ceased and maintenance of pavements and bridges was also overdue. Action taken by municipalities and operators to stop the deterioration of urban roads and public transport included experimenting with transport management models and significant deregulation, opening up the market for private operators. However, this process takes time and most services are still provided by city-owned companies largely financed from the city budget. The regulatory regime has become a mixture of deregulation and partial regulation, with bidding for contracts gradually becoming common practice.

A clear transport policy is now widely accepted as a priority to avoid a transport crisis. Shaped by international trends, Krakow City Council was the first to introduce a sustainable transport policy in 1993, when Warsaw began preparing its transport policy which was adopted in 1995 (Resolution on Transportation Policy of Warsaw City Council).

The situation of urban roads and public transport started gradually changing from the mid 1990s. By this time traffic volumes in some large urban areas had exceeded 400 cars per thousand inhabitants, resulting in rising congestion seriously affecting public transport, particularly buses. Trams suffer less from congestion as most run on separate tracks. In the largest urban areas traffic congestion, road accidents and parking are considered the most critical problems together with deteriorating pavements and tracks, and ageing trams and buses. Awareness of the severity of the problem in five Polish cities is presented in Table 25.

However, this rating does not necessarily reflect the real situation. Studies which measure travel speed in different societies have shown that when congestion is recent, perception of the problem is exaggerated. Cities where congestion has been experienced for a long time and where travel speed is much lower than those measured in Warsaw or Poznan, have lower scores than those found in these five Polish urban areas.

After Krakow and Warsaw, other urban areas including Bialystok, Lodz, Gdynia, Nowy Sacz, Poznan and Wroclaw, formulated transport policies with targets, directions for development and operating principles for the urban transport system. In general, urban areas favour sustainable transport policies with priority for preserving and promoting urban public transport.

Table 25. **Transport situation in five Polish cities in 1992 and 1999**

Problem	Congestion		Noise		Air pollution	
	1992	1999	1992	1999	1992	1999
Scale of the problem 1 – very local 4 – widespread	2.25	3.25	2.75	3.25	3.25	3
Severity 1 – no problem 4 – very serious	3	3.75	3	3.5	3	3.25
Trend : 1 – major improvement 4 – sharp deterioration	3.25	3.5	3	3.25	2.75	2.75

Annex: Resolution No. XXVI/193/95 of the City Council of the Capital City of Warsaw of 27 November 1995 regarding Transportation Policy for the Capital City of Warsaw.
Source: ECMT.

In summary, after a transition period (1989 to 1995) which was very difficult for urban transport, the period between 1996 and 2000 gave reasons for some optimism:

- Increasing understanding of the importance of urban transport is manifested by: *a*) widespread adoption of transport policies which favour public transport, *b*) increased funding for fleet purchase and tram track repair, *c*) new funding methods, *d*) visibly changing attitudes to existing tramway systems, which are less affected by the disturbance caused by increasing car traffic, and *e*) more road traffic management policies giving priority to public transport vehicles (separate lanes, actuated traffic lights).

- Declining passenger numbers have been stabilised and a small growth in numbers was recorded in some areas.

- Quality of service has improved; overcrowding and time loss have ceased to be the main problems (except for areas affected by road congestion)and greater importance is being given to previously ignored factors, such as cleanliness, courtesy, personal safety and quality of information.

- Rationalisation of operator organisation and management has improved management effectiveness and productivity.

- Progress is visible in fare systems and quality control.[1]

- Limited state assistance has improved co-operation (mostly organised by the Chamber of Urban Transport) between companies.

Despite these positive signs, the following problems remain:

- widespread congestion is affecting public transport operating conditions, particularly buses; the lack of a generalised priority system for buses reduces operational speed, affecting punctuality and regularity of service;

road congestion, previously restricted to large urban areas now also affects small and medium urban areas and its extent and duration is increasing;

- there are inadequate financial resources to renew ageing tramway and trolleybus rolling stock, repair tracks and introduce modern traffic management and control, though bus fleet replacement has improved;

- unequal competition between public and private operators which conduct activity beyond the regulated services means that the legal basis of competition must be improved urgently;

- the widely practised annual municipal budgeting approach makes long-term funding decisions for purchase and modernisation-development investment impossible, though some municipalities now use multi-year budgeting approaches (Szczecin and Krakow);

- resolving inter-municipal transport service problems is difficult, co-operation between neighbouring municipalities is rare and although administrative reform will probably resolve the problem of co-ordination at county and province level, co-ordination between the activity of Polish State Railways and urban and suburban transport companies remains a problem;

- the conservative attitude of public transport staff and trade unions focussed on temporary goals can be a deterrent when changes must be made to achieve long-term positive effects.

The urban transport financing system is a priority. Self-financing in the Polish urban transport system is considerably higher than in EU countries and neighbouring Central European countries, apart from smaller urban areas in Hungary. Self financing has been achieved by higher ticket prices and improved performance, at the expense of excessive savings in fleet and infrastructure maintenance (tram systems) and modernisation investments. The small share of private sector, including foreign operators, reflects the unattractive and risky investment market of the urban transport sector.

Transport problems in Polish cities will increase without policy changes. Financial solutions must be found to compensate the shortfall due to ticket subsidies (discount fares, right to free trips), surcharges from municipalities, counties and provinces for providing "socially desirable" services (in sparsely populated areas). Funding must also be found for tram infrastructure investments (tracks, power supply) to enable more equal competition for trams which despite environmental and operational advantages (independence from road traffic) cannot compete with buses, because bus operation costs do not include the cost of using urban roads. Financial resources for roads are also insufficient.

Land use and transport

Transition has strongly influenced the spatial development of cities, with both positive and negative impacts on transport. Positive changes include: diversifying single function areas (for example, large residential areas without jobs and services) by introducing commercial and other activities, increasing the density of activities in city centres and well served public transport corridors. Urban sprawl is a visible negative symptom, as populations have stabilised in city centres but are growing in low density development in the suburbs. Large hypermarkets and shopping/service centres mushroom at peripheral locations which are well served by roads, but not necessarily by public transport. More than 25 such centres have been built in Warsaw in the last ten years. Parking policy needs to be adopted and implemented not only for hypermarkets and related activities but also for city centres.

2.   Institutional Framework

Although the central administration has totally withdrawn from urban transport ownership and funding, it still has some control over urban finances, as it decides on fare discounts for senior citizens, students, handicapped people and other groups and has a restricted owner/manager role for main urban roads (national and regional roads). It occasionally funds major investments, such as the Warsaw metro. The national budget also finances some road investments such as the urban sections of national roads.

There is no national agency or ministry for urban public transport. Urban area representatives participate in various national commissions, or through organisations such as the Union of Metropolitan Cities, the Association of Polish Cities, the Chamber of Urban Transport (IGKM), or the association of urban public transport operators. This situation has often been commented on by foreign experts and the International Finance Institute. According to a 1994 World Bank report, the absence of any explicit state interest or action related to public transport is anomalous and means many worthwhile projects are not carried out. The Ministry of Transport should be re-engaged as the functional sponsor of public transport. This would not be a return to old paternalistic ways and purse-holding, but would embrace an agenda common to ministries of transport in industrial economies. Similarly, according to a 1999 World Bank memorandum (Poland: Strategic Priorities for the Transport Sector), the state has gone too far in decentralising all public transport responsibilities to urban areas and has not addressed the complicated issues of urban roads. If Poland is to harmonise its urban public transport policies and practices with those of the EU, the Ministry of Transport should increase its capacity to help urban areas make strategic decisions in competitive tendering, subsidy reform, road and public transport investment policies, and road use pricing,

161|

as well as accessing capital in the period before urban areas reach financial self-sufficiency. It was also stressed that the revised road financing system, based on an allocation formula applied to a portion of fuel taxes, may be biased against urban roads, and in principle has limited use as a tool to manage urban traffic and modal split.

The role of the Chamber of Urban Transport is important. This autonomous organisation established in 1991 by public transport companies now represents 130 public and private member companies and institutions. It collects and distributes information, including statistical publications and a bi-monthly information bulletin. The organisation is lobbying to include urban transport under the responsibility of the Minister of Transport and organises working groups and committees on planning and economic affairs, operation, power supply systems, maintenance of buses and tramways, track maintenance and operating practices.

In 1995, the Chamber of Urban Transport commissioned a study on behalf of urban transport companies, entitled Programme for Urban Transport Development in Poland. The study includes a critical assessment of the situation, future public transport demand, foreign urban transport trends, recommended policies, suggested directions for desirable technological progress and formulated programmes for rolling stock acquisition and infrastructure investment. The report ends with suggestions for funding and legal and institutional changes, including the role of the central administration.

After years of underfunding, the situation for urban roads and transport is changing and efforts to amend the law seem effective. In 1998, the parliamentary transport lobby was created and some positive changes introduced, including:

- local government compensation for lost revenues from discount fares and free trips; further detailed legal regulations will be necessary to compensate for discount fare privileges established at central administration level;

- revision of timetable co-ordination; in 1999 co-ordination was taken over by municipalities (*gmina*), counties (*powiat*) and self-governed provinces (*voivodships*);

- the inclusion of public transport in the transport sector (Act on sectors); in the future, the Ministry of Transport and the Ministry of Maritime Economy should share responsibility for urban transport.

The central administration should soon assume its new role as functional head of urban transport, with responsibilities common to ministries of transport in OECD countries. The scope of these responsibilities would include relevant legislative activities and initiatives; formulating basic regulations and transport policy recommendations; technology development policy for both imports and domestic industry; labour relations; the collection and maintenance of sectoral databases; design of transport planning procedures; research and development. The government has clearly shown its intention to move in this direction with the 2000 national draft transport policy.

3.   Policy framework

3.1. *National transport policy*

The 1999 draft transport policy was prepared by the Ministry of Transport and Maritime Economy. Promotion of public transport, especially in urban areas, was one of the four main challenges, with a number of possible policy options:

- continuation of present trends leading to uncontrolled growth of road transport and no accompanying road infrastructure development;
- a modified development policy following EU experience to adjust the capacity of the road system to growing motorization;
- the sustainable development option.

The sustainable development option was chosen as a basis for the national transport policy for sustainable development for 2000 to 2015 which includes detailed policy objectives and measures for urban and regional transport. The policy gives a higher priority to sustainable development, harmonising the transport system with the requirements of the European Union and balancing the growth of the car fleet with road infrastructure development.

To tackle emerging urban transport problems, the central administration will grant municipalities financial assistance for major capital-intensive investment public transport projects (starting with rail systems in large urban areas), provide loan guarantees for system upgrading, and supply information and promote best practices in urban transport including non-mechanised means of transport (cycling walking). The Ministry of Transport will work to ensure that local and regional development plans and programmes are co-ordinated to facilitate decisions on items such as roads which involve different administrative levels (national, regional, county, local). New legislation will enable municipalities to generate financial resources to develop, maintain and operate transport systems. Parking charges, tolls for using bridges and entering city centres, and congestion charging were mentioned as examples. Measures are urgently needed to allow the Ministry of Transport to promote the reform of local transport management systems and the co-operation of municipalities to organise urban transport systems.

The Ministry of Transport, working with environmental and technical groups, has proposed legislation to reinforce public transport with a clear division between the provision of transport operations and the organisation of public transport services. The public sector is responsible for organising services (including tendering for operators), financing and operational obligations, while operators work on clear

163

commercial basis. The 2000 law to restructure and privatise the Polish State Railway Company also reflects this approach. It provides a legal framework for a modern, commercially oriented rail service and proposes the commercial/public split for urban and regional rail services. Parliament has allocated funding for the next three years to support the development of this service.

The latest legislation and the draft national transport policy reflect central administration support for local governments to improve urban transport and roads. This support will depend on the extent to which local transport policy for a given urban area is consistent with the principles of overall efficiency and sustainable development.

3.2. Local transport policies

The transport policies adopted in recent years by some municipalities are based on the principle of sustainable development. The term "sustainability" is used in its broadest sense, i.e. social, economic and environmental sustainability. These policies address:

- the integration of land use and transport planning;
- promotion of public transport;
- reducing car use in urban areas, first of all in city centres;
- traffic management;
- traffic calming measures for the city centre and residential districts;
- promotion of cycling;
- traffic safety measures.

This does not mean that there is no intention to improve and develop road networks and parking facilities. However, in most places it has been decided that priority should be given to develop roads to reduce through-traffic in central and high density areas.

Krakow

Krakow (750 000 inhabitants) was the first urban area to introduce car traffic restrictions in the historical city centre and parking charges (1987). The 1993 transport policy was co-ordinated with the 1994 Local Land Use Development Plan with common objectives such as curbing urban sprawl, traffic zoning and calming, priority for public transport and parking policy. The potential of the existing tramway was recognised and in 1996, the City Board adopted a medium and long-term programme (in co-operation with the European Bank for Reconstruction and Development) to upgrade and develop the tramway and build a new fast tram line. The programme targets extensive fleet replacement and providing tram priority on the most congested sections of the network, using advanced quality management methods through contracts with the operator(s). Unlike most urban areas, over the past decade the Krakow municipality has implemented a multi-annual financial planning system for infrastructure development. This has resulted in increased public transport use, new investment (infrastructure and rolling stock, including low floor trams) and traffic management initiatives (bus / tram lanes, exclusive bus lanes, etc.).

Warsaw

Warsaw (1.65 million inhabitants) illustrates current trends. The draft transport policy was prepared using the results and recommendations of the first ECMT/OECD project on sustainable urban travel.[2] The municipality considered a number of options ranging from "the motorised city" to "the car free city". The sustainable transport policy option was retained after an 18 month review and approval process and the 1995 Resolution on Transportation Policy was unanimously adopted by Warsaw City Council.

The general objective of Warsaw's transport policy is a sustainable development strategy for the city by creating efficient and safe conditions to transport people and goods, with guaranteed priority for public transport. The development of transport should stimulate economic development and spatial organisation in the city; it should improve city prestige, reduce the differentiation in development and quality of life in specific areas of the agglomeration and satisfy requirements to reduce the environmental impact of transport (under existing and projected economic conditions).[3]

Full implementation of the 1995 Warsaw Transport Policy is proving slow and further legislation will be needed to enable full implementation. The highest priority has been given to metro construction but despite considerable resources (including from the central administration) the construction of the first line has been delayed. Limited progress has been made in improving bus and tram transport, and suburban railway services continue to deteriorate. Traffic priorities for trams and buses have been little developed. The annual budgeting system in Warsaw makes it difficult to implement larger projects requiring medium and long-term strategy planning.

However, despite implementation difficulties, the objectives and general directions of the policy have not been challenged in most recent planning studies and programmes. Indeed the conclusions and recommendations of the 1998 Study on Conditions and Directions of Spatial Development. were fully consistent with Transport Policy adopted three years earlier.

Public opinion of public transport is still good. The results of two travel surveys (1993 and 1998) (Table 26) show that the majority of people are in favour of priorities

165|

Table 26. **Percentage of people in favour of bus/tram priorities even to the detriment of car driving conditions**

	1993	1998
Total	64%	66%
Car owners	59%	61%

Source: ECMT.

for buses and trams (*e.g.* exclusive bus lanes), even if this adversely affects traffic conditions for the private car.

The same survey showed a shift from buses to tramways, despite the modernisation of the bus fleet and an ageing tram fleet. This trend would no doubt be stronger if plans to renew the tramway fleet and upgrade tracks and power supply system were implemented.

Warsaw has started experimenting with a new technique of consultation and negotiations between stakeholders (Warsaw Transport Roundtable) to address controversial issues and gain public support for ambitious ideas.

Katowice

The city of Katowice (350 000 inhabitants) is a special case as it is a part of the largest urban area in Poland (Upper Silesia) with over two million inhabitants. While the city successfully manages to formulate land use and transport development policies and plans, urban transport system planning and management is proving difficult. The well developed railway service could serve the conurbation of Upper Silesia better if all levels of government (local-city, county and region) co-operated. Ongoing upgrading of the existing main tramway, serving the most developed corridor Katowice-Chorzow-Bytom is of primary importance. If successful, this project could play a great role in demonstrating the potential of tramway systems. In fact, the cost of upgrading the 22 kilometre line to fast tram standards (tracks, power supply, low-floor trams, traffic management and information system) is equivalent to the cost of building 500 meters of underground metro system.

Poznan

Poznan (580 000 inhabitants) has also co-ordinated transport policy and development plans with land use plans and multiannual investment programmes. The overall objective of the municipal transport policy is to build a balanced city transport system taking into consideration economic, spatial, environmental and social factors, on the basis of politically agreed priorities and available instruments. In 1999, the completion[4] of transport policy and development plans co-ordination with land use plans and investment programmes were preceded by consultation with the public, professionals and interest groups. It was considered important to obtain the approval of all political parties and social communities using mechanisms to balance the demand for transport services with the possibilities for meeting demand within overall development objectives. Different forms of business activity were taken into account – location, stimulating business ventures in various sectors of the transport services, etc. Other objectives included:

- minimising conflicts between transport facilities, traffic and land-use development;
- reducing the negative impact of transport services on the natural environment;
- rationalising transport needs of the population, especially reducing individual car traffic;
- providing equal opportunities on the employment market and equal access to education and services (social aspects);
- financial and budgeting feasibility (realistic programs and plans).

Key aspects of the land use and transport plans are the following:

- departure from the concept of a circular city propagated in the 1970s to the notion of a compact city;
- use of existing resources (natural, infrastructure, economic);
- city zoning for transport.

Transport specific objectives include:

- increasing the efficiency of the transport system with priority for public transport users and creating better conditions for cycling and walking;
- effective reduction of heavy goods through-traffic;
- maintenance and rehabilitation of transport infrastructure;
- better access to the transeuropean and national transport system.

The municipality has set up a system to monitor transport policy implementation and must prepare a detailed ten year implementation timetable. Poznan is the only Polish urban area with an extended Area Traffic Control system, which operates with a central unit and over 90 connected intersections out of the planned 200.

Public transport organisation and management policies

Operating companies are being restructured to improve their performance and/or reduce costs. The public transport operators in several urban areas are now corporate organisations, to be run under commercial law. At present, they are still completely owned by municipalities, but their managerial independence has

167|

been increased and are seeking private partners and investors. The current model is that municipalities retain the regulatory function (service patterns, schedules, fares), often run by a specialised transport authority, leaving operations to company management. Relations between operators and municipalities are increasingly regulated by service agreements, based on fixed rates for agreed vehicle kilometres of service and stringent performance control.

Quality is a growing priority for both municipalities and operators with quality requirements included in recent contracts. Simple quality parameters, such as punctuality, are being replaced by more complex methods of quality evaluation, with multi-criteria and advanced statistical methods of quality control. Financial incentives (bonuses and penalties) for operators have been introduced and marketing studies and stated preference surveys are becoming popular.

New consultation initiative

Experience in Warsaw demonstrates that it can be difficult to implement even the best concepts which have authority approval. In the new political framework, inadequate co-operation between authorities, interest groups and the general public slows down resolution of transport problems in urban areas. A Canadian style multi-stakeholder consultation process has been introduced by some municipalities to improve co-operation. With the assistance of the Polish Institute for Sustainable Development, the Warsaw Transportation Round Table (WTRT) was established in early 2000 based on the experience of the International Center for Sustainable Cities in Vancouver.

The WTRT makes recommendations to the City Board, adoption of any proposal being by consensus. The WTRT has 17 members representing five sectors: business, local government, universities, environmental consulting, NGOs and the general public. Members are selected/nominated by stakeholders from these sectors. WTRT discussion topics are decided by common agreement.

The first session in 2000 was devoted to traffic zoning in Warsaw, to clarify issues for the general public and interest groups. It was recommended that zoning be implemented more energetically. Policies for the development of the urban road system were discussed during the second session (October-November 2000). No consensus was reached for the most controversial issue namely the location of the transeuropean A-2 motorway, but other crucial issues such as investment priorities and two city ring roads were approved. Generally, the recommendations of the WTRT have supported and gone beyond Warsaw's 1995 sustainable transport policies. Although it is too early to tell how these recommendations will accelerate the implementation of sustainable transport policy, there is already evidence that decision-making has been improved by increasing communication and understanding between different sectors. With greater stakeholder involvement in the decision-making process, the likelihood of reaching better and more publicly acceptable decisions is increased. It is hoped that other urban areas will see the WTRT as a good example for a more transparent and democratic process engaging the public and various interest groups.

4. Conclusions

Urban areas are adopting sustainable development strategies, based on a compromise between social, economic and environmental protection targets. The basic principles of sustainable urban transport are:

- limiting the role of the car in urban areas, particularly in city centres and giving priority to public transport and pedestrian and cycle traffic;
- eliminating or reducing through-traffic by building by-passes and ring-roads;
- rehabilitation and more effective use and modernisation of existing infrastructure and equipment; this includes better use and upgrading of existing tramway systems;
- growing interest in advanced traffic management systems;
- priority in traffic for public transport;
- extending the scope of financial instruments: first using parking charges and later congestion charges in gridlocked urban areas.

With limited financial resources for public transport, almost all urban areas are giving priority to fleet repairs, tramline modernisation and equipment, and software to assist in operation, maintenance and management. This includes management and passenger information systems. Warsaw is an exception with a strong policy giving priority to metro construction. Nevertheless, ambitious policy is not enough, as the implementation of sustainable transport policies in urban areas is slow. The main negative factors in implementing transport policies seem to be:

- the high priority of personal car ownership in transition country consumer patterns. Constraints on car use are very unpopular so policy and decision makers are concerned about public reaction to radical measures such as giving priority to tramways and buses in urban traffic, traffic calming, strict enforcement of traffic rules and parking and road charging;
- as in other countries, spectacular capital intensive investment projects attract more attention than more efficient but less visible options such as maintenance and modernisation of existing equipment and infrastructure and better traffic management. With limited financial resources, new projects which drain the city budget are implemented slowly, sometimes with unpredictable results. As a general rule, the financial and economic viability

169

of competing projects and actions under effective project management is not always taken into account;

- inexpensive and feasible solutions such as upgrading existing tramway systems tend to be disregarded due to the conservative attitudes of professionals. For decades, tramways were considered as old-fashioned and no competition for the car;

- inadequate communication between the public and policy-makers makes even the best concepts and proposals difficult to implement. The role of mass media is crucial in this respect.

The role of the central administration is changing. In the first years of the transition period, it delegated the entire responsibility for urban transport to municipalities. Emerging problems have led to a new approach. A new law has defined government responsibility for urban transport and a draft national transport policy shows clear intention to provide some support to municipalities. This assistance will be dependent on the extent to which local transport policy is consistent with principles of overall efficiency and sustainable development.

Notes

1. IGKM – Izba Gospodarcza Komunikacji Miejskiej.

2. Summarised in *Urban Travel and Sustainable Development*, ECMT/OECD (1995), Paris.

3. See Resolution N° XXVI/193/95 of the City Council of the Capital city of Warsaw, November 27, 1995 Regarding Transportation Policy for the City of Warsaw ANNEX I.

4. Transport Policy for the City of Poznan (Resolution of the City Council of Poznan No. XXIII/269/III/ 99 of 18 November 1999); Study of Spatial Development Conditions (Resolution of the City Council of Poznan No. XXII/276/ III/99 of 23 November 1999); Long-term Investment Programme for 2000-2004 (Resolution of the City Council of Poznan No. XXVIII/336/III/ 99 of 22 December 1999).

References

BPRW (1993). *Warszawskie badanie ruchu* – 1993 (Warsaw Traffic Survey – 1993). Warszawa.

BPRW (1998). *Warszawskie badanie ruchu* – 1998 (Warsaw Traffic Survey – 1998). Warszawa.

ECMT/OECD (1995). *Urban Travel and Sustainable Development*. Paris.

European Communities (1998). QUATTRO: *Quality Approach in Tendering Urban Public Transport Operations*. Final Report. Transport Research Fourth Framework Programme. Brussels.

Friedberg J. (2000). *Menace of Transport Underdevelopment and Directions of counteractions in State Policy*. In: Proc. of SITK Congress Transport 2000. Krakow-Zakopane, 14-16 September 2000.

IGKM. Komunikacja miejska w liczbach : 1990-1991, 1992, 1993, 1994, 1995, 1996, 1997, 1998,1999.

Ministry of Transport and Maritime Economy (2000). *National Transport Policy for the period 2000-2015 for Sustainable Country Development*. Draft for public consultation. In: Proc. of SITK Congress Transport 2000. Krakow-Zakopane, 14-16 September 2000.

QUATTRO (1998). *Urban Transport in Poland*. report WP7/D8/PL. IGKM.

Roczniki Statystyczne (1990-1998) *Annual Statistics*. GUS Warszawa.

Roszkowski M., Suchorzewski W. (1999). *Ocena stanu i funkcjonowania komunikacji w Warszawie oraz ocena realizacji polityki transportowej zatwierdzonej w 1995 roku wraz z propozycjami jej modyfikacji*. (Evaluation of the State of the Warsaw Transport System, Assessment of Implementation of Transport Policy Adopted in 1995). Proc. of the SITK Conference "Transport in Warsaw". Warsaw, 18.06.1999.

Rozkwitalska C., Suchorzewski W. (1997). *Komunikacja miejska w Polsce w 1996* (Urban Transport in Poland – 1996). IGKM Warszawa.

Rozkwitalska C., Suchorzewski W. i in. (1999). *Komunikacja miejska w Polsce w 1998* (Urban Transport in Poland – 1998). IGKM Warszawa.

Rozkwitalska C., Rudnicki A. i Suchorzewski W. (1995). *Program rozwoju komunikacji miejskiej w Polsce w latach 1995-2000 i po roku 2000* (Programme for the Development of Urban Public Transport in Poland in 1995-2000 and after 2000). IGKM Warszawa.

Rudnicki A. (1992). *Obs?uga komunikacyjna w obszarach zurbanizowanych w Polsce* (Transport Serving Urban Areas in Poland). Transport Committee of the Polish Academy of Science. A. Rudnicki (ed.).

Rudnicki A. (1999). *Kryteria i mierniki oceny miejskiej komunikacji zbiorowej* (Criteria and Measures to Assess Urban Transport). IGKM Warszawa.

Suchorzewski W. (1999), *Transportation Policy for the Capital City of Warsaw – 3 years after adoption*. ECMT/OECD International Workshop: Implementing Strategies to Improve Public Transport for Sustainable Urban Travel, Athens, 3-4 June 1999.

Suchorzewski W. (1999) *The funding of public transport investment in Central Europe.* Proc. UITP/ECMT Seminar on Financing Urban Public Transport, Paris, 13-14 1999.

World Bank (1994). *Poland: Urban Transport Review.* The World Bank Report No. 12962-POL, October 1994.

World Bank (1999). *Poland: Strategic Priorities for the Transport Sector.* Report No. 19450-POL, June 1999.

Portugal

1. The Context

1.1. Key trends in urban travel

Portugal's 10 million inhabitants are concentrated on the coast. Coastal cities have grown with rural migration, while inland areas are increasingly sparsely populated. Those remaining in rural areas tend to be older and do not usually own cars. As public transport access is limited, using taxis is a necessity rather than a luxury in these areas. In cities, the influx of population has pushed up land prices, forcing people into outlying suburbs where land is cheaper but public transport services are poor. This pattern is most obvious in Lisbon and Oporto, where the suburbs sprawl and the population lives in flats in dormitory towns, commuting to work for two to four hours a day. Small and medium size towns (with populations of 10 000 to 50 000) face similar problems. Cities are becoming polycentric, with workplaces and industries on the periphery. This trend creates new mobility patterns, increasing private car use, and complicating transport problems and policy responses.

Despite a significant effort to improve public transport in recent years, car ownership has continued to grow and the modal split has shifted from public transport to private cars. Concern about environmental sustainability in urban transport has increased. This concern is apparent for instance in the POLIS programme which deals with land use in most of northern and central Portugal, and part of southern Portugal, where the population pressures are greatest. The programme aims to remove cars from historic city centres, create pedestrian areas, renovate urban areas to attract population to city centres, create cycle lanes and paths, improve public transport and upgrade parks.

Road safety is also a major concern for both local and central government authorities. Municipalities are responsible for urban safety and most cities have implemented traffic calming measures, such as roundabouts, speed bumps and speed sensitive traffic lights. The central administration sets the maximum speed on national roads and urban areas (where they can be lowered by municipalities).

It also runs extensive information campaigns on the use of safety belts and appropriate child restraints, and on preventing drinking and driving.

The public is increasingly concerned about air pollution, which some municipalities have tried to address through parking policy, the improvement of public services to encourage modal shift and the use of alternative fuels for local and urban buses. A significant number of buses use a sunflower oil mixture (biodiesel) and liquefied petroleum gas to reduce CO_2 emissions. Experiments to build and operate an electric bus driven by fuel cells are supported by the EU's THERMIE programme. EU Directives regulating fuel quality and vehicle emissions are contributing to reducing transport emissions, notably NO_x.

The extension of paid parking in most cities has reduced traffic in central areas and improved traffic flow, though it has increased traffic in outlying areas. Some low cost peripheral parking located near transport hubs has been built, notably in the Lisbon Metropolitan Area (LMA).

There are few studies of urban transport in Portuguese cities. Information on sustainable urban transport measures is available for Lisbon, as an example of a large metropolitan area, and for Evora, a medium size town.

1.2. Evora

Overview

Evora has a population of just over 50 000 inhabitants. Evora's city centre, with about 18 000 inhabitants, was designated as world heritage site by UNESCO in 1987. The city has 40 neighbourhoods around the city centre. Major urban improvement has taken place both in the centre and in the suburbs. In 1977, the Evora Urbanisation Plan was Portugal's first urban master plan. Inspired by the Besançon experience, it considered future traffic problems alongside urban planning. It forecast a spectacular increase of the car ownership rate, from 110 cars per 1 000 inhabitants in 1973 to 150 cars in 1980 and 350 cars in 1995, one of the highest rates in Portugal. As most streets were narrow (46% of the streets are less than 3.5 meters wide), a ring road was needed for transit traffic, which in the 1970s represented about half of total traffic, allowing the creation of a pedestrian area within city walls. Urban transport measures developed as follows:

- 1979: development of the Traffic and Transport Plan;
- 1980: first pilot measures: changes in the city entrance and creation of pedestrian areas;
- 1988: first traffic management measures, which were restrictive: roundabouts were built between the inner and outer city to channel a flow of some 2 000 vehicles per hour;

- 1995: with 70% of jobs, almost one-third of the population and only 3 000 possible parking places in the centre, parking was created outside the city walls and paid parking was instituted in centre.

The strategy of the municipal authorities was to divert part of the traffic to the ring road, whilst encouraging drivers to use parking places outside the city (park and ride) and public transport for their daily trips into the centre. In 1995, 72% of the working population used a car to go to work but not to enter the city. Some 1 200 parking places in the centre (about half of those available) are paid, and the rest reserved for residents. The implementation of the Integrated System of Transport and Paid Parking led to a reduction of traffic flows in and out of the city at the main roundabouts. It increased the traffic within the city, though only for short periods (parking for more than one hour is forbidden in some places), and balanced the number of cars going in and out of the city.

Traffic plan

The city within the old walls was organised into four traffic areas separated by a mainly pedestrian central area. Under this new traffic plan, drivers had to park at the entry closest to their destination and crossing the centre was made more difficult. Another positive change was that the public bus network was redefined, increasing the offer with the same number of buses. Outer ring road traffic increased by 70 to 90%, whilst traffic fell in the centre, except around the university, where the number of students tripled and traffic increased by 7.5% in the morning peak hours.

The plan was approved by municipal authorities in 1980 and the first measures taken in December 1981. The later stages of the plan are still being implemented today. The ultimate goal of the municipal authorities is to charge for motorised entry into the city centre, though such road pricing has yet to be introduced, one of the main obstacles being concern over public acceptance.

Public transport (buses)

In the early 1980s the bus network consisted of 20 lines operated by a public company (which has since been privatised). Those lines provided 8 200 journeys, 73.5% of which served the inner city. Four large neighbourhoods were not connected to the centre. Service frequency was low, with no week-end services and week services ending at 9 p.m. The fleet of large buses slowed and sometimes blocked the traffic in the city centre. Trips on foot were an important part of mobility, though as the city grew, private cars became the main means of transport (about 4 times public transport). In the early 1990s bus lines were redesigned, but financial resources were inadequate to renew the fleet and make public transport more attractive.

As a result, the municipal authorities purchased a fleet of 6 mini-buses, using less polluting biofuels and with an improved level of comfort to attract new users. They

175|

also increased service frequency to every 15 minutes in peak hours and to 60 minutes at other times. These new buses were able to move around the narrow streets in the centre more easily. Ticket prices were frozen for three years, which also attracted new passengers. As the urban transport system works as a whole (paid parking and public transport) and is operated by the same entity (public/private partnership), the income from paid parking can be used to subsidise public transport.

The main problems faced were:

- delays in building parking places outside the city walls due to problems with land purchase;

- growth of economic activity outside city walls attracting central residents and changing mobility patterns;

- enforcement, despite local police co-operation, and some fraud on resident parking permits (people no longer residing in the centre registering as residents).

1.3. Lisbon

Facts and figures

In 1991, only 34% of the Portuguese population lived in urban areas (*i.e.* towns with a population of over 10 000 inhabitants). Most of these (55%) were concentrated in the LMA. The LMA became a legal entity in 1991 (Law No. 44/91), though it was not provided with the financial resources needed to carry out its own programmes or support co-ordinated action taken by all of the LMA's 19 municipal authorities (including the capital city Lisbon). The LMA covers around 3 115 km² with a 1991 population of 2.5 million. The city of Lisbon covers 84 km², with a population of 680 000. In 1991, the car ownership rate was 293 vehicles per 1 000 inhabitants, double the figure a decade earlier. The development of the LMA has not followed communication axes. It was governed by the individual action of private investors, giving rise to random urban development excessively dependent on private cars.

The main economic activity is services, which account for 75% of employment, generating a pendulum commuting movement. In 1990 almost 700 000 people entered the city each day, of which 47% used public transport and 53% private transport (around 300 000 vehicles). Daily trips per capita grew from 1.6 in the 1970s to 2.4 in the 1990s, a 44% rise.

Some 90% of the most important foreign and Portuguese companies have their headquarters in the LMA. Some 40% of all companies registered in Portugal are located there. Of these, 85% are small companies with less than 10 employees. Half these small companies are located in Lisbon and the rest in other LMA municipalities.

While the population of the LMA continues to increase, the population of Lisbon itself is shrinking and growing older because younger residents are forced out by rising land prices. Between 1980 and 1991 the centre lost about 120 000 of its residents, or 79% of the 150 000 inhabitants lost by the city. In 1991, the centre provided 73% of the total employment of Lisbon.

Lisbon has undergone significant changes in the last few decades, notably the expansion of tertiary activities from the original downtown area to other areas, pushing residents into outlying areas.

Institutional issues

Historically, municipal authorities, public transport operators (under the authority of a number of ministries) and some central government institutions have had conflicting responsibilities in the area of urban transport. This has led to inefficiencies in the development of road and railway infrastructure, with road infrastructure being given greater importance, constraining the economic and social development of the city and making Lisbon one of the most congested cities in Europe. The use of public transport has been declining in Lisbon (with the exception of the subway, called metro), notably due to a rise in private cars ownership (120% between 1970 and 1993). For LMA public transport, only river transport increased between 1980 and 1990, while rail transport fell, especially after the motorway was built in the west (the A5 to Cascais). In recognition of these problems, in 1994 municipal authorities adopted the Letter of European Cities for Sustainable Environment (Aalborg Letter), and established a Long Term Local Action Plan.

The main characteristics of Lisbon at the beginning of the 1970s were:

- slower demographic growth and ageing above the national average;
- a growing services sector;
- 24% of the workforce employed in industry;
- low unemployment;
- industrial growth at the periphery of the city beginning to saturate transport infrastructure;
- concentration of administrative and economic decision-making in the city.

In the second half of the 1980s, the main characteristics were:

- industrial relocation to the periphery, made possible by improved transport infrastructure;
- renovation of market and production activities in the riverside area;
- expansion of tertiary activities, forcing some other activities as well as residents out of the centre.

177|

At this time, planning documents dated back to the 1960s: the Lisbon General Urban Plan (1967) and the Master Plan of the Lisbon Area (1964), which suffered from institutional problems that hindered their application. In particular, there was no co-ordinating body for their implementation and public transport operators acted autonomously. The Municipal Master Plan and the Lisbon Strategic Plan were completed in 1989 to address existing issues and prevent problems likely to arise in the 1990s. The Strategic Plan was intended to involve all relevant parties: public operators with monopoly franchises, businesses, schools and universities, municipal managers and all involved, interested citizens. These plans were applied to transport and mobility measures in the 1990s, notably through the following measures:

- expansion of the metro, tripling its size in the last 12 years;
- building of a railway crossing on the Tagus river (under construction) and improvement of suburban, regional and national railways;
- rehabilitation and modernisation of the tram network (partly achieved);
- modernisation and reinforcement of fluvial transport;
- development of interfaces between different transport modes, along with supporting parking places;
- completion of two ring roads (CRIL and CREL).

Concerning urban planning, these measures have had the following effect:

- renewal of the city centre;
- population recovery for Lisbon, attracting younger people;
- linking of the city to its river;
- development and integration of the eastern side of the city.

The 1998 Lisbon Universal Exhibition resulted in a significant development of transport infrastructure and accessibility, as well as the installation of telecommunication and exhibition facilities that remained after the event. It also renovated a very degraded area of the city.

Bus lanes

A survey of mobility in the LMA has recently been completed and is expected to yield significant quantitative data. Because urban space is scarce and private car use growing, the Lisbon municipality decided to encourage public transport, notably through the creation of bus lanes in the main arteries connecting shopping areas. In the absence of light railway systems and given the poor performance of trains (although they are improving), bus flows reach 100 buses/hour in either direction in morning peak hours, or even 200 buses/hour in some exchange areas such as Campo Grande. Competition from private cars had reduced the commercial speed of buses by 10% before bus lane policies were implemented.

The main purpose was to raise the commercial speed of buses, thereby increasing service frequency, reducing waiting times and improving overall bus service availability, quality and image, leading ultimately to increased use of public transport. First, 40 kilometres of bus lanes were developed, though they were not respected over 6 kilometres because of poor sign-posting. Another 8.6 kilometres were added in 1995. Commercial speed increased in some arteries from 9 km/hour to 14 km/hour in morning peak hours.

The introduction of bus lanes is closely coordinated with other public space management measures (traffic light systems and parking policy) taken by the municipality. The process began in the early 1980s and is still under way. New bus lanes, combined with traffic light systems giving priority to buses, were recently implemented on the avenue along the river leading to the east of the city. In the near future bus lanes will be created from outside Lisbon (Algés) into the centre and from the north-west periphery (Pontinha) to the east (Areeiro).

Difficulties encountered included:

- practical difficulties in separating and organising bus traffic (some stops had to be located in the middle corridor);
- financing problems;
- frequent invasion of private cars in bus lanes, sometimes due to insufficient signalling;
- high enforcement costs, especially initially, though enforcement proved essential.

Priority to public transport

There has been a slight increase in the use of public transport in recent years, as shown by the following indicators:

- the Carris bus company saw its occupancy coefficient grow in 1997, mainly due to the new tramway;
- the Lisbon metro is the only mode that grew regularly between 1970 and 1995 (1.4% annual increase in the number of transported passenger-kilometres);
- Transtejo (the main fluvial transport operator) saw a growth of 9.4% in passenger-kilometres in 1996.

In the early 1990s, Carris started renovating the tramway lines on the waterfront corridor. Articulated cars with a total capacity of 210 passengers started to operate in 1995 on a 15.4 kilometre line known as the Belem line, the largest operated by Carris, conveying up to 4 000 passengers per hour in each direction at peak times. It is a key interchange with other transport modes (ferries at Belem, and suburban trains, buses and ferries at Cais do Sodré). This route is due to be extended to the outer suburbs of Lisbon, to Cruz Quebrada where there is a new park and ride terminal with capacity for 4 500 cars.

The metro was also extended in the early to mid-1990s and the stations improved (aesthetically and practically). At the end of 1997 and in 1998, for to the Lisbon Universal Exhibition, six stations were opened and important line connections were made.

Work started on the old Tejo bridge to enlarge it for a railway crossing. The fleet of river crossing ships was improved and ferries were replaced by catamarans that halved travel time and improved comfort. These measures were accompanied by the construction or extension of parking capacity to 6 650 places at ferry terminals in 1997.

Finally, Carris is improving its buses in terms of comfort and switching to less polluting fuels, as fleet renewal progresses.

Parking policies

In drawing up urban plans for the 1990s, the municipality of Lisbon was faced with the need for parking places to avoid chaotic parking along main streets or sidewalks. The intention was also to reduce traffic in the historic centre by moving parking to other areas and converting the centre to pedestrian areas or areas that could be used for cultural events.

The creation of underground car parks near residential and shopping areas was vital, as was the introduction of paid parking at road level. This would to liberate space in streets and sidewalks, making traffic easier for cars, and, above all, for public transport, and putting an end to the encroachment of pedestrian space by drivers. The idea was to make these parking places rotational, with progressive pricing to discourage longer use. Several such car parks, mostly near subway stations, were built and sidewalks emptied of parked cars.

In the early 1990s a car park with a 2000-car capacity was built near a major transport interface (Campo Grande) and the capacity of the existing car park near another interface (Colegio Militar) was increased. Another car park was built in a shopping area (Chiado) with 600-car capacity, absorbing the parking capacity of an area intended for pedestrian use in the core of the city, near the river. This was a compromise solution, since shop owners opposed the conversion of a major parking area into a pedestrian area, arguing that they would lose customers.

At the same time, field trials were conducted in Lisbon with an Automatic Debiting and Electronic Payment for Transport project, a new parking management and control system improving the management of available parking spaces and providing information to drivers who can pay for parking electronically.

It should be noted that underground car parks get more expensive closer to the city centre, where the cost of parking over one hour is very high.

In 1996, after a change in the presidency of the municipality, parking meters were introduced and gradually extended to the outskirts, generalising paid parking. This measure, though long planned, had been considered politically unpopular. Surprisingly, residents thought it one of the most useful taken by the municipality, even asking for it to be extended further. Enforcement is carried out by the private companies operating the parking meters, with police co-operation to issue fines. Lisbon has a differentiated tariff system applied from 8.00 a.m. to 8.00 p.m. on weekdays and from 8.00 a.m. to 1.00 p.m. on Saturdays.

Pedestrian policy

The municipality decided to improve and create pedestrian areas to raise the quality of life of the residents of Lisbon and those who commute there to work. The Municipal Director Plan together with the Regional Land Use Plan for the LMA made up the relevant legal framework.

In 1990, with the Municipal Order P241/90, the riverside central western area became a shopping and recreation pedestrian area, linking the city to its river. In 1992, together with a central Government authority, the municipality converted a dock and warehouse area into a pleasant pedestrian area where restaurants and bars attract people at night. Some shopping areas in the centre destroyed by fire in 1986 have been renovated and converted to pedestrian areas, where luxury shops and a range of services are located. With the extension of the metro network, the first station located right in the core of the city opened, encouraging the use of public transport instead private cars. Parking is not available, except for a couple of paid parking areas, and enforcement is efficient. Nevertheless, underground car parks nearby make it possible to park for short periods at reasonable cost, with charges increasing markedly beyond one hour.

Park and ride

In the mid-1990s, mobility was improved in the LMA, not only through infrastructure, but also transport mode management. Public transport can be made more attractive in peripheral zones if drivers can park safely and cheaply (a daily fee of EUR 0.75). At city limits, near bus, train and metro stations, parking was provided, some of it free. This measure was accompanied by :

- the improvement of transport interfaces (some yet to be completed, for instance the Cais do Sodré interface, intended to link trains, metros and ferries, has only been completed for train and metro connections);

181|

- the expansion of the metro network (6 more stations, a new line and an increase from 19 km in 1993 to 31 km on 1998).

These measures were made possible by political will and through negotiations between the municipalities involved.

2. Institutional Framework

Portugal is a republic. Legislative powers are held by the Parliament and executive powers by the government. Within continental Portugal (*i.e.* excluding the autonomous islands of Madeira and the Azores), there are only two levels of government: the central administration and the municipalities. There are also administrative regions, but they have no legislative or executive powers.

In urban areas, municipalities have extensive powers, some granted by the Constitution of the Portuguese Republic, though the central administration is mainly responsible for surrounding areas, as well as interurban road transport, railways and ferries.

There are over 300 municipalities with powers to intervene in urban transport. These responsibilities were extended by law No. 159/99, which entrusts municipalities with local and urban transport planning, management and investment over the whole of a municipal area (not just the city area, as in the past). Municipalities also have responsibilities in land use and environmental protection. However, some of these powers can be overridden by central government projects such as infrastructure development. There are also some grey areas where responsibilities are shared. Transport plans are seldom covered in land use master plans, which are subject to public hearings and usually revised every five years (though some municipalities have realised the importance of transport plans and are incorporating them in land use plans). Municipalities have to consult the central administration on issues relating to infrastructure development, protected areas or historic buildings. Municipalities also interact with each other, through municipal associations.

Concerning the organisation of urban transport, there are currently several possible approaches:

- 6 municipalities have their own transport service (the municipality being the operator);

- 23 municipalities have contracts with operators for the provision of public transport;

- one municipality has a mixed public-private company for the provision of urban services (made up of the municipality, a private bus operator and a private firm operating the paid parking computerised management system);

- the two main cities (Lisbon and Oporto) have public bus operators with exclusive rights within the city, plus metro (in Lisbon) and rail operators (two companies for the LMA, one of them private).

Other cities have one or several operators for urban and suburban transport (about 130 companies, with small operators being found mostly in the northern part of the country). The larger operators in terms of fleet and services are in the Lisbon area.

3. Policy Framework

The main examples of urban transport policies in the POLIS programme are provided below.

- Viana do Castelo: removal of car traffic from the historic centre and creation of pedestrian areas; urban renovation to attract residents to the city centre; construction of bicycle lanes (mostly for recreational purposes);
- Bragança: extension of the pedestrian area;
- Vila Real: traffic management, introduction of paid parking, improvement of public transport, extension of green areas;
- Vila do Conde (Oporto Metropolitan Area [OMA]): renovation of the Atlantic waterfront by traffic management (road redesign), creation of pedestrian areas, creation of a bicycle path and implementation of alternative mobility projects;
- Matosinhos (OMA): public space renovation; rehabilitation of degraded industrial areas; extension of pedestrian areas;
- Oporto (OMA): traffic management (road redesign), redefinition of urban uses (mixed with beach use);
- Vila Nova de Gaia (OMA): road redesign; industrial building rehabilitation; creation of a pedestrian street; renovation of the historic centre;
- Aveiro: urban renovation around the wholesale fish market; incentives for river transport; rental bicycle parking in the centre and bicycle paths;
- Coimbra: city centre renovation and accessibility improvements with the construction of a ring road to divert traffic from the city centre;
- Viseu : street /roundabout redesign; creation of a city plaza as a new central area, mixing several activities (business, shopping, housing and parking);
- Guarda: connection between the planned urban green park and the city centre by alternative transport modes; creation of bicycle paths and pedestrian areas; improvement of the city's image;

183|

- Covilhã: clean-up of the city's small rivers, which had been polluted by industrial discharge (from textile plants), enabling the development of green areas along the riverside; possibly also industrial building renovation;

- Castelo Branco: creation of a pedestrian area between the church and the castle; redesign of the centre through traffic management (planned intro-duction of paid underground parking), enabling the conversion of the main square into a large pedestrian area;

- Leiria: cleaning and maintenance of pedestrian areas by the riverside, where a bicycle path is planned; inner centre traffic management and underground paid parking;

- Sintra/Cacém (LMA): prioritisation of roads to regulate city access; pedestrian protection in the inner centre, as well as the creation of a pedestrian path along the river; redesign of the transport interface to remove heavy vehicle traffic and connection of road and rail transport networks by pedestrian paths; creation of a city park;

- Almada /Costa de Caparica (LMA): renovation of the Atlantic waterfront; improvement of degraded buildings; enlargement and improvement of the waterfront pedestrian path, connecting it with pedestrian streets; connec-tion with the Transpraia light train along several beaches; creation of a bicy-cle path between beaches (the bicycle lane was not separated from other traffic); regulation of paid parking and traffic management;

- Beja (in the south Alentejo region): improvement of central accessibility and creation of pedestrian paths connecting cultural areas and monuments; renovation of inner centre; traffic management;

- Albufeira (in the Algarve region in the south of the country): creation of a pedestrian and cycling path connecting the new port infrastructure to the city centre; construction of two peripheral car parks, one at the city entrance on the main road and the other near the football field (for eastern traffic), close to the pedestrian path connecting to the city centre, to reduce traffic in the centre; enlargement of pedestrian and green areas.

Beyond these examples from the POLIS programme, Beja has introduced a pilot-project for collective taxis (taxis on call) with the involvement of the munic-ipality, the central administration, the local transport company and the taxi asso-ciation. Some buses use alternative fuels (mainly in major cities), and there are some electric vehicles, for instance for postal delivery in Evora. Cycling is encouraged by making it easier to load bikes on trains and the metro (at week-ends), and in most cities bicycle paths have been built, though mainly for leisure purposes.

Concerning real time information, a number of screens provide customers with public transport information (schedules, delays, etc.) in the LMA. Screens showing televised information on traffic congestion are installed on main access roads. The possibilities offered by GPS are also being used to improve security in buses and taxis. The AMMOS project tested telematic applications (mainly during the Lisbon Universal Exhibition) in public transport in the LMA and will be extended to other cities. The public could consult screens to plan the most suitable itinerary, connections, prices and predicted travel time, as well as alternative options. The use of (contact free) electronic ticketing was tested in a pilot project shared with other western European cities (ICARE and CALLYPSO projects), though it has yet to be fully implemented.

Although tolls are paid on motorways and on the two bridges leading into Lisbon to recover building and maintenance costs, they have had little effect on modal shift to public transport. There is no urban road pricing.

In October 2000 the Parliament adopted a resolution (No. 68/2000) promoting the use of public transport, in which it recommended that the government:

- create mechanisms for the co-ordination of transport systems to ensure appropriate articulation between modes, and improve accessibility and mobility;

- reinforce measures to promote high quality public transport services, especially those that are more environmentally friendly;

- and reinforce energy policy to save energy and reduce the environmental impact of transport.

The document states that the measures needed to meet these targets include:

- the creation of metropolitan transport commissions;

- incentives to create transport tickets integrating private and public transport, relying on peripheral car parks near mass public transport networks;

- improvement of public transport quality in terms of regularity and comfort;

- strengthening of the interface between public and private transport modes;

- incentives to improve security in public transport;

- incentives for multimodal ticketing systems, including electronic ticketing;

- incentives for less polluting alternative energy sources, especially in city centres;

- increasing support for innovation and new technologies in public transport, as well as telematic technologies for real time information to the public.

Despite this resolution, the measures have not yet been implemented and a legislative proposal concerning the creation of metropolitan commissions was disproved by the national association of municipalities.

185|

4.   Conclusions

Although there are still many difficulties in urban transport planning and man-agement (mostly due to poorly defined or overlapping responsibilities), there is a will to shift policies to favour of public transport. However, many administrative obstacles are difficult to overcome because the parties involved are reluctant to give up their responsibilities. Furthermore, new responsibilities require new fund-ing, even though most municipalities can only raise taxes on property and the con-struction industry, which might not be sufficient to finance public transport systems.

A further administrative difficulty is the lack of effective, competent authori-ties for the organisation of transport in the two main metropolitan areas, where responsibility is shared by 14 and 19 municipalities respectfully. In addition, tasks carried out by public transport operators, such as urban public transport planning and financing, are shared with the central administration.

References

Levy, Maurício (1995), *Articulated cars to serve Tagus waterfront*, in Railway Gazette International, Vol. 151, No. 4 , April, pp. 203.

Viegas, J.M. and Mexia, A (1993), *Lisbon Metro Expands its Network*, in Public Transport International, No. 4 , 1993, pp. 33-37.

Teles de Menezes, Jose (1992) *Gestão Equitativa do Espaço Urbano – corredores BUS em Lisboa*, Seminário Transcomunitário: Transportes Eficientes em Cidades de Média Dimensão (Thermie), 14 May, Coimbra.

Direccao-Geral de Transportes Terrestres (1997), *Transporte Ferroviário e Fluvial : Informação Estatística* 1970-1995, June, Lisbon.

Transtejo, SA (1997) – *Relatório e Contas* 1996 (Report and Accounts 1996), Lisbon.

Carris (1998), *Companhia de Carris de Ferro de Lisboa, S A – Relatório e Contas* 1997, Lisbon.

Hirschfeld, Charlotte (1998), *Lisbonne, ou comment sortir du libéralisme pur et dur*, in Transport Public, February.

Neves, Antonio O. (1996), *Planeamento Estratégico e Ciclo de Vida das Grandes Cidades – Casos de Lisboa e Barcelona*, Ed. Celta, Lisbon.

Stathopoulos, G. and Papachristou, N. *et al.* (1994) *Automatic Debiting and Electronic Payment for Transport- The ADEPT Project: Lisbon Field Trials: Car Park Booking, In-vehicle Guidance and Information, and Fee Collection*, in Traffic Engineering and Control, Vol. 35, No. 6, June, pp. 368-372.

Da Silva, Nunes F. (1992), *Sistemas Integrados de Transporte e Estacionamento: a Proposta de Évora* (*Integrated Transport and Parking Systems: Evora's Proposal*), Seminário Transcomunitário: Transportes Eficientes em Cidades de Média Dimensão (Thermie), 14 May, Coimbra.

Direcção-Geral do Ordenamento do Território (1997), – *Cidades Médias e Dinâmicas Territoriais*, in Sistema Urbano Nacional, Vol. II, October.

Câmara Municipal de Evora (1980), *Plano de Circulação e Transportes de Evora*, May, Evora.

Câmara Municipal de Evora (1992), SITE – Sistema Integrado de Transportes e Estacionamento na Cidade de Evora, Relatório e Caracterização do Sistema, April, Evora.

Russia*

1. The Context

Some 73.2% of the Russian Federation's 146.3 million inhabitants live in urban areas (1998 census). Over 35% of the population lives in urban areas of more than 500 000 inhabitants. Complex social and economic trends are defining the development of urban public transport. In recent years the worsening social and economic situation, with job and production losses, a reduction in the average income and a simultaneous rise in prices (including fuel, energy and transport service prices) has led to a steady reduction in mobility (Figure 26).

Figure 26. **Trends in mobility**

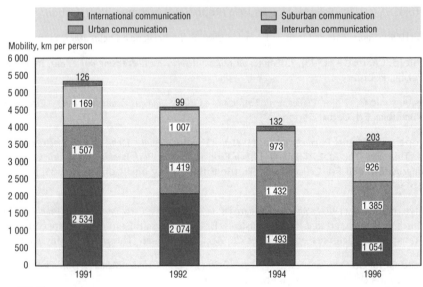

Source: ECMT.

---

* Report written by Vadim Donchenko, State Scientific and Research Institute of Motor Transport, Moscow.

Despite the consequences of the 1998 economic crisis, the growth of the car fleet has remained high because Russian-made new and second-hand cars and imported second-hand cars which fell sharply in price. The highly urbanised population and low car ownership (less than 40% of households own a car) makes Russia more dependent on public transport than other countries of similar average income. The rate of urban public transport use is about 85% in Russia, compared with 20% in Western Europe and about 3% in the United States. Cars represent about 9% of total passenger traffic in Russia. As a result, a reliable urban public transport system remains a major factor for social stability.

The economic reforms transferred responsibility for urban public transport and management of bus services (as well as trolleybuses and trams) from the state to the municipalities, but did not allocate sufficient funding. Municipal budgets made no provision for fleet replacement, previously funded by the state, which resulted in the loss of quality and quantity of public transport services at a time when demand was increasing in urban areas. Consequently, more affluent users switched to car use: between 1995 and 1999 the modal share of cars increased from 15-20% to 30-35% (in some urban areas 50%).

Reform of the transport management system began in 1991 and removed public transport management from the central administration. Despite major changes in social and economic conditions and rising standards of service quality, no fundamental reform was made to the main instruments for regulating public transport operation. Only very small changes in the use of specific indices were made in the legislative and normative base of public transport management. Besides the partial transfer of powers to municipalities, no institutional reforms were made. Processes involved with motorization also remained unregulated at national level. The private car fleet is not considered as an object for state management under the competence of the Ministry of Transport.

As a result car traffic has significantly increased in urban areas. In large urban areas, motor transport accounts for 80 to 90% of total air pollution emissions. Investigations have shown that in Moscow, cars contribute 64% of the total emissions from motor transport (buses less than five%). The contribution of cars to emissions of hydrocarbons (HC), nitrogen dioxide, benzene, toluene, acetaldehyde, xylene and styrene exceeds 70%, and their contribution to emissions of benzene vapour is as high as 90%.

1.1. *Key trends in urban travel*

In 2000, the urban passenger vehicle fleet comprised 15.3 million cars (77.7% of the total number of cars), including 14.4 million private cars and 490 700 buses (77.5% of the total number of buses). Although the 1998 economic crisis caused a slowdown in car growth (Table 27), numbers of cars remain high and are expected

Table 27. **Car fleet (1992 to 1999)**

	Number of cars	Annual growth (%)
1992	10 797 522	–
1993	11 781 818	109.1
1994	13 223 507	112.2
1995	14 727 755	111.4
1996	15 814 988	107.4
1997	17 631 626	111.5
1998	18 819 558	106.7
1999	19 717 782	104.7

Source: ECMT.

to rise in the near future. The motorization rate (number of cars per 1 000 inhabitants) varies regionally due to economic differences. In 1999, the average motorization rate was 130, below developed countries, though the difference is reducing very quickly.

Table 28 shows the wide regional variability in the number of private cars. Car ownership in various urban areas is also very different:

- 220 cars per 1 000 inhabitants in Moscow;
- 178 cars per 1 000 inhabitants in Voronezh;
- 150 cars per 1 000 inhabitants in Ufa;
- 120 cars per 1 000 inhabitants in Nizhny Novgorod;
- 200 cars per 1 000 inhabitants in Toliatty;
- 110 cars per 1 000 inhabitants in Novosibirsk.

In some regions with no developed industry and poor incomes, the motorization level is less than 100.

Car use has intensified with the growth of the fleet. Average use of private cars increased by 50% between 1993 and 1999 (10 to 15 thousand kilometres). The average age of cars in urban areas is 10.8 years. However, this average varies from

Table 28. **Distribution of cars in Russian regions**

Motorization rate (cars per 1 000 inhabitants)	Number of regions	Number of cars	% of the total car fleet
< 80	13	1 105 663	6
81-100	22	2 696 066	17
101-180	39	10 538 438	60
> 181	4	2 780 361	17

9.5 years in Moscow to 13.8 years in the urban areas of the Republic Mari El. At present most cars are Russian made and do not meet modern environmental requirements. Only 14.5% of cars are foreign (new and second-hand). It has been estimated that only 4 to 7% of the fleet meets EURO 1 requirements.

In 1999 urban bus traffic was organised into 1 315 urban areas and grew 2%. In the last two years trends have returned to levels at the beginning of the 1990s. Urban electric transport operates in 113 urban areas (tramways in 27 urban areas, trolleybuses in 46, tramways and trolleybuses in 41, metros in six). The new economy is reopening the market for taxis which now operate in 149 urban areas. A new kind of transport service is emerging with the use of cars and minibuses on demand for passenger transport. Inland water transport also carries a small volume of passenger traffic.

The most important trend in urban and suburban traffic is the constantly increasing participation of small businesses which operate on an equal basis with state and municipal companies. About 20 000 buses belonging to such companies now run on regular routes.

1.2. Urban public transport infrastructure and fleet

At the end of 1999 there was 9 845 kilometres of trolleybus lines, 6 491 kilometres of tramway lines and 398 kilometres of metro lines. The public transport fleet comprised 57.7 thousand buses, 12.2 thousand trolley buses, 12.0 thousand tramways and 5.8 thousands metro wagons (Table 29).

A significant proportion of vehicles are used beyond their standard lifetime :

- more than 40% of buses;

- 39.3% of trolley buses;

- 36.4% for tramways;

- 5.6% of metro wagons;

- 30% of electrical railway wagons.

Table 29.   **Urban public transport fleet**

	1991	1992	1993	1994	1995	1996	1997	1998	1999
Tramway vehicles	14 737	14 326	13 913	13 499	13 263	13 013	12 731	12 392	11 950
Trolley buses	13 980	13 894	13 827	13 469	13 161	12 752	12 500	12 257	12 190
Metro wagons	5 373	5 509	5 573	5 662	5 745	5 785	5 801	5 781	5 763
Buses	59 800	56 100	56 600	59 700	56 800	56 700	58 400	57 900	57 700
Taxis (thousands)	52	32	25	18	14	12	9	7	8

The average age of buses in 1998 was 9.9 years, metro wagons 15 years, trolley buses about eight years. The condition of the public transport fleet is critical, as no capital renewal is possible due to the absence of investment mechanisms. When creating such mechanisms not only must the possibilities and interests of urban transport companies and local authorities be taken into account, but also the strain on the transport engineering industry. Public transport vehicles are mainly bought with regional and local budgets. In 1999 the investment for buses was RB 1 950 million (US$70 million), for trolley buses and tramways RB 408 million (US$14 million) and for the metro RB 100 million (US$3.5 million). Investment from central administration was zero and US$0.7 million came from foreign investment.

With urban public transport companies short of investment capital, the production of trolley buses, tramways and metro wagons fell sharply in the 1990s (Figure 27).

Although the fleet of urban buses is about 60% below the socially required level of production, bus imports stabilised in the 1990s (Figure 28). This trend may be explained by the limited purchasing capacity of public transport companies and private firms. The market for urban buses offers new Russian made buses, new and second-hand imported buses and buses assembled in Russia from imported components. In practice the most frequently purchased vehicles are

Figure 27. **Production of public transport vehicles**

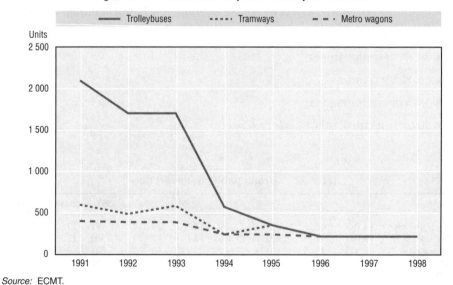

Source: ECMT.

Figure 28. **Production and imports of buses in the 1990s**

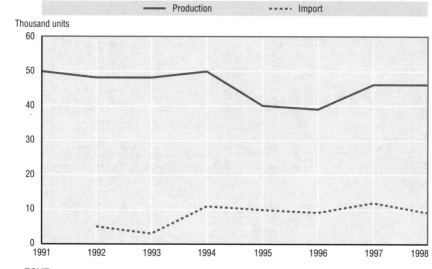

Source: ECMT.

obsolete Russian models and imported second-hand buses which are over six years old.

1.3. Urban public transport

In spite of the considerable growth of private motor transport (mainly cars), public transport still retains the largest market share in urban areas. The total number of urban and suburban public transport routes, which was reduced during the first years of the economic reforms, has stabilised at 15.8 thousand. Urban public transport volumes grew in 1999, with a total of 40.1 billion passengers representing a total of 205.0 billion passenger kilometres travelled, of which:

- buses: 19.4 billion passengers representing 104.4 billion passenger kilometres;
- trolleybus: 8.9 billion passengers representing 28.6 billion passenger kilometres;
- tramway: 7.7 billion passengers representing 26.2 billion passenger kilometres;
- metro: 4.1 billion passengers representing 45.8 billion passenger kilometres.

Suburban passenger traffic also grew in 1999, with about 3.9 billion people transported, representing 56.2 passenger kilometres (Table 30).

193|

Table 30. Urban and suburban public transport passenger statistics

	1991	1992	1993	1994	1995	1996	1997	1998	1999
Number of urban areas with public transport, mode of transport, units									
Tramway	70	70	70	68	68	68	68	68	..
Metro	6	6	6	6	6	6	6	6	..
Trolleybus	86	86	86	85	85	85	87	87	..
Bus	1 387	1 293	1 321	1 286	1 249	1 266	1 250	1 289	..
Taxi	465	442	365	241	222	186	169	157	..
Number of routes – mode of transport, units									
Tramway	..	695	696	686	677	681	664	649	..
Trolleybus	..	891	907	916	923	925	932	920	..
Bus	28 545	26 960	26 304	26 929	25 973	25 342	25 806	25 384	..
Total number of passengers – all modes of transport (millions)	45 962.1	44 919.4	45 320.2	43 825.3	42 809.8	43 390.0	43 959.4	43 468.3	44 095.5
Of which :									
Tramway	7 619.5	8 070.6	8 125.2	7 644.4	7 563.9	7 510.8	7 481.0	7 481.0	7 710.0
Metro	3 229.0	3 567.5	4 212.1	4 224.4	4 149.9	4 173.3	4 128.2	4 146.2	4 087.1
Trolleybus	8 004.9	8 619.1	9 101.6	8 751.3	8 546.6	8 681.0	8 812.9	8 852.3	8 925.7
Bus	26 511.8	24 352.4	23 703.7	23 078.5	22 458.5	22 963.5	23 480.5	22 947.0	23 331.4
Taxi	525.6	265.7	139.3	98.4	66.0	43.4	33.1	24.1	20.8
Maritime	13.2	8.4	6.1	4.2	3.2	2.1	1.5	1.2	0.8
Internal water	58.1	35.7	32.2	24.1	21.7	15.9	22.2	16.5	19.7
Passenger turnover – all modes of transport, million passenger kilometres	29 497.5	275 230.8	274 469.0	269 214.8	264 907.3	263 843.2	263 652.9	258 744.1	261 768.6
Of which:									
Tramway	24 101.2	25 961.9	26 326.1	25 869.5	25 356.7	25 238	25 035.8	25 483.3	26 214
Metro	35 571.8	39 589.4	46 754.7	47 000.7	46 180.3	46 622.3	46 195.4	46 458.8	45 775.4
Trolleybus	23 918.5	26 161.8	28 280.3	27 154.1	26 852.3	27 330.1	27 872.7	28 185.9	28 562.3
Bus	202 454.9	179 048.4	170 601.1	167 386.2	165 229.8	163 747.0	163 818.4	158 065.0	160 704.7
Taxi	7 883.5	3 773.4	1 977.9	1 406.6	950.3	624.3	476.8	345.4	306.7
Maritime	221.3	124.5	92.0	83.5	64.6	84.2	16.7	16.3	16.3
Internal water	824.3	571.4	436.9	314.2	273.3	199.1	237.1	189.4	189.2

Source: ECMT.

Table 31. **Comparison of urban public transport use in Russia
and some western countries (1996)**

Country	Total annual distance covered by public transport vehicles, (million kilometres)	Average distance covered by public transport vehicles/ inhabitant/day (kilometres)	Average number of passengers/vehicle
Great Britain	4 600	79	9
Italy	5 186	91	10
USA	9 851	38	10
Germany	4 714	58	15
Russia	7 536	51	38

Source: ECMT.

Table 31 compares the data for urban public passenger transport services in Russia with other Western countries.

1.4. *Fares, fare privileges and the financial state of public transport companies*

The income of specialised state and municipal public transport companies does not usually cover operational costs (Table 32). The main reasons for this and the management inefficiency of enterprises are fare limits and the large number of people with fare privileges.

Trip fares are revised annually by regional authorities on the basis of population solvency and the social situation of the region. The frequency of fare revisions is inadequate in view of the constant growth of direct expenditure on transport which influences primary costs. Fares vary considerably from region to region and some (Irkutsk Region, Ulyanovsk Region, Altai Krai, Republic of Dagestan, Chuvash Republic) urban bus fares can remain unchanged for more

Table 32. **Share of operational costs covered by fares
(nine months of 1999)**

Mode of transport	Share of operational costs, covered by fares (%)
Urban buses	58.2
Suburban buses	61.3
Tramways	43.3
Trolley buses	49.8
Metro	69.3

Source: ECMT.

Figure 29. **Regional distribution of the average urban public transport fare**

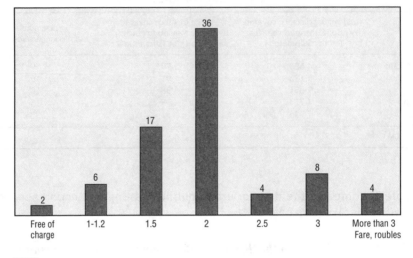

Source: ECMT.

than a year. Figure 29 shows the regional distribution of the average amount paid for urban public transport fares.

Granting reduced or privileged fares can be justified for social reasons. However the problem of fare privileges is caused by a lack of harmonisation between the legislation and the economic situation coupled with a lack of instruments to cover the shortfall incurred by the transport of passengers granted reductions for social or professional reasons. Moreover, the number of categories of "privileged" passengers is increasing. There are now fifty privileged traveller categories compared with nineteen a decade ago. Some 80% of the passengers who pay less for their trips (privilege tickets, free tickets) do so under privileges defined at national level (16% for professional reasons and 84% for social reasons including invalids, pensioners and students). In addition 15% of passengers travel illegally due to high ticket prices. The resulting share of passengers who pay for their tickets in urban and suburban public transport has halved in recent years and is now only 38%.

Regional and local budgets only partially cover the income loss for public transport companies caused by reduced fares, which further aggravates the financial position of such companies (Figures 30 and 31). In 1999, the shortfall for public transport companies had risen to RB 16.6 from RB 15.1 in 1998. On average annual

Figure 30. **Comparison of public transport company losses and budget subsidies, 1997-1999**

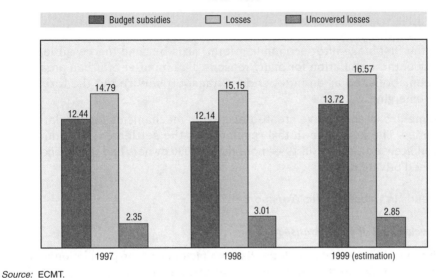

Source: ECMT.

Figure 31. **Comparison of public transport losses by mode and budget subsidies (1999)**

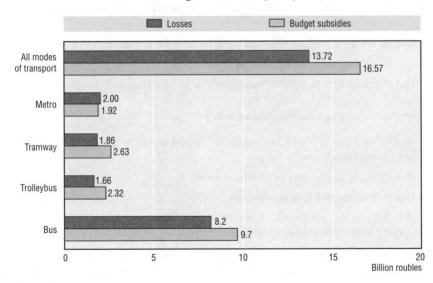

Source: ECMT.

subsidies paid by city administrations to public transport companies in 1996 was about US$20 per urban inhabitant.

1.5. Taxis

In the first stage after economic reform, taxis became inaccessible for the majority of the population for many reasons. In a number of urban areas, taxis had been abolished as an independent transport service but the taxi fleet is now re-emerging.

Some urban areas have created economic mechanisms for regulating taxi companies. The key issue in taxi regulation is the settlement of competition between licensed carriers (in 1999 more than 30 000 owners had taxi licences) and unlicensed private drivers.

2. Trends in Urban Public Transport

2.1. Development of public transport

Urban public transport is dependant on factors such as population mobility, competition between different modes and private cars, the unpredictability of demand, lack of profitability of services and funding. The transport mobility of Russians in 1996 was 5 122 kilometres per person per year, 20% less than in 1990. In 1996, average public transport mobility was 3 568 kilometres per person per year, 33% less than in 1990. Figure 26 illustrates the changes in average mobility and the decreasing trend of urban public transport use between 1990 and 1996, when:

- use of urban travel decreased by 8.1% and suburban travel by 21%;
- use of private cars increased by 48%;
- the average urban public transport trip length decreased by 30%.

2.2. Correlation between income and mobility

The loss of market share for public transport services observed over the past years can be explained by:

- the difficult social and economic situation;
- the reduction in living standards;
- the worsening economic state of public transport companies and loss in quality of urban public transport services;
- the rapid growth in the number of private cars.

The social and economic situation and reduction in living standards sharply restricted demand which in turn reduced both the average number of trips by all modes of transport per person (in urban areas 600 trips per person in 1996) and the average trip length. This trend which continued between 1997 and 1999 has affected the geographical distribution of passenger flows and redistributed the market share of the transport modes.

Since the economic reforms, the share of the monthly wage spent on transport has increased from 2% in 1993 to more than 7% in 1997 and in the largest urban areas now exceeds 10%. Between 1992 and 1997 the fares for urban public transport grew almost four times faster than the average income and almost ten times faster than the average minimum monthly income. The situation is most difficult for those with earnings at the level of the average income. The cost of 50 monthly trips has increased from 5% of the average income between 1992 and 1993 to 17% in 1997.

Estimation of the elasticity of demand for public transport according to income reveals a high correlation between the income level and trip length (Table 33). It has been shown that the greater the need for a trip, the lower the elasticity of demand. Demand is least elastic for all business and recreational trips in suburban areas (for example, weekend trips to secondary homes). Recreational (for example, summer holidays) and long-distance trips are the most sensitive to variations caused by changes in fares.

Growth in the use of private cars for non-commercial purposes has reduced solvent demand for all modes of public transport because the incomes of car owners and their families tend to be above average. This makes it more difficult to raise transport fares (especially for urban and suburban travel) and increases pressure on national and local budgets for subsidies to cover the growing expenses of public transport.

The largest passenger volumes are in urban areas. In large urban areas, public transport includes: buses, trolley buses, tramways, (including high speed trams),

Table 33. **Correlation between income and trip length**

		1993	1994	1995	1996	1997
Real income	Index	100.0	66.2	47.7	50.1	51.8
Long-distance passenger turnover (rail+plane)	Billion passenger kilometres	263.4	212.8	187.1	168.4	154.5
	Index	100.0	80.8	71.0	63.9	58.7
Suburban passenger turnover (rail+bus)	Billion passenger kilometres	181.6	169.7	158.6	151.9	147.2
	Index	100.0	93.4	87.4	83.7	81.1

Source: ECMT.

metro, electric railways, private cars, taxis and "route taxis" (small or medium size buses which are operated on regular routes with no fixed stops). In the smaller urban areas, passenger transport is usually by bus and private car. Demand for travel has low elasticity linked to price and income but high cross elasticity.

2.3. Quality of service and competition

The quality of urban bus services considerably deteriorated during the period of economic reform. In a number of urban areas bus waiting time can be up to 70 minutes and passenger density on buses more than 10 people per square metre (the norm is six passengers per square metre). As a result walking has become a common mode for short distances (up to two kilometres).

Lack of systematic research and great differences in the degree of development of private and privatised bus companies between urban areas makes it very difficult to estimate the market split between the different types of bus ownership. In urban areas where the administration creates favourable conditions for private owners to operate, the market share for private buses can be between 35 and 40%. The development of competition between different forms of ownership, a sufficient number of private owners and efficient regulation of transport by municipalities has considerably improved the quality of passenger transport services. For example, in 1994 the World Bank qualified development of the public transport system in Cherepovets (Urals) as one of the worst in Russia. The municipality's efficient transport policy (support of private bus companies, contracts of carriage decided on the basis of competition by municipal order) has significantly changed the situation. By 1998, the number of buses had increased from 0.3 buses to 1.4 buses per 1 000 inhabitants, with an average waiting time of 3-5 minutes (maximum 10 minutes) and an average passenger density of 0.1 passengers per square metre.

2.4. Subsidies and special services

The high level of subsidy for transport companies from national and regional budgets is the important feature of the public transport market. On average 5 to 6% of municipal budgets goes to finance public transport companies. This level of subsidy reflects the importance of a good public transport system in maintaining regional social and economic stability as well as the impossibility to set economically viable fares due to low income levels. Under subsidy conditions there is practically no competition between the modes of urban public transport and market share depends on municipal policy. In addition to economic instruments (e.g. fixed fares for each mode of transport) municipalities often use direct administrative pressure to guarantee service. For example in some urban areas, private bus owners are only granted licences provided they ensure "socially important" services. Almost 30% of licences given to bus owners between 1994 and 1998 had special conditions attached. The list of these special conditions is constantly growing: to the traditional conditions such as peak hour services and services for schools and hospitals, have been added others such as the carriage of war veterans and services for schools and colleges from the suburbs.

2.5. Taxi traffic

One of the negative consequences of the economic reforms on the transport sector was a sharp reduction in taxi operators. The taxi fleet has fallen to 9 000 vehicles (six times less than in 1990). The number of urban areas with a taxi service has fallen from 550 to 169, the volume of taxi traffic has been reduced almost 17 fold and some areas taxis have practically disappeared. Privatisation of the majority of state taxi enterprises by lease or sale of the cars to the drivers, inability to renew and replenish the car fleet, and shortcomings in licence and fare systems for private taxi owners has made taxis inaccessible for the majority of Russians. At the same time the need for this kind of service is satisfied by the unregulated and unlicensed work of private car owners, which removes a significant portion of urban passenger traffic from state control and taxation.

3. Institutional Context

3.1. National level

Ministry of Transport of the Russian Federation (MoT)

The MoT is responsible for state transport policy, which aims to satisfy the transport needs of the population and the economy. The MoT's main tasks are regulation, management and control, to ensure the safe, efficient and sustainable functioning of transport networks (except railways) and co-ordinate the relevant supervisory bodies.

The MoT presents draft laws to the Legislative Assembly of the Russian Federation. It is responsible for implementation (standards, rules and requirements), development and completion of national programmes and projects and the organisation of the necessary scientific research related to transport legislation. The MoT has its own regional inspection body (Russian Transport Inspection) which, together with other state control bodies, ensures that transport legislation, traffic safety regulations and environmental requirements are observed.

Russian Federation Building and Communal Housing State Committee

The committee carries out interdepartmental co-ordination and regulation in building, architecture, town-planning, housing policy and communal housing in

201

co-operation with regional administrations. This Committee has regional architecture and town-planning bodies across the entire Russian Federation.

Ministry of Internal Affairs of the Russian Federation – State Road Inspection Division

The division enforces compliance with road safety regulations, conducts traffic engineering and control work (including technical facilities and automated systems), takes measures to improve motor vehicle and pedestrian traffic, approves road building, reconstruction and maintenance projects and the construction of urban electric transport lines (traffic safety issues). It approves the opening of regular public transport routes. The State Road Inspection Division acts at national level and in every region.

Ministry of Natural Resources

In 2000 the Ministry of Natural Resources took over from the Environmental Protection State Committee. It has responsibility for the development and realisation of national environmental protection policy and for compliance with environmental legislation and regulations. The Ministry is represented in each region.

3.2. Regional level

At regional level, the development of transport infrastructure and the drafting of regional transport and town planning policy is the responsibility of 89 regional administrations. Each administration has departments managing transport and building projects and enforcing housing and land use policy. At the same time, regional bodies of the central administration work in each region to ensure national and regional co-ordination.

3.3. Local level

Municipalities are responsible for the practical management of urban transport development and land use. These administrations are entirely responsible for:

- implementing legislation to develop urban land use plans and programmes for urban transport and road traffic;
- ensuring the smooth operation (including funding) of environmental safety improvements in urban public transport;
- repairing, building and maintaining the urban road network and traffic engineering.

Each municipality has specific departments to take decisions and municipal companies are set up to implement practical measures.

3.4. Interaction of authorities

Interaction of urban transport and land use management authorities is based on mutual co-ordination of the decisions and project development (programmes). The legislation defines when investigations must be conducted by the state control bodies (environmental assessment of building projects, examination of town planning documentation). Meetings are organised by the different levels of government to discuss concrete projects and programmes, with the participation of representatives from all interested authorities and organisations.

3.5. Institutional problems in urban transport management and land use

Unfortunately the existing institutional framework does not provide for efficient management of urban public transport. The main cause of the failure is not poor co-ordination between ministries, committees and organisations at national, regional and local levels but the lack of a common legal policy basis to develop urban transport. Governmental monitoring and management of mobility is inadequate and the instruments for central management of town planning and urban transport are not designed to meet sustainable urban transport objectives.

The main town planning legislation is the Town Planning Code which merely outlines the need to observe environmental requirements when developing town planning documents for building and renovating urban areas. The code specifies that the planning of an urban area and bordering areas must include provision for public transport and the urban road network. However, the state town planning policy defined by this Code gives no clear guidelines on the ways to achieve a reasonable reduction in transport demand through land use planning, restriction of private car use and supporting the development of public transport and non-motorised modes of mobility.

On the whole the weight of difficult urban transport decisions falls on municipalities which tend to operate according to their funding possibilities and their (often inadequate) understanding of the ways to solve the problems they face.

4. Policy Framework

4.1. Urban transport and land use planning

There is no integrated national policy for urban travel. The Ministry of Transport has developed and is implementing the Federal Programme for the Development of City Bus, Trolleybus and Tramway Production, financed by the federal budget.

At national level the General Territory Settlement Scheme for the Russian Federation and the Principal Proposals for Development of Town Planning for

203|

Different Parts of the Russian Territory are being developed. In the regions, complex programmes for environmental protection and the use of natural resources are also being developed. In practice, each municipality has a public transport development plan. It is the responsibility of urban municipalities to design and implement urban road plans and programmes which aim to improve road network capacity and traffic conditions. Unfortunately the realisation of most measures suffers from lack of funding.

4.2. Improvement in legislation and regulations in urban transport management

Three new laws have been passed by central administration, one to serve as a basis for a state policy in urban public transport , the second on motor transport (commercial transport only) and the third to ensure the environmental safety of motor transport.

The next phase of national laws will target sustainable development in urban transport; environmental assessment; local government; the land code; air protection; the health of the population; road safety; and the town-planning code.

4.3. Integration of land use and transport planning

Measures in this field are carried out at regional and local levels. Planning public transport development is a major feature of development plans for large urban areas. Forecasts for motor fleet and traffic volume changes are used as the basis for street infrastructure planning.

4.4. Development of public transport

At present the main problems affecting the development of public transport are the following:

- lack of funds to support urban public transport. In many cases budget planning and estimation of losses is carried out without sufficient data; specific assistance from the federal authorities is seldom sought;
- the absence of a simple urban public transport fare policy which can be broadly applied;
- rising fares in a context of income reductions which has reduced the willingness of passengers to pay for transport;
- the problem of finding a way to recoup the losses from privileged fares;
- the lack of an effective system for traffic registration and accounting expenditure and income, the practice of drawing up contracts between transport companies (owners) and municipalities, and the use of an index system which defines urban public transport in contradiction with market economy

instruments and conditions. In fact, there is no control on real transport expenses and no systematic audit of the transport system. Available data on traffic transport mobility and shortfalls in transport profitability are in many cases incorrect and excessive;

- financial restrictions seriously undermining the development of the transport engineering industry which is in urgent need of modernisation;

- inadequate communication systems to ensure minimum passenger information on service changes and poor timetable co-ordination.

As a result transport companies have been forced to raise fares whilst simultaneously cutting down the route network and reducing service quality (regularity, number of vehicles in service and the technical condition of vehicles).

Measures proposed to improve urban public passenger transport include the creation of a three-level system (national, regional, local) of special funds for urban public transport. Subsidies should cover 40% to 45% of the real expenses of urban public transport (15-20% of this will be from a national fund, 80% to 85% from regional and local funds) and the remainder has to be earned from ticket sales. The special funds will be sourced from:

- additional taxes on gasoline, and changes in the taxes and duties on car sales and obtaining number plates;

- an urban charge for car owners (introduction of local car owner tax, or a municipal parking tax).

Other measures include exemption of urban transport companies from specific transport taxes, and reform of the urban public transport management system to create a more commercial relationship between municipalities, urban public transport planning organisations and transport companies with different patterns of ownership. Improvement of the contract form of interrelations would include municipal regulation of social transport fares. The State will decide on the degree of competence of municipal authorities to regulate fares.

Urban public transport income could also be increased by reviewing the customer base and legal regulation of privileged trips. Legislative instruments will determine compensation levels for budget losses incurred through fare privileges granted to the socially needy, and also review the definition of reasonably grounded levels of compensation. Compensation will be paid into local budgets to ensure these funds are only spent on urban public transport. The proposals also include the introduction of a simple bus pass for privileged categories of passengers (this system has already been introduced in some urban areas such as Nizhny Novgorod and Krasnodar).

Modernisation of the urban public transport fleet is also needed as is constant monitoring of the supply and demand for urban public transport, and the

205|

development and implementation of a registration system for urban public transport traffic.

Strong legislative and executive policy at national and regional levels is indispensable to resolve urban public transport issues, in particular privileged categories of passengers and mechanisms for compensating the real cost of their transport.

4.5. *Reduction of car use in urban areas*

The main factors reducing car use in the largest urban areas are the extreme congestion which reduces the average speed to between 10 km/h and 15 km/h, and parking restrictions in the centre of urban areas. Administrations have also introduced traffic restrictions in the largest urban areas:

- prohibiting motor vehicles from entering certain specially registered natural zones;
- prohibition of truck traffic through city centres;
- prohibition of truck traffic in some urban artery roads at set times;
- prohibition of stopping in the busiest urban roads.

In Moscow, proposals are being developed for the "environmental classification" of motor vehicles with restrictions on the registration and operation of lower "environmental class" motor vehicles in some urban areas (Figure 32). These proposals are formulated in the draft city law on the environmental safety of motor vehicles. The proposals are being considered both by the Moscow Government and by the State Duma (Russian Parliament). Any measures taken to limit the use of some categories of private car and increase car owners' responsibility to comply with environmental regulations meet with strong opposition from the media and politicians trying to gain favour with the car owner lobby. In many cases this obstructs decision-making.

4.6. *Traffic management*

The main local road traffic management measures being taken to increase the average speed and smoothness of traffic flow and reduce intersection delays are:

- implementation of modern traffic light management systems (green wave for co-ordinated regulation of traffic lights);
- building multi level road junctions and underground pedestrian crossings;
- introduction of traffic engineering measures (road marking, road signs) directed at smoothing the traffic flow and increasing network capacity;
- implementation of a parking policy.

Figure 32. **Environmental classification of motor vehicles (extract)**
Motor vehicles

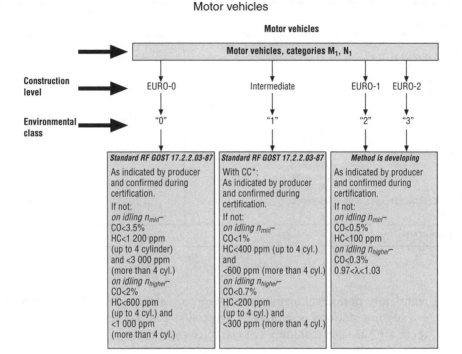

Source: ECMT.

4.7. Other measures

Other measures are also being introduced to improve sustainable urban transport:

- converting vehicles (including municipal vehicles) to compressed natural gas (CNG) using local budgets, special extra-budget funds and contributions from the Russian Joint-Venture Company GAZPROM. At present about 50 000 motor vehicles run on CNG. Further expansion is restrained by the lack of effective economic and administrative support mechanisms;

- retrofitting vehicles to reduce pollutant emissions; for example in Moscow between 1997 and 1999 more than 14 000 buses and trucks were fitted with oxidising catalytic converters using a special fund set up by the Moscow municipality;

207|

Table 34. **Schedule for EU regulations and their introduction in Russia**

Regulations	Russia		UN EEC	
	Application date	End date	Application date	End date
83-01B (EURO 1)	–	–	30.12.92	2.07.95
83-02 (EURO 1)	01.01.99	–	2.07.95	7.12.96
83-03B,C (EURO 2)	–	–	8.12.96	–
EURO 3	–	–	2000	–
EURO 4	–	–	2005	–
49-00	–	–	15.04.82	14.05.90
49-01	01.04.96 (1year)	31.12.97	14.05.90	01.07.92
49-02A (EURO 1)	1.01.98 (1 year)	–	01.07.92	04.10.95
	1.04.96 (3 years)	1.01.99		
49-02B (EURO 2)	1.01.99 (3 years)	–	01.10.95	1999-2000
EURO 3	–	–	2000	–

Source: ECMT.

• mandatory periodical inspections for motor vehicles in service using modern testing stations operated by specialist companies. In Moscow alone there are 123 such test lines for cars, trucks and buses;

• banning the sale of leaded petrol in some regions and urban areas (Moscow, Saint-Petersburg, Samara, Nizhny Novgorod, Moscow Region, Sochi...); production of low sulphur content diesel fuel (Moscow); control of fuel quality at filling stations;

• certification of car industry production to ensure compliance with international standards (the schedule for implementation in Russia of EU environmental Regulations is shown in Table 34).

5. Conclusions

In the Russian Federation policy to ensure the sustainable development and operation of urban transport is not clearly formulated at any level, national, regional or local. Governmental bodies do not have the competence to take decisions to regulate the urban passenger traffic demand and manage car use. At present, the main tasks of the transport management authorities and municipal administrations only cover the operation of public passenger transport. The main priorities for immediate action in favour of sustainable urban transport are:

- improving existing legislation and introducing new laws to regulate urban transport, town planning, transport activities and the environmental quality of vehicles;
- creating effective mechanisms for the funding and management of urban public transport;
- implementing measures and decisions at municipal level to limit the use of private cars in urban areas whilst simultaneously improving the quality of public passenger transport services and ensuring that all groups of the population have equal access to urban public transport;
- creation of guidelines to monitor passenger demand and the public transport system in urban areas.

References

Шефтер Я., Шмитьков А., Трякин К. "Состояние и проблемы развития общественного пассажирского транспорта". Информавтотранс, Москва, 1997. (Shefter Y. Shmitkov A., Tryakin K., "Current state and problems in the development of public passenger transport", Informavtotrans, Moscow, 1997.)

Винокурова Т., Овчинникова И., Транспорт. Наука, техника, управление, №7-8, Москва, 1999 (Vinokurova A., Ovchinnikova I., Transport. Science, Engineering, Management, No. 7-8, Moscow, 1999.)

Donchenko V., Incentive schemes for motor cat fleet renewal for improved environmental protection in the Russian Federation. ECMT Document CEMT/CS/ENV (99)2, 1999.

Иванов А. И другие. "Тенденции, проблемы, перспективы автомобилизации в России" от чёт по теме "Разработка комплексного прогноза автомобилизации в России и её социально-экономических последствий", Книга 1., Москва, 2000. (Ivanov A. and others. "Trends, problems and perspectives of motorization in Russia" book 1, Moscow, 2000.)

Итоги социально-экономического развития транспортного комплекса в 1999 году. Материалы по расширенному заседанию Коллегии Минтранса России, Москва, 2000. (Social and economic results of the development of a transport system in 1999. Materials for the meeting of an extended board of the Ministry of Transport of the Russian Federation, Moscow, 2000.)

Брурсма К. Проблемы городского пассажирского транспорта в России. Журнал "Русский ямщик", №2, Москва, 1999.(Brursma K, Problems in the urban passenger transport in Russia, magazine "Russky Yamshchik" No. 2, Moscow, 1999.)

Родионов А. Повышение эффективности городского пассажирского транспорта: опыт г.Череповца. Москва, Журнал "Автомобильный транспорт" №7, 1999г. с.17.(Rodionov A How to increase efficiency of the city passenger transport: practice of the city of Cherepovets. Magazine "Abtomobilny Transport", No. 7, page 17, Moscow, 1999.)

Российский статистический ежегодник. Статистический сборник Госкомстат России. Москва, 1998 и 1999. (Russian statistics annual. Reports of the State Department of Statistics of Russia. Moscow, 1998 and 1999.)

Транспорт и связь в России. Госкомстат России. Москва, 1999.(Transport and communications in Russia. State Department of Statistics of Russia. Moscow, 1999.)

Автомобильный парк России. Журнал "За рулём" №1, Москва, 1998.(Road vehicle fleet in Russia, magazine "Za Rulyem" No. 1, Moscow, 1999.)

Городской общественный транспорт. Отчёт проекта TACIS, Москва, 1998. (Urban Public Transport, TASIC report, Moscow, 1998.)

Донченко В., Петрухин В. и другие Анализ и оценка современного загрязнения окружающей среды автотранспортом в Северо-Западном Административном округе г. Москвы. Научно-технический отчёт, НИИАТ, Москва, 1999. (Donchenko V., Petrukhin V. and others. Analysis and evaluation of the current state of environmental pollution from road vehicles in the North-West Administrative district of Moscow. Technical report. NIIAT, Moscow, 1999.)

Switzerland*

1. Introduction

Post-war transport in Switzerland has gone from constraint to constraint:

- first constraint: insufficient carrying capacity of the road network, resulting in congestion; remedy: road construction, financed by fuel taxes and road tolls;

- second constraint: insufficient environmental carrying capacity, resulting in public opposition to road construction and still more congestion; remedy: promotion of public transport;

- third constraint: insufficient public transport serving isolated settlements, despite investment efforts, resulting in continuing congestion and environmental damage; remedies: demand-oriented transport policies combining public transport development and car restraint measures (push and pull strategy); mobility management by public authorities, transport operators and private enterprises as well as integrated traffic management to make best use of existing infrastructure and reach sustainable mobility.

Regional and local transport policy is mainly defined by the cantons and municipalities. The federal government is not directly involved in urban transport policies, though it has a substantial impact in three areas:

- national transport policy is an important functional framework for regional and local mobility because it influences the long-distance modal split. For instance the Rail and Bus 2000 concept introduced a minimum hourly frequency for public transport all over the country. In addition, a recent national ballot approved significant investments in rail infrastructure, notably for two alpine tunnels, while the distance-based heavy vehicle charge promotes to the internalisation of external costs of transport;

- the federal government sets standards for the implementation of cantonal transport policy which regulates local traffic. The National Clean Air Act and the Clean Air Concept are particularly relevant in this respect;

---

* This report was prepared by Mr Peter Güller (Synergo).

• funding for individual and public transport is shared by the three levels of government. Reforms are under way or discussion on separating railway infrastructure and operation, balancing revenues and responsibilities across the three levels, and providing support to regional transport policy.

2. Context

2.1. Socio-economic trends

Switzerland covers 41 000 km², with a population of 7.1 million. Two-thirds of the country is mountainous, limiting population density to an average 172 inhabitants/km². Population densities vary from 26 in the alpine canton of Grisons to 687 in that of Zurich (which covers the city as well as rural areas), 1 413 for Geneva and 5 218 for Basle-Town. The Central Plateau separates the Alps in the south and the lower Jura mountain range in the north. International freight transport flows mainly from north to south, while domestic passenger largely follows a west-east axis, linking the large urban areas.

Compared with the EU (Table 35), Switzerland is characterised by:

• a similar average age structure;

• a slightly above average population density and employment rate;

• a different economic structure, with a smaller contribution from agriculture;

• a high per capita gross domestic product and a very low unemployment rate.

The Swiss economy is highly dependent on foreign trade. In volume, imports amounted to 42 million tonnes in 1998 and exports to 12 million tonnes. In value terms, imports amounted to SF 116 billion and exports to SF 114 billion, pointing to the high added value of exports compared with imports.

Table 35.   **Comparison of Swiss and EU socio-economic parameters**

Swiss levels with EU = 1

Population density	1.2	Share of agricultural employment	0.6
Population under 25	0.9	Share of industrial employment	0.9
Population over 65	1.0	Share of tertiary employment	1.1
Employment rate, male + female	1.2	Per capita gross domestic product	1.4
Employment rate, female	1.1	Unemployment rate, male + female	0.4

Source: ECMT.

2.2. Key developments in the transport sector

The expansion of car traffic and its environmental impact

Table 36 shows the variety and intensity of factors behind traffic growth, pointing to the following trends:

- population growth is not the main cause of traffic growth;

- motorization and traffic are growing more than personal income;

- the number of cars has increased more than trips and distances; the availability of cars has increased;

- average trip length has fallen, possibly as a result of the increasing number of very short trips;

- the average annual distance covered by cars has decreased as more cars are available to meet mobility needs;

- the occupancy rate of cars has fallen and vehicle-kilometres (the indicator relevant for congestion and environmental impact) have increased more than travel demand, expressed in person-kilometres;

- fuel consumption has not followed vehicle-kilometres, as the fleet is using less fuel; the reduction is smaller than technical progress would have allowed because of the increase in the proportion of heavier vehicles, though the proportion of small vehicles has recently begun to increase;

- CO_2 emissions are fully correlated with fuel consumption increases;

Table 36.   **Factors behind traffic growth**

		Unit	Change 1970/1990
1	Population	Million	+8%
2	Disposable income per inhabitant	SF. (1980 real prices)	+36%
3a	Motorization	Cars per 1 000 inhabitants	+99%
3b	Car fleet	Million	+116%
4	Trips	Persons-trips (million)	+95%
5	Average distance per trip	Km	−10%
6	Total driven distance	Persons-kilometres (million)	+75%
7	Occupancy rate of cars	Persons/car	−6%
8	Total distance covered by vehicles	Vehicle-km (million)	+82%
9	Fuel consumption per km	Petrol + diesel (kg/100 litres)	−16%
10	Fuel consumption	Petrol + diesel (1 000 tonnes)	+54%
11	CO_2 emissions	CO_2 emissions (1 000 tonnes)	+54%
12	NO_x emissions	NO_x emissions (1 000 tonnes)	+17%

Source: Güller P. *et al.* (1998) Gaining Breath ... and Time. Learning Scheme for the Assessment and Shaping of Environment-Oriented Urban Transport Policies. COST Action 616, Luxembourg.

- NO$_x$ emissions initially increased with fuel consumption but this relationship was uncoupled with the installation of catalytic converters.

Challenges for public transport

Switzerland is known as a country of rail travellers. Distances covered per inhabitant by rail are by far the highest in Western Europe (Table 37). Yet between 1970 and 1995, the share of rail transport in total passenger-kilometres travelled decreased from 16% to 13%, while public road transport remained at 5% and the share of cars rose from 77% to 79%. In the last ten years, however, rail transport has increased by 32%, substantially more than road transport, as the RAIL 2000 measures to improve public transport started to pay off (see below). Nevertheless, private road transport remains the dominant transport mode, except in urban areas.

Table 37. **Distance travelled annually by rail per inhabitant, 1995**

	Switzerland	Germany	France	Italy	Austria
Distance per capita (km)	1 717	744	952	867	1 198

Source: ECMT.

The number of people travelling regularly on public transport has sharply risen in recent years. Almost half the population has some sort of season ticket, one fourth has a half-price pass and over 200 000 have a general pass. Service has considerably improved in recent years, especially for railways (Switzerland has one of the busiest timetables in Europe), as well as for buses. The average public transport load factor has declined since 1970, though inter-city load factors are considerably higher than on regional lines and capacity on urban lines is fully used. For instance the services provided by the Swiss Federal Railways in the area of the Zurich Transport Association were stable at 13 million kilometres between 1993/94 and 1998/99. This association covers the whole agglomeration, including parts of neighbouring cantons. The number of daily passengers crossing the boundaries of the city of Zurich in the same category of services increased by one third between 1989 and 1999.

Trends in investment

In the decade after World War II, investments for road and rail were similar. Road network investments took a strong lead in the 1960s, with the construction of highways (Table 38). Compared with other European countries, road infrastructure investments in Switzerland represent the highest share in GDP, the highest ratio per capita and the highest cost per kilometre. As for public transport, the share of

Table 38. **Road and rail investments in Switzerland**

Investment (SF million)	1960	1980	1998
Road investment, including renewal and maintenance	490 (78%)	2 576 (83%)	3 815 (61%)
Rail investment, including improvements and maintenance	140 (22%)	519 (17%)	2 408 (39%)

Source: LITRA.

investments in GDP and costs per kilometre are average, while investment per capita is the highest.[1]

In 1960, the total cost of planned motorways was estimated at SF 6 billion. This estimate had to be corrected upwards on several occasions. In the fifth construction programme of 1995, it stood at SF 62 billion. The federal contribution to these costs (about 85% of the total) was financed by the revenue from a fuel tax. The cantonal part was covered partly by dedicated road funds. In the 1986 Clean Air Concept, the Federal Council slowed the extension of the network. In a 1994 ballot on the Alpine Initiative, voters ruled against the expansion of transit highways in the Alps. The policy of the Ministry for Transport is to maintain the quality of the highway network. Concerning cantonal and communal roads, fewer roads are being built than in the 1960s and 1970s, while maintenance and operation costs are rising. The policy focus is on more "intelligent" roads, optimising existing capacity using modern information technology and integrated traffic management.

In the railway sector, a key project of the 1970s was a high-speed trunk line across the Central Plateau. This idea was replaced by the RAIL 2000 concept. The goal was no longer to maximise speed in inter-city traffic, but to improve the efficiency of the network all over the country. Connections in all directions are now possible in most larger towns at 60 or 30 minute intervals. Two major projects (Rail 2000 and Alpine Transit[2]) with connections to the European high speed train network, as well as extensive measures to reduce noise, should make rail more attractive and environmentally friendly. Around SF 30 billion is to be invested in these projects over the next 20 years. From this, some SF 6 billion is allocated to the second stage of Rail 2000, funded notably by mineral oil taxes, some of the revenue from the Distance and Weight-Based Heavy Goods Vehicle Charge and VAT, as well as loans on capital markets.

These far-reaching decisions for public transport have been approved by voters. Nevertheless, political circles defending car use have launched a new initiative (called Avanti) to increase the capacity of the highway network.

Striving for subsidies

Some 75% of road infrastructure and maintenance is financed by special taxes (mineral oil tax, highway vignette and heavy vehicle charge, and cantonal vehicle taxes), the rest by the general budget. Expenditure on roads by the Federal Government is lower than the revenue from the mineral oil tax and highway vignette. The difference is to a large degree used for cantonal roads, balancing cantonal expenditure and revenues. There is a substantial distortion for municipal spending, as most road investment and maintenance is funded from the general budget.

The Confederation is increasingly involved in the financing of roads. The share of federal contributions has grown between 1986 and 1995 from 32% to almost 40%, while the share of road traffic expenditure in total cantonal expenditures has remained stable. Some cantons find it politically difficult to increase such expenditure. A peculiarity of road infrastructure and maintenance funding is that contributions from national and cantonal levels are increasingly interwoven. The share of cantonal financing of national highways has increased, and as has the share of federal contributions to cantonal roads. To clarify this situation, the Federal Government is preparing a new model for "financial equalisation".

In contrast to private transport, public transport does not have any dedicated source of income. Infrastructure and operation costs are met by the general budget. On the average, 45% of public transport costs are covered by user charges (which is more than in France and Germany, but less than in the United Kingdom and the United States). Since 1990, federal contributions to public transport have increased from SF 2.1 billion to over 5 billion. The self-financing capacity of Swiss Federal Railways has been stable since 1982 at over 80%, an average between very profitable inter-city traffic and low profit regional services. The self-financing capacity of private railway undertakings ranges from 45% to 65%. Federal and cantonal contributions roughly doubled between 1982 and 1997. The financing of local public transport is different, as the federal government does not subsidise this category of transport.

Price developments

Public transport prices have increased in line with the index of consumer prices, whereas the price of petrol has risen considerably less (Table 39). Swiss transport prices are high by international standards (Table 40).

Congestion – not only a matter of road capacity

The Federal Roads Office started recording road congestion in January 1993, on the basis of radio bulletins. Since May 1996, traffic bulletins have also been

Table 39. **Swiss price index for consumption
and passenger transportation**

Basis: 1972 = 100

	1972	1999
Total consumer		
prices	100	244
Public transport	100	259
Railway	100	246
Regional public		
transport	100	290
Individual transport	100	208
New vehicles	100	174
Transport taxes	100	141
Attendance and		
maintenance	100	408
Fuel prices	100	185

Source: Dienst GVF (2001) Die Preisentwicklung im Persononverkehr, 1972-86, Studie 4/86 und 1987-94, Studie 258, sowie Abay G., Preisentwicklung im Personenverkehr, 1994-99. ARE, Bern.

Table 40. **Transport prices, 1996**

	Switzerland	Germany	France	Italy	Austria
EU = 1	1.23	1.04	1.06	0.88	1.17

Source: Federal Office of Statistics (1999) Statistisches Jahrbuch der Schweiz 2000. Zürich.

collected by the Swiss Touring Club, though only for major traffic jams on main roads. Data on urban congestion are not collected.

Some 80% of congestion occurs on highways. Statistics of the Federal Roads Office (Table 41) show that:

• 20% of all congestion hours on motorways are attributable to road works;

• over 30% of congestion is due to road accidents;

• 40% is the result of heavy traffic;

• two thirds occur on weekdays.

Case studies and model calculations confirm high time losses in urban traffic, with minor delays making a significant contribution: about half of all delays are attributed to additional travel times of less than 5 minutes per journey. So the calculation of costs relating to traffic congestion depends to a considerable extent on whether such delays are taken into account.

217|

Table 41. **Number and duration of congestion on highways
and main roads**

	1993	1996
Cases of congestion	921	2 072 (+125%)
Duration of congestion, in hours	2 399	4 121 (+72%)

Source: ASTRA/Infras (1998) Staukosten im Strassenverkehr, Bern.

User perception of traffic problems

A selection of survey results for 500 people in urban regions shows that Swiss cities have a low level of complaints regarding congestion in road traffic, parking fees and parking space (Table 42). There is, however, a difference between German and French speaking areas. With regard to public transport, there are few complaints about travel time and the level of comfort, but more about price levels.

Table 42. **Traffic problems as perceived by inhabitants
of urban regions**

Percentage mentioning road problems:	Congestion	Lack of parking	Level of parking fees
Zurich	63	75	69
Bern	42	66	55
Geneva	76	84	77
Lyon	91	86	90
Barcelona	89	93	84
Rotterdam	36	51	65
Stockholm	61	72	67

Percentage mentioning public transport problems:	Travel time	Level of comfort	Level of fares
Zurich	29	17	51
Bern	26	16	45
Geneva	45	33	67
Lyon	69	88	80
Barcelona	77	58	65
Rotterdam	23	26	42
Stockholm	44	27	26

Source: Güller P. *et al.* (2000) Road Pricing in der Schweiz, Bern. And: Güller P. *et al.* (2000) Pricing Measures Acceptance: Surveys, Interviews and Media Analysis. EU project on Pricing Measures Acceptance (PRIMA), Zurich.

2.3. *Externalities: accidents, air pollution and noise*

Safety

Between 1980 and 1996, road accidents increased less than motorised traffic. The number of injured fell by 18% and fatalities by 51%. This confirms the success of measures taken in the last twenty years to improve safety, including better training and information for vehicle users, technical improvements to vehicles, the extension of the motorway network, as well as regulations such as the use of safety belts and speed limits.

Air pollution

Concentrations of nitrogen dioxide and lead are falling as a result of the introduction of emission standards for transport sources, controls on industrial and waste disposal facilities and the introduction of low-NO_x combustion technologies. Nevertheless, emission standards in urban areas and along roads with heavy traffic are often still massively exceeded for these pollutants as well as for particulates (PM_{10}). Ozone limits are often exceeded in summer in all regions, especially at medium altitude in the Prealps and Alps.

One third of CO_2 emissions and 60% of NO_x emissions are due to transport activities (Table 43).

Noise

Around 30% of the population is exposed to critical levels of noise from road traffic. In the city of Zurich, this figure reaches 40%. With increasing train frequencies, noise impacts have increased. The costs of rail noise protection measures are estimated at SF 3 billion, *i.e.* about a tenth of planned rail investment.

Environmental costs

Considerable progress has been made in calculating the external costs of transport (Table 44). Concerning environmental costs, car traffic caused the largest

Table 43. **Trends in NO_x and CO_2 emissions, 1950-2000 (tonnes)**

	1950	1970	1980	1990	2000
NO_x	31 300	134 000	170 000	166 000	117 000
CO_2 total	10 000 000	40 000 000	n.a.	40 700 000	38 600 000
CO_2 due to terrestrial transport	n.a.	n.a.	n.a.	14 670 000	15 280 000

Source: Federal Office of Statistics (1999) Statistisches Jahrbuch der Schweiz 2000. Zürich.

Table 44.   **External environmental costs of transport, 1995**

Million SF

	Road passenger	Road freight	Rail passenger	Rail freight
Accidents				
Incl. insurance charges	5 830	730	58	13
Excl. insurance charges	1 560	130	31	7
Noise	670	300	134	28
Health impacts of air pollution	895	520	4-11	2-6
Reduction if climate change measures are taken:	−450	−350		
Construction damages of air pollution	340	235		
Reduction if climate change measures are taken:	−170	−160		
Damages of air pollution to vegetation	230-600	120-315	6-15	3-7
Reduction if climate change measures are taken:	−115/−300	−80/−205		
Avoidance of climate change	1 300	400	3	3
Other environmental costs	110-180	100-170	63-93	54-84
Total external environmental costs	**4 370 to 4 630**	**1 210 to 1 350**	**240 to 290**	**100 to 140**

Source: Maibach M. *et al.* (1999) Faire und effiziente Preise im Verkehr. Bericht D3 des NFP 41, Bern.

share (SF 4.5 billion in 1995). Despite a reduction in emissions, total environmental costs are not falling because traffic volume is still growing.

3. National Policies

3.1. *Institutional framework*

Subsidiarity, democracy and financial equalisation

In accordance with the Swiss federal system, political responsibility is shared between the federal government (the Confederation), 26 cantons and 2 900 municipalities, following the subsidiarity principle, which means that the more decentralised levels should be given responsibility as far as possible. Even in areas where the Confederation has been given formal responsibility, the cantons and municipalities are likely to have considerable freedom for implementation.

Another important feature of the Swiss institutional framework is the use of direct democracy at all three government levels. The possibilities for recourse and participation by private organisations and interest groups must be taken into account when analysing policy making in Switzerland. Every constitutional amendment is subject to a mandatory vote and every new law is subject to an optional referendum which can sanction parliamentary decisions.

At the same time, each level (Confederation, cantons and municipalities) has its own tax structure and base. The revenues of the Confederation are higher than its expenditures, the difference being mainly used for contributions to lower government levels and for the so-called "financial equalisation" that is carried out among the cantons. The federal government is preparing a new model of this equalisation, considering both allocation of tasks and financial flows.

Interrelations between different levels of government

The Confederation, cantons and municipalities share responsibility for land use policies. The federal level plans and authorises federal land use activities, approves cantonal planning guidelines and supports land use planning research and public information. The cantons set general land use guidelines and are responsible for regulating construction and planning, setting land use development objectives and establishing zoning plans. Municipalities are responsible for detailed land use planning, including binding regulations separating building from non-building zones, and for the use of and access to land.

Concerning transport, the Confederation deals with emission standards for road traffic, mineral oil taxation, heavy vehicle taxes, the planning of the highway network, speed limits on highways,[3] and the organisation of long distance and regional public transport and combined freight transport. It does not provide subsidies for local transport but it cofinances regional transport. Until recently, it has generally covered the deficits of the Federal Railway Company, thereby indirectly subsidising railways in urban regions. Financial support to the Federal Railway Company is now only provided on the basis of specific service agreements with the authority (Confederation, canton or transport association) concerned.

The cantons are responsible for the construction and maintenance of highways and cantonal through-roads (using revenue from the mineral oil tax), for motor vehicle taxation, for regional public transport, and for parking and traffic regulation. Regional public transport services are contracted to transport operators by cantons or by regional transport associations on the basis of service agreements. Cantonal laws regulate the allocation of responsibilities between the canton and municipalities.

Almost 90% of the costs of local urban roads are paid by municipalities from local tax revenue. As a rule, local public transport does not receive federal support. The Confederation can only contribute to investments aimed at separating public and private transport on roads, such as level crossings and bus lanes. Expenditure for transport per capita in larger cities is roughly twice that in smaller cities. The Confederation expects municipalities to implement Clean Air and Noise Regulations, further

221|

burdening their budgets. There are therefore parliamentary proposals to provide federal support for urban transport.

3.2. National transport policy

National transport policy is guided by the overall objective of sustainable mobility. Backed by the Constitution and a series of laws, the Federal Department of Environment, Transport, Energy and Communication understands by this objective:

- environmental protection based on the principle of precaution and the polluter pays principle;
- economic efficiency, ensured by service optimisation, the application of market rules and contractual service agreements;
- social solidarity, providing mobility and access for all population categories all over the country.

The implementation of this policy requires action in various areas, such as transport policy in the narrower sense, land use policy, fiscal policy, environmental policy and energy policy. Swiss transport policy is also co-ordinated with the EU.

From a comprehensive transport concept to pragmatic partial reforms

Due to the growth of (motorised) transport and its impact, the Federal Council recognised the necessity of establishing a Comprehensive Transport Concept in the 1970s, though in a 1988 ballot, voters refused to accept its main outcome: the Principles of a Co-ordinated Transport Policy, and a new formulation of the section on transport in the Federal Constitution. Nevertheless, transport policy discussion in the 1980s and 1990s was largely influenced by the proposals of the Comprehensive Transport Policy, notably better transport co-ordination, greater emphasis on environmental problems, support for public transport, a more logical division of responsibilities between the Confederation and the cantons, and more equitable funding of transport by those responsible for its (external) costs. In recent years reaching an international consensus in transport policy has become increasingly important.[4]

A key element of modern Swiss transport policy is the Rail and Bus 2000 concept, aimed at increasing the network effect of public transport country-wide. It was developed in the early 1980s, as a solution to a politically unacceptable high-speed railway project linking the large cities on the Central Plateau. In the framework of Rail 2000, cities act as "transport spiders", with connections to long distance and regional transport every hour, or even every half hour in larger agglomerations. The nation-wide timetable has gained regularity, offering time-saving transport chains. Public transport users can step into a bus in any village and are sure to get to any point in the country without interruption. The 1998 ballot on financing public transport provides the funding for the second stage of the Rail 2000 concept.

Large investments in railways have been supported by railway reform. The 1996 revision of the Railway Statute had the following objectives:

- clearer allocation of responsibilities for transport: national transport is the responsibility of the Confederation, regional transport is the joint concern of the Confederation and the cantons, and local transport falls to the cantons and municipalities;

- financing harmonisation: each canton receives support for all transport undertakings on the same basis, abolishing distinctions between federal and private railways;

- refinancing of federal railways through debt relief and interest-free loans;

- service contracts: payments from the government to the railways are only made for compensation that has been agreed in advance in a contract between the Confederation, the canton and the transport company defining services and costs.

On a larger scale and in the longer term, railway reform includes:

- separation of infrastructure and operating costs for larger railway undertakings;

- free, open access to the network, for freight and some passenger traffic;

- separation of management tasks and political interests in railway operations;

- new procedures for financing investment in federal railways;

Regional transport services are contracted by the cantons who pay for the deficits, together with the federal government. There is a long standing dispute on financing urban public transport. To finding a solution, a recently established high-level study group is dealing with:

- defining regional and local public transport in agglomerations, examining possibilities for the federal government to engage more actively in urban transport policy;

- widening the scope of federal financial involvement in urban public transport, for instance by using revenue from the mineral oil tax for investment and operation;

- balancing federal support to roads and rail;

- examining conditions for federal contributions: formation of regional transport associations, elaboration of comprehensive regional mobility concepts, and the role of different government levels and urban regions in implementing such concepts;

- parking charges and road pricing.

223|

The proposed New Model of Financial Equalisation also examines changes with a view to disentangling federal and cantonal responsibilities:

- the operation and maintenance of national highways as well as extensions of the network should be entirely a federal responsibility, the Confederation then handing such tasks over to third parties, be they public, private or mixed;

- the maintenance, operation and extension of cantonal main roads would remain a cantonal responsibility, though federal cofinancing would no longer be a general rule and should be possible for individual projects that cannot be entirely financed by the cantons;

- federal contributions to urban traffic separation (bus lanes, railway crossings etc) should be increased.

According to the Federal Constitution, traffic on roads that are open to public use cannot be charged, though the parliament can provide permits in special cases, thereby making road charging legally possible. But in principle, road charging would require a change in the Constitution, along the lines of the articles regarding highway vignettes and the heavy vehicle charge. A federal law would also be needed to provide the general legal framework and cantons could then develop their own rules and regulations, though country-wide harmonisation of road charging would be necessary.

Land use policy

Land use policy is defined in the 1979 Federal Spatial Planning Law and the 1996 Basic Lines of Spatial Development. The connection between land use policy and transport is evident: urban sprawl and its excessive use of valuable land. Key elements of the Basic Lines of Spatial Development are therefore the development of public transport (local to international) and a land use policy that follows the principle of urban networks, settlement concentration, better structuring of agglomerations and urban renewal. At the same time, the attractiveness of rural areas for housing and employment should be increased.

Environmental protection policies

A revised Federal Constitution came into force on January 1st, 2000. It states the following ecological principles which guide all national policies, not only policies on environmental protection:

- sustainability;

- the principle of precaution and the polluter pays principle;

- economical land use.

By explicitly introducing the notion of sustainability and the polluter-pays-principle, environmental policy has significantly changed in the past few years: the former policy relied mainly on regulations and subsidies, whereas the new approach focuses on economic instruments, individual responsibility and co-operation. The 1983 Environmental Protection Act (last revised in 1997) provides for measures protecting human beings, animals and plants, as well as their habitats from damaging impacts such as air pollution and noise. It contains some important measures:

- an environmental impact assessment for large infrastructure projects, for instance car parks for more than 300 cars;

- the right of appeal in the planning stage of construction projects to environmental organisations designated by the Federal Council;

- the obligation for public authorities to co-operate with trade and business organisations to encourage initiatives implementing the Environmental Protection Act.

Air quality policy

The 1998 Clean Air Ordinance sets maximum limits for NO_x, CO, O_3, SO_2 and PM_{10}, charging the cantons with the task of defining action plans for areas with high pollution levels. The canton of Bern for instance elaborated its first action plan against air pollution in 1990, presenting measures to reach air quality standards. The measures were developed and implemented in a close co-operation between the canton of Bern and the relevant municipalities.

As road transport emissions are a major source of air pollution, and as parking has been recognised as a major factor determining car traffic, parking management is a central instrument for the cantonal and municipal action plans against air pollution.[5] Depending on the availability and quality of the public transport system in a given area, (new) parking places can be more or less restricted or taxed.

Energy Policy

Federal energy policy is defined in the 1990 action programme Energy 2000. The adoption of an energy article in the Constitution, a referendum-based moratorium on new nuclear power plants and the Federal Council's declarations at the 1990 International Climate Conference in Geneva and at the 1992 UN Conference on Environment and Development provide a new framework for Swiss energy policy.

In addition to economic instruments (an energy tax and an ecological tax reform), the government is pursuing the aim of sustainable development through voluntary measures for rational and renewable energy use, outlined in Energy 2000 and its successor Energy 2000+. This programme is led by the Ministry for Environment, Transport, Energy and Communications and composed of representatives from all three government levels and of business, interest groups (notably consumer and environmental organisations) and research. Measures relevant for transport policy are for example ECO-drive courses, the promotion of local car sharing and combined traffic, as well as mobility management and the promotion of consumer awareness.[6]

The 1999 Energy Law is the legal basis of Energy 2000+. The most important changes are the possibility to contract out certain tasks to private organisations, and fund cantonal sustainable energy programs (instead of promoting only single projects). In January 2001, the Federal Council launched a successor programme (Swiss Energy) which brings together businesses, cantons, municipalities and environmental NGOs in actions to reduce CO_2 emissions.

Fiscal policy

Revenue for road construction and maintenance is principally generated by road users, through motor fuel taxes, motorway user badges (vignettes), the distance-and weight-based charges on heavy goods vehicles and the cantonal vehicle license charges.

Around 30% of the revenue from motor fuel taxes goes to the general budget of the Confederation. The rest is reserved for roads, especially motorway construction and maintenance. It also finances projects that are less directly connected with road construction (*e.g.* environmental and landscape protection, combined transport). By contrast, municipalities have to finance their roads mostly from their own resources, *i.e.* local tax revenue.[7]

The distance-and weight based heavy vehicle tax was introduced on 1 January 2001. In September 2000, a proposal to introduce an energy tax for non-renewable energy resources to raise finds for solar energy was put to the vote. At the same time voters had to decide on an alternative proposal for an energy tax with a lower rate and time limitation to raise revenue for the promotion of all renewable resources. Voters were also asked to decide on a constitutional amendment that would lay the foundation for an ecological tax reform raising energy taxation and lowering payroll taxes. This ecological tax reform would raise taxes on non-renewable resources, and lower non-wage labour costs (such as social security contributions), while existing taxes and subsidies would have to be checked for providing environmental incentives. For motorised transport, the approval of any of these proposals would increase higher fuel prices[8] and generate resources to promote measures such as car-pooling, car-sharing, ECO-drive and non-motorised traffic (bicycles, pedestrians) in combination with public transport. All proposals were rejected, voters following the argument that there are already too many taxes and that alternative energy technologies should not be subsidised.

The next effort in this direction will be a CO_2 tax. The 1999 Federal Law on the Reduction of CO_2 provides for a number of measures to reduce emissions of CO_2 to 90% of the 1990 level by 2010, including a CO_2 tax only if emission reductions are not being made, at the earliest in 2004.[9]

Research policy

Transport has been dealt with in two national research programmes in the last decade. Programme No. 25 focused on urban transport and programme No. 41 on the relation between transport and the environment. The programmes have resulted in recommendations, concerning notably:

- indicators of sustainable mobility;

- linkages between spatial development policy and transport policy;

- the internalisation of external transport costs;

- mobility management for commuting, shopping and leisure traffic;

- using telematics in road and rail transport;

- the interaction of the three government levels in transport policy;

- new approaches to transport funding;

- international considerations in Swiss transport policy.

Research has brought significant progress in policy implementation, key topics being institutional reforms, participation processes, public/private partnerships, public acceptability, project monitoring and assessment.

4. Cantonal and local policies in urban areas

As mentioned in the previous section, there is no federal policy for urban transport. The national level has only recently started to elaborate a position on urban development issues. Yet federal policies – and among them national transport policy – have great influence on what goes on in urban areas and what other levels of government should and can do. The main responsibility for regional and local land use planning and the implementation of transport policy rests with cantons and municipalities.

227|

4.1. *Trends in urban development and transport*

Growth in urban population

Generally speaking the share of the largest urban regions on total population has recently slightly fallen and the share of the largest cities has fallen even more (Table 45). Demographic growth is larger outside the largest urban areas than inside and is generally negative in larger cities (with the exception of Geneva), whereas it is positive in their suburbs. Though this trend is not yet visible in statistics, some recent indicators point to urban areas becoming more attractive, with large investments in housing and a process of gentrification.[10] Environment-friendly transport policies (traffic calming in residential areas and parking restrictions for non-residents) may have contributed to increasing the attractiveness of urban areas.

Urban land use patterns

Data on land use trends show that areas within reach of large cities have been significantly developed in the last two decades (Table 46), though there is

Table 45.   **Growth and share of urban populations**

	1990	1998	Change (%)
Total population	6 750 700	7 123 500	+5.5
Population in 16 cities with over 30 000 inhabitants	1 449 600	1 420 800	−2.0
Share of 16 cities with more than 30 000 inhabitants	21.5%	20.0%	−1.5 percentage points
Five largest cities	937 300	915 800	−2.3
Zurich	341 300	336 800	−1.3
Basle	171 000	168 700	−1.3
Geneva	167 200	172 800	+3.4.4
Bern	134 600	123 300	−8.4
Lausanne	123 200	114 200	−7.3
	1994	1998	Change (%)
Total population	7 019 000	7 123 500	+1.5
Population of the five largest cities	2 376 600	2 393 200	+0.1
Share of the five largest agglomerations	33.9%	33.6%	−0.3 percentage points
Zurich	924 000	935 100	+1.2
Basle	405 200	402 400	−0.7
Geneva	441 700	452 200	+2.4
Bern	321 488	317 367	−1.3
Lausanne	284 301	286 106	+0.6

Source: ECMT.

Table 46. **Land use for settlements**

Canton	Period	Change (%)
Zurich	1982/84-1994/96	+8.5
Zug (next to Zurich)	1982/83-1994/96	+14.5
Basel Stadt	1982-1994	+0.5
Basel Land (next to Basel Stadt)	1982-1994	+10.2
Bern	1979/82-1992/94	+11.0
Freiburg (next to Bern)	1979/82-1990/94	+19.6
Geneva	1980-1992	+9.5
Vaud (with Lausanne, next to Geneva)	1979/81-1990/93	+14. 1

Source: ECMT.

Table 47. **Land prices in the Zurich urban area, 1998**

Average price of unbuilt residential land, in SF/m^2	> 900	700-900	600-700	500-600
District (city) of Zurich	X			
Neighbouring district of Zimmerberg (lake side west)		X		
Neighbouring district of Pfannenstil (lake side east)		X		
Neighbouring district of Furttal			X	
Neighbouring district of Glattal			X	
Neighbouring district of Limmattal				X

Source: ECMT.

no degradation of inner suburbs. Obviously there are differences in income among the outer urban areas, reflecting land prices in particular.

Urban employment

In some large cities (such as Zurich and Geneva), there has been a slight decline of the number of fulltime employees, whereas in others there is still slight growth (*e.g.* Basle and Bern). Surrounding areas show large increases in employment (Table 48). Such fringe developments may bring workplaces closer to inhabitants of suburban belts, though they are often poorly served by public transport.

229|

Table 48. **Spatial development of employment, 1985-1991**

	Increase in the number of full time employees, 1985-1991	Change (%)
Switzerland	211 500	+8
Canton of Zurich	30 500	+6
District of Zurich	−4 600	−2
Neighbouring districts	900 to 9 800	+6 to +32
Neighbouring Canton of Zug	7 000	+19
Canton of Basle	2 600	+2
Canton of Basle	10 700	+15
Canton of Bern	15 900	+5
District of Bern	6 200	+5
Neighbouring districts	700 to 1 600	+6 to +18
Canton of Geneva	5 600	+3
City of Geneva	−4 300	−4
Neighbouring district of Meyrin	5 500	+66
Canton of Vaud	21 500	+10
District of Lausanne	4 600	+5
Districts between Genf and Lausanne	300 to 5 400	+12 till +26

Source: ECMT.

Table 49. **Cars per 1 000 inhabitants, 1999**

	351-400	401-450	451-500	501-550	551-584
Switzerland			484		
Canton of Bern		445			
City of Bern	370				
District (city) of Zurich		X			
Neighbouring district of Zimmerberg (lake side west)			X		
Neighbouring district of Pfannenstil (lake side east)				X	
Neighbouring districts of Furttal, Glattal and Limmattal					X

Source: ECMT.

Trends in car ownership

Car ownership has grown, especially in suburban areas (Table 49). Car ownership is lowest in core cities that have poorer populations and excellent public transport as well as facilities for bicycles and pedestrians.

Public transport use

The data available on transport use for Zurich, Bern, Basle does not yield overall conclusions.[11] Generally speaking there are positive and even impressive developments in railway transport in urban regions:

- Zurich: success of the S-Bahn;
- Basle: slight reduction in local public transport, but increase in regional rail transport;
- Bern: better results for local public transport demand than in Basle.

4.2. Transport policy and its implementation in Zurich

Involvement of cantonal and local levels of government: current transport policies

The 1975 Cantonal Law on Planning and Construction set the principles for planning at cantonal, regional and local level. In accordance with this law, the Canton

Table 50. **Public transport use in urban areas**

Daily passenger load on Zurich S-Bahn. crossing Zurich city boundaries	1989	1998	Change (%)
S-Bahn in total	170 700	239 600	+40
Transport corridor	1997/1998	1999/2000	
Lake-side west	44 861	50 527	+13
Lake-side east (based on a strong increase in frequency)	16 440	19 831	+21
Furttal	6 188	6 919	+12
Glatttal	33 132	34 306	+4
Limmattal	20 036	21 852	+9
Bern public transport company (SVB)	1998	1999	
Passenger-kilometres by tram, bus and trolleybus (million)	160.7	161.4	+0.4
Kilometres driven by tram, bus and trolley bus (million)	8.8	9.0	+2.3
Number of passengers	1990	1997	
Pax (million)	98.7	117.8	+19
Passengers of public transport operators in **Basle**	1990	1998	
Basle Transport Services	Index 100	95	
Railway Services in Basle tri-national region	Index 100	103	
In comparison:			
Car traffic on urban main roads	Index 100	107	
Car traffic on highways in Basle region	Index 100	110	

Source: ECMT.

231

of Zurich developed the 1987 Cantonal Master Plan providing partial plans of settlements, landscape, transport, and public utility provision. The municipality of Zurich, which has the status of a region, submitted its Regional Master Plan twice to voters (in 1982 and 1983), both times with a negative result. The cantonal government therefore overruled the municipality and adopted a plan in 1984, at least for its land use and transport components. In 1990, the municipality of Zurich proposed a transport plan which was accepted by the canton in 1992. The municipality has also completed a communal law on zoning and construction that was approved in 1992, though there were many appeals mainly regarding the conversion of industrial land to tertiary use and the density allowed. The cantonal government therefore adopted a 1995 law on zoning and construction for the city of Zurich, with fewer land use and density restrictions. In 1998 the municipality drafted its own master plan, which has since been adopted.

This history shows the kind of ping-pong played between cantonal and municipal governments, possibly due to the notorious power game between the canton and its largest city, as well as to a difference in political allegiance, the canton being rather conservative, the city more socialist and green.

In parallel with land use planning efforts and in accordance with the 1986 Federal Clean Air Ordinance, the canton of Zurich completed a Cantonal Action Plan against Air Pollution (1988/89). To improve local acceptability, the canton of Zurich formed nine regions (groups of communities) for the action plan. The municipality of Zurich has long taken a pioneering approach to stationary sources of air pollution, though the canton has been strictest with mobile sources. When the municipality submitted its plan, the canton made a series of amendments, mainly to reduce speed on through roads in the city, the capacity for car traffic on the urban road network and parking space in the inner city.

While the urban municipal government was fighting to improve environmental quality, the canton took up the position of suburban residents that wanted free access to the core of the agglomeration, though at least municipalities from the inner suburban belt became more aware of traffic problems when they were working out the regional Action Plan against Air Pollution with the city.

Transport demand policies

The main goals of transport policy in Zurich are to improve mobility while curbing the use of private cars, enhance the city's image, improve the quality of urban life and reduce air pollution and noise, while meeting the needs of industry and commerce. The municipality followed these principles in its 2001 Mobility Strategy, characterised by:

- combined mobility, with operational transport chains;
- mobility management and consulting services for sustainable transport;

- promotion of public transport for all travel purposes (commuting, shopping and leisure);

- promotion of walking and cycling;

- better integration of main roads into urban life;

- combination of by-passes creation and road calming;

- definition of large areas with no through traffic, including measures to improve the attractiveness of public areas;

- parking management by regulation, guidance and pricing;

- combined traffic and land-use planning.

Public transport improvements (dedicated tram tracks and bus lanes and preferential treatment at traffic lights) play a key role, supported by traffic control and restrictions. Vehicle entrance to the city is limited when the automatic monitoring system indicates that congestion is unacceptably high. The number of public parking spaces in the centre has been reduced and attempts are made to cut down on private parking (which has trebled over the last 20 years). Planning policy aims to encourage new housing and commercial developments along corridors that are well-served by public transport and channel as much traffic as possible on the main road network, leaving residential areas relatively free from traffic. Extensive 30 km/h speed limit zones have been introduced in almost all residential areas.

With some 300 million passengers a year, public transport remains the dominant mode of travel in Zurich. Between 1985 and 1990 (when the S-Bahn was opened), use of municipal services alone increased by over 30% to 470 public transport trips per inhabitant per year (about twice the level of most comparable western European cities). The authorities intend not only to maintain this high level, but to raise it to stop the growth of car travel. Very positive results have been achieved with every improvement in the service. In addition public transport operators have a wide range of mobility management measures and offer combi-tickets.[12]

The policy has certainly improved overall mobility, but despite everything that has been done, there has been no change in the volume of car traffic in Zurich itself nor in any of the radial corridors along which the new S-Bahn lines run. Car traffic has remained constant during peak hours since the mid-1980s and has actually risen during off-peak hours. In the rest of the canton, mainly in the neighbouring districts of the city, car traffic has been increasing steadily. The main congestion problems are on the tangential highways, around large traffic generators (such as shopping centres) and on the access routes to the city.

233|

Public transport

In popular ballots in 1962 and 1993, underground public transport projects were rejected and a completely different concept brought a breakthrough in public transport policy. In 1977, voters accepted a SF 200 million budget for increasing the speed of tramways and buses, and in 1979 the municipality advised all its departments to give priority to public transport over car traffic. The so-called SESAM-System allows to tramways or buses to get preferential treatment at junctions.

In 1981 voters in the Canton of Zurich approved the budget for the S-Bahn system which started in 1990. The key element was a through traffic arrangement under Zurich Main Station, until then a cul-de-sac station. At the same time urban public transport services were extended and almost all the residents of the city can reach a stop within 300 metres. Services run at least from 6.00 a.m. to midnight at 30 minute intervals. During daytime intervals on tramway lines are 6 to 8 minutes.

Road traffic

For years the municipality of Zurich has refrained from developing the main road network to prevent traffic from increasing and having an undesirable effect on the modal split. This principle was broken in 1985 with the opening of two national road segments, the northern bypass and a radial tunnel leading to the core of the city, though accompanying traffic control measures were taken, including reducing the number of lanes on the existing network and shortening green light times for cars. The overall capacity increase of the road network remained within limits, though difficulties experienced in implementing traffic control measures, show that in the future (especially when a bypass is completed) accompanying measures must be included in the project from the outset. The western bypass is under construction. The whole bypass will consist of a ¾ ring linking traffic from all parts of the canton and the whole of Switzerland, even without a tunnel under the lake of Zurich (southern bypass) which is being kept as an option in the cantonal road master plan.

The main road network has been cut back in the last decade by cycle tracks, pedestrian crossings, banning night driving on roads through residential areas, etc. Many technical measures to restrain traffic in residential areas were supplemented in 1991 by extensive 30 km speed-limit zones.

Integrated traffic management

Though extensions of the highway and main road networks are proposed by right wing members of the cantonal and municipal parliaments, both governments have in recent years developed a policy of making better use of existing road and rail networks, as well as road-bound public transport by integrated traffic management. In accordance with the National Master Plan for Telematics in Transport, a comprehensive approach is being taken. The Mobility Strategy of the municipality of Zurich goes beyond the cantonal approach in that it involves various forms of mobility management on the basis of innovative co-operation with transport operators and traffic generating private firms.

Parking policies

In 1994, the municipality was required by a popular ballot to implement a new parking charging policy, not only to cover installation and control costs, but also taking into account the shortage of road space, problems with bringing goods to downtown businesses, congestion, air pollution and the high uncovered cost of maintaining of urban roads. Car drivers from around the urban area should pay for the use of the urban network. In 1996 another important decision was taken: parking lost to pedestrian areas could be compensated by new underground car parks, thereby overcoming the long-standing opposition to additional parking. For new buildings, the minimum number of parking spaces has been replaced by a maximum number depending on location and public transport facilities.

The municipality has entered into a number of agreements with traffic generators in and around the city. For instance in 1998 the municipality and the Swiss Federal Institute of Technology fixed a limit on the number of vehicles entering the campus ever day, considering mainly environmental issues. They also agreed on a control mechanism and on action to be taken from both sides in case the number is exceeded. The municipality and a large site developer are negotiating an even more promising solution to private business parking: all private parking facilities in the area are treated like public car parks, following the same pricing principle, with an annual parking licence and a number of vehicles allowed into the parking area set according to the capacity of the surrounding road network. The site developer has to pay a basic fee according to this contingent. The number of entries is measured in six-month periods. If it exceeds the amount agreed, the developer has to pay for each additional entry.

Political acceptance for car traffic reduction

The objectives of municipal transport policy are regularly approved by clear majorities in opinion polls. About 65% of the population is also in favour of reducing car traffic in the town. However, conflicting results were obtained in two referendums.

In June 1988, Zurich voters rejected a funding package of SF 42 million proposed by the municipality to support the regional S-Bahn system and transfer more traffic from cars to rail. The opponents of this proposal argued that the package was too vague and that although they could appreciate the need for traffic restraint, individual measures had to be stated in detail with reference to their

235|

location and organisation. As a result, the cantonal government rejected traffic restraint measures on cantonal, *i.e.* main roads.

In November 1989, the population approved municipal transport policy by clearly rejecting (70% of the vote) an underground road project strongly supported by businesses, car user groups and non-socialist parties. This outcome swept aside the claim by opponents of the municipality's transport policy that the solution was not to restrain private car traffic but to develop main roads (underground roads being deemed more environment-friendly) to improve traffic flows.

Current and expected conditions for traffic, environment and economic resources

Road traffic conditions within the city are not critical due to a well managed traffic restraint policy in the inner suburban belt. The main feature of Zurich's transport system is its excellent public transport. Users of public transport move in peak times more quickly than cars and at other times almost as fast. The use of public transport in the city is supported by an excellent regional railway system and by easy pedestrian access.

Air pollution peaked in the canton of Zurich in 1985. Since then fuel composition and engine improvements have sharply reduced air pollution.[13] Nitrogen dioxide concentrations are now mostly within quality standards (annual mean of 30 $\mu g/m^3$) in rural areas and away from busy roads. In exposed urban areas, air quality targets for NO_2 and ozone are still not met. Compared with 1995, NO_x emissions need to be reduced by 30% for both cars and lorries. Within the municipality of Zurich the downward trend of the end of the 1980s for nitrogen dioxide pollution has flattened in recent years, while the share of freight traffic in overall pollution has increased. Short-term pollution levels have been reduced substantially and standards (24 hrs-daily mean of 80 $\mu g/m^3$) are only seldom exceeded. PM_{10} values have been collected since 1998 and show that both the annual mean (20 µg/m3) and the daily mean (50 $\mu g/m^3$) are exceeded in many areas, even away from busy roads.

Noise from road traffic has recently shifted to national highways, especially in Zurich. In some other access roads and on local roads traffic noise has been reduced by local and cantonal measures. Anti-noise measures along national highways are feasible, but along cantonal roads they are technically more difficult and costly.

The canton of Zurich has in recent years submitted to popular ballots two proposals for raising the motor vehicle tax. The answer was twice "no". Many road projects, including incomplete highways, are blocked. Both the canton and the municipality are in a difficult financial situation. Concerning the canton, this is due to the recession. As for the city of Zurich, structural causes are more important, notably social problems (old people, unemployed, foreigners, marginalised groups, etc.) and the movement of high taxpayers to surrounding communities. Community taxes are therefore higher in Zurich than nearby. In February 1999 a cantonal ballot on financial equalisation brought a large permanent contribution of the canton to the city for central service and special expenditure (social, cultural and police services). The future financial situation of the canton and the city looks brighter, but higher revenues will be used to reduce debt. At the same time the restructuring of public transport due to changes in federal law will bring more responsibility to the canton for contracting and financing regional public transport services.

Description of an actual decision making process: Closing the Limmatquai (an inner city main road)

To illustrate the complex transport policy decision making process in Zurich, a description is provided below of the closure of the Limmatquai, an important road along the main river crossing Zurich. The closure of the road has become symbolic for urban transport policy because it reduces traffic in a core part of the network. The decision making process brings to light the relationship of the municipal government with its parliament and with the cantonal government.

In 1987 the voters of Zurich city rejected two proposals to close the Limmatquai for through traffic. The first proposal, stemming from an individual initiative in the municipal parliament, was to ban traffic between the lakeside and the central station (about 1 kilometre) and reserve the road for pedestrians. It was rejected by 58% of voters. The second proposal, brought by the municipal parliament, was to limit traffic restraint measures to the core part of the Limmatquai, where urban quality and cultural heritage is concentrated. This proposal was also rejected, but only just. The idea of freeing the Limmatquai from through traffic returned in a new form, accompanied by a proposal from a member of the local parliament to build a bypass tunnel parallel to the Limmatquai. That proposal was also rejected in a popular vote.

In 1990, the central stretch of the Limmatquai was classified as an access road with through traffic in the communal transport master plan. The fact that the road and its function was set in the plan meant that a change in the function of the road (for instance closing it to through traffic) was a matter for the communal parliament and should be approved by the cantonal government.

Subsequently there were several other municipal parliament proposals aimed at freeing the Limmatquai from car traffic and providing space for pedestrians and public transport. In 1996 the municipality proposed a pedestrian area with car access in the core part of the Limmatquai only. This proposal was supported by shop owners, who had become aware that in other parts of the urban area where pedestrian zones were already established, business was flourishing. The proposal was also backed by the fact that a full closure of parts of the Limmatquai 237|

in 1993 and 1995 for maintenance work did not result in unbearable traffic conditions in other roads. In addition, 30 km/hr speed zones were introduced in most residential areas around the central business district. The municipality organised an architectural competition for reshaping the embankment and its road space.

Nevertheless, it took three more years for the parliament to move to close the core part of the Limmatquai. Beforehand the municipality had to carry out a public consultation[14] because the closure of the road implied a modification of the city's transport master plan, and counter objections raised by citizens. On 7 April 1999, the municipal parliament decided to close the core part of the Limmatquai, though only after it had improved traffic on bypasses and submitted the proposal to a popular vote, which took place on 13 June 1999. While the municipal parliament was discussing the proposal in the spring of 1999, the cantonal parliament was active. The cantonal government was asked for its position, and the somewhat ominous reply was that the cantonal government would wait for the results of the vote, which approved the proposal by a majority of 60%. As of February 2001, the Limmatquai is still not closed. There are still private appeals and political controversies going on.

This case of closing the Limmatquai shows how complicated and long decision making in urban transport policy can be. This also applies to road building proposals. The fight generally opposes left-wing to right-wing militants in the city itself, and the majority leftist/green government of the municipality of Zurich to the majority right-wing government and parliament of the canton.

4.3. Transport policy and its implementation in Bern

Current transport policies[15]

In the last decades, Bern has also experienced a transformation of transport planning principles. Until the 1970s, the transport planning process was mostly geared to satisfying demand. If there was a bottleneck, capacity increases were sought, the limiting factor being financial. This demand-oriented strategy led to a vicious circle. With improved transport infrastructure distances travelled between home, work and leisure activities increased, traffic volumes rose, and noise and air pollution became serious, strengthening the incentive to move out of the city. This process of suburbanisation was quite strong: between 1970 and 1990, the population of the town of Bern dropped from 160 000 to 135 000 residents, while workplaces increased from 118 000 to 126 000 and the number of people commuting from suburbs to the city increased from about 40 000 to 60 000.

In 1983 the municipality of Bern introduced new transport planning principles with the Environment, City and Transport report which no longer advocated increased road capacity but focused on a reduction of the harmful effects of traffic. The new objectives were:

- promoting public transport to encourage as many motorists as possible to switch to public transport;

- channelling motorised traffic onto the main road network, bypassing residential areas;

- calming and reducing traffic in residential areas;

- setting up new park and ride facilities at the periphery of Bern and in the region, together with a strict control of inner-city parking.

Today, urban transport policy in Bern is not only concerned with financial resources, but also by standards of air quality and noise levels set by federal law. The 1995 Traffic Concept outlines the measures needed to meet these objectives.

The 1995 Traffic Concept of the city of Bern

In 1995 the municipality approved the Urban Spatial Development Concept, which includes an Urban Planning Concept and a Traffic Concept. The latter includes objectives and measures for every mode of transport and differentiates between infrastructure and traffic management. Its main objectives are:

- to improve the quality of urban life and the environment;

- to maintain the operational functionality of the transport system;

- to increase safety and speed.

Starting from these general goals, specific objectives for public transport, motorised private road transport (including parking), bicycle and walking policies were formulated.[16] The objectives for motorised road transport are:

- to define a hierarchy of roads and a traffic system that helps reduce motorised road traffic;

- to introduce an integrated traffic management system;

- to regulate traffic to reduce air pollution and energy use;

- to restrict public and private parking locally and follow a parking charging strategy that encourages public transport and cycling.

In particular, the canton of Bern developed a strategy of Priority Development Sites near public transport stations in the whole agglomeration, where new workplaces and residential areas should be concentrated.

Traffic management

The transport policy of Bern is governed by the federal environmental legislation, mainly the Federal Clean Air Ordinance and the Federal Noise Protection Ordinance.

239|

For Bernese traffic planners the answer to this challenge was an integrated traffic management system, aimed at avoiding, shifting and guiding traffic by:

- protecting residential areas from through traffic, while maintaining traffic flow on the main network;

- moving parking in pedestrian areas of the central business district to outlying car parks, with parking guidance reducing search traffic;

- road pricing with differentiated fees according to the area, road and level of congestion.

Road pricing has not yet been implemented. Voters rejected an urban tunnel project that was to be financed by road pricing, mainly because they felt the project was not well integrated into the urban road network.

Public Transport

The guiding principle of Bern's transport policy is to promote traffic that is adapted to the city rather than to adapt the city to the traffic.[17] Therefore, the main element of Bern's urban traffic planning is public transport. The city and region have an intricate network of tram, bus, trolley bus, light rail transit and urban railway lines. Almost all of these lines feed directly into the city centre and offer frequent services. Not surprisingly, Bern has one of the highest modal shares of public transport in western Europe for trips to the city centre. The advantages offered by public transportation are complemented by attractive promotional measures, *i.e.* an integrated regional fare system for season tickets. Motorists are encouraged not to drive into the city centre by park and ride facilities at rail terminals throughout the region or at bus or tram stops at the periphery. Examples of projects to improve public transport include the Bern-West tram and the new S-Bahn stations co-ordinated with spatial development projects (Wankdorf, Brünnen).

Parking policy

Bern has an active and well documented parking policy strategy (for a more extensive discussion see section below).[18] It is a comprehensive strategy comprising many types of parking policy measures:

- in the central districts of the city of Bern the parking fee is SF 2 per hour. The municipality intends to introduce spatially differentiated fees, including a doubling of fees. Parking time restrictions are the other main instrument of parking policy in the central districts of Bern;

- visitors to events in the main sports stadium or the exhibition centre have to pay parking fees of SF 5 per half day and SF 10 per day;

- a blue zone has been introduced in almost all residential areas. Parking time for non-residents is limited to 90 minutes and residents can buy a park card for SF 20 per month or SF 240 a year;

- guidance is provided to operators of park and ride facilities, notably criteria that should be taken into consideration when the provision of new facilities is planned.

The canton of Bern has drawn up guidelines for parking policy measures (*e.g.* parking fees that include the cost of land use, maintenance and investment) for public car parks. As there is no legal basis for forcing private firms to take parking policy measures on existing car parks, public authorities have completed a handbook for firms that intend to introduce voluntarily parking policy measures. The provision of new parking spaces is restricted according to the availability of public transport the area concerned.

Improvements for pedestrians and cyclists

Since 2001 Bern has invested SF 4 million a year for measures in favour of pedestrians and cyclists, notably to make public areas more attractive and improve connections.

Improvement of road safety

Bern has a special plan for reducing the number of accidents by 20% within 10 years.[19] This plan includes measures such as the systematic protection of crossings and a speed limit of 30 km/h in residential areas.

Problems of perception and acceptance

In 1996 the inhabitants of Bern were asked about their perception of traffic problems.[20] Some results are mentioned below:

- for 50% of pedestrians the most important problems were noise and air pollution;

- around 60% of cyclists listed as large or very large problems noise and air pollution, the lack of bicycle lanes, the risk of accident and fear of theft;

- the most important problem for users of public transport were prices (60% of public transport users);

- 60% of motorists put the problem of parking first and 50% were concerned about parking fees;

- in residential areas, 50% of inhabitants ranked air pollution problems as rather large to very large, 40% made the same judgement for noise and for land used by road traffic.

241

Current and expected conditions regarding traffic, the environment and economic resources

Since 1990, average daily traffic on urban main roads in Bern City has remained below the level of 1980, though average daily traffic on highways in the urban region has increased annually by 5%. This trend slowed only between 1993 and 1995. In exposed urban areas air quality standards for NO_2 and ozone are still not met and NO_x emissions need to be further reduced from mobile sources.

The canton of Bern and the city of Bern are in a difficult financial situation. Deficits are rising and taxes are among the highest in Switzerland. The deficit of the city of Bern is partly structural, as in the case of Zurich. In addition, it is the seat of the large federal administration that does not pay taxes. In the future the city will get some SF 20 million per year from the canton for social, cultural and police services, and public utilities, thereby reducing the city's debts.

Description of an actual process: parking policy

In 1983 the municipality of Bern defined four objectives for parking policy:[21]

- reducing traffic volumes in residential areas;
- stabilising private car traffic in rush hours;
- maintaining the attractiveness of Bern as an economic and cultural centre;
- providing park and ride facilities on the outskirts of the city centre.

In accordance with the 1985 Federal Act on Air Pollution, the air pollution action plan for the urban area of Bern[22] was published in 1992. As transport is a major source of air pollution, the plan contains a large number of policy measures concerning car and heavy vehicle traffic. Parking policy measures and regulations are the main instruments to reduce emissions from cars. The reduction targets of the plan are ambitious: NO_x and VOC emissions from transport should be reduced by 60% by 2005[23, 24]. The plan is the basis for parking policy in the urban area of Bern.

The authorities have created a special organisation to design and implement parking policy measures. Five working groups have dealt with issues related to existing and new public parking spaces, private company parking, park and ride at S-Bahn stations, and parking at public administrations. The organisation was useful because it brought together all those concerned.

In 1990, voters approved a proposal for more restrictive parking policy measures to reduce the flow of commuters entering the city each day. The main parking regulations were:

- no new multi-storey car parks in or close to the city centre. Locations on the outskirts or at motorway exits must be well served by public transport and

242

new multi-storey car parks must displace existing parking spaces in the city centre;

- a change from a legal minimum of parking spaces for new buildings to a legal maximum of one parking space per 10 workplaces.

The initiative was launched by the social democratic party, with strong opposition from representatives of local businesses and especially the Chamber of Commerce and associations of retailers.

After the popular ballot, both sides launched new and contradictory proposals. The main controversy was the number of public parking spaces in the city centre. As the situation became very unsatisfactory, in spring 1994 both sides agreed on a compromise stating that the number of the public parking spaces would be unchanged, but public parking in the historical part of the town would be reduced. At the same time the capacity of multi-storey car parks will be increased.

The introduction of parking policy measures was accompanied by a broad communication strategy. The starting point was the impression that people are very critical of each intervention in private car traffic. Therefore, the main objective of the public relations strategy was to generate a positive attitude with regard to the parking policy measures to engender a "win-win" situation. In the case of Bern, the communication strategy comprised the following elements:

- a brochure[25] showing the impact of car traffic on air quality and describing parking policy measures planned for the urban area of Bern; it encouraged awareness in transport choices without demonising car use;
- media events, rather than press conferences: the first was a race on a typical commuter trip between journalists and municipal officials using different means of transport;[26] the destination being the conference hall of a large private company where the communication strategy and parking policy measures were presented to the press;
- advertisements to raise public awareness and motivate car users to change their driving behaviour;
- information flyers for households: at the end of the advertising campaign each household received an a flyer summarising the message of the advertisements;
- public events in residential areas: local markets or fêtes were organised to inform the population and demonstrate alternative parking strategies, allowing people to experience the advantages of the parking policy measures;
- posters to communicate the main message of the parking policy ("less traffic – more quality of life") and to advertise local events.

The style, tone and appearance of the different parts of the strategy were co-ordinated to create a recognition effect and ensure continuity.

243|

The position of stakeholders

Whenever public authorities plan restrictive parking measures strong opposition can be expected. Businesses frequently believe such measures will affect the attractiveness of a location for private companies, while environmentalists and often a majority of residents support such measures.

In the urban area of Bern opponents to the parking policy argue that restrictive parking measures on public and private commuter car parks impair the position of private companies on the labour market compared with other companies not affected by such measures, and that any reduction in the accessibility of shops and companies will reduce custom and therefore turn-over.

There are several reasons why these potential disadvantages did not prevent these measures. In the case of commuter traffic the following points should be mentioned:

- in the urban area of Bern parking measures are part of a comprehensive traffic and land use planning strategy. The S-Bahn and park and ride facilities will considerably improve opportunities to switch to public transport and growth of industry and especially services will be concentrated in locations close to the S-Bahn stations;

- a large part of industry and services is located in the city of Bern, the best served by public transport;

- commuter traffic can be organised as car pools (same destination, acquaintance of the employers, existing internal information channels, etc.);

- other factors such as the unemployment rate, wages and working conditions have more influence on the attractiveness of a job than the availability of parking at work;

- in the urban area of Bern it is up to the companies to take parking measures in their car parks; these companies will not introduce parking measures that deteriorate their competitiveness on the labour market.

In the city of Bern (as probably in every urban area) retailers are among the strongest opponents of parking policy measures (especially parking fees and restrictions). They point to the strong competition between retail trade in the city centre and suburban shopping centres, arguing that parking restrictions in the city centre weaken the position of urban retail trade and destroys jobs.

The possibility of increasing parking fees has been discussed between researchers and public authorities. In official publications[27] a fee system that is differentiated according to location and type of parking and that internalises external costs is a long term objective for Bern's parking policy strategy. On the other hand, the traffic compromise mentioned above shows that retailers are aware of the fact that the attractiveness of shopping in the city centre depends on many factors, accessibility for car users being just one. Therefore, the following points were important in the discussion:

- accessibility: normally, if opponents to parking policy measures speak of accessibility they only think of private car traffic. The importance of public transport and infrastructure for pedestrians and cyclists is often under-estimated;

- attractiveness of public space: parking policy measures – especially the removal of existing parking spaces – can be an opportunity to redesign urban public space (using trees, benches and sculptures), as streets can be developed more creatively if there is no need to accommodate rows of stationary cars.

Public opinion polls in several Swiss cities (Zurich, Bern, Biel and Solothurn) have shown that visitors rate the attractiveness of public space higher than the availability of parking.[28] With regard to the political acceptance of parking policy measures, a major problem is that the rating of the important pull-factors by the owners of retail facilities is in contradiction with preferences expressed by public opinion.

New developments

Several lessons can be drawn from the implementation of previous clean air action plans in Bern. While technical measures in heating, industry and automobile technology have contributed to reducing air pollution and energy consumption, these improvements have been partially compensated by traffic and energy use increases. Although this problem was known, measures were insufficient. The 2000 Action Plan on Clean Air covers the whole of the Canton of Bern, not only poor air quality areas.[29] Furthermore it provides for improved co-ordination of clean air policy with land use planning by adjusting the planning horizon to 15 years.

To implement this new approach, the plan uses so-called road performance models. According to the cantonal 1995 emissions balance, the road performance of motorised passenger traffic (measured as daily vehicle-kilometres) must not rise by more than 8% between 2000-2015 to meet clean air and climate protection objectives.[30] The largest share of this growth potential is allocated to urban areas (maximum 11% growth). In the region of Thun for example, five municipalities have developed a regional road performance model: 40% of the additional road perfor-mance is allocated to locations with big traffic volumes, the rest to the whole region. The planning authorities welcomed the flexibility given by this approach, though no one really knows how to control road performance! This new concept has to prove its feasibility.

Another element of parking policy is in a critical phase. In accordance with the 1990 Action Plan, the canton limits the number of parking places. This regulation was heavily opposed by representatives of trade and industry, and was replaced in the 2000 Cantonal Construction Decree by a range of parking allowances. The maximum number is therefore no longer determined by the accessibility of a site by public transport, but by investors.[31] In addition, municipalities will no longer be allowed to adapt the allowance in certain areas. For the city of Bern, this means that stricter existing parking regulations might be loosened in the future.

4.4. *Transport policies in other urban regions*

Similarities

When comparing transport policies in different urban regions in Switzerland, one can mainly see similarities. These similarities are based on common trends in the development of traffic and its problems. Strong motorization has led to highway development through and around all larger agglomerations and to urban sprawl. Promotion of public transport and non-motorised transport has become a top priority. Parking policy aims to protect residential areas from through traffic and limit parking in central areas. It has also aimed at setting maximum parking for new housing, business and entertainment developments, and parking policy everywhere faces similar difficulties in implementing these measures.

Similarities are also due to a common legal base, notably the federal law and ordinance on spatial planning and the federal law and ordinance on clean air, which set clear objectives for transport planning: less sprawl, less air pollution. Both laws require cantonal laws and plans that bring policy making closer to the level of implementation and give more power to municipalities.

Finally, there is all over urban areas an intensive debate on transport policy issues in professional organisations, allowing some benchmarking and experience sharing with regard to innovation.

Differences

Differences among urban regions concern scheduling and emphasis in transport policy. Some are still at the stage of completing the highway network. Others find the existing highway network through or around the city is clogged by transiting traffic, using up space for regional traffic and are considering large scale integrated traffic management, involving both individual and public transport. While some urban areas have a high level of S-Bahn services, others are just about to launch such developments. The same is true for the integration of urban centres into the high speed railway network. Providing priority to public transport on urban roads and junctions by telematics has not reached the same level in all cities. Park and ride policies are not seen everywhere as a solution to traffic problems. Road pricing has been proposed in two large cities to finance an inner-city tunnel or a bridge over a lake and was rejected by voters, though this could be due to the projects rather than the funding source proposed.

Reasons for political success or failure

Transport policy in Switzerland still favours public transport, especially in urban areas. After a long period of successful policy making in this respect, there are now voices calling for a new generation of road investment. This movement, which can be identified nationally and locally, is counterbalanced by the will of many to continue softer transport policies: integrated traffic management, mobility management and structural reforms in public transport. Scarce financial resources tend to push in this latter direction. On the other hand, heavy investment in public transport has to prove its worth. It seems therefore that policy making is in a waiting and exploring stage, after a long period of clear-cut attitudes.

5. Lessons learned

Lessons learned from urban transport policy implementation are outlined below:

- municipalities are only partially autonomous in handling local transport problems. They need to negotiate with cantons and neighbouring communities. Grouping the communities of an urban area into a regional body with specific responsibilities may become a condition for the allocation of federal assistance addressing urban transport problems;

- municipalities are closest to local interests. Transport policy needs public participation in defining problems, setting goals and strategies, designing measures and involving local partners. Good mobility management results have been achieved on the base of direct co-operation between municipalities, transport operators and private companies;

- the recent re-urbanisation trend may counterbalance urban sprawl. Making better use of road and rail infrastructure by traffic management and telematics can help especially in urban areas where space and financial resources are scarce. New transport projects will need to be accompanied by measures that aim at limiting road traffic and reducing car dependency;

- urban transport policy in Switzerland has for many years been favoured by a focus on sustainability, though it can do little to solve basic problems such as CO_2 emissions, unless there is action at national and international level.

Recommendations for increasing financial support for sustainable transport stem from two large research programmes, one on urban transport and the other on the environmental impact of transport. Taking a broader perspective, as well as in day-to-day life, it is apparent that we have a "lose-lose" situation and we must (and

247|

Figure 33. **From a "lose-lose" to a "win-win" situation**

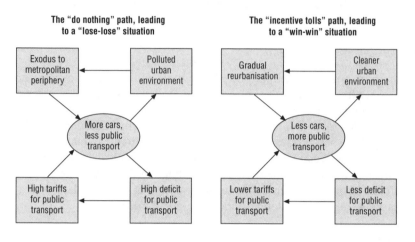

The "do nothing" path, leading to a "lose-lose" situation

The "incentive tolls" path, leading to a "win-win" situation

can) get a "win-win" situation (Figure 32). A majority of people and businesses should be convinced that they and society as a whole are winning more than they lose by accepting measures that are geared to achieving sustainable mobility.

There is no doubt that for all involved in policy making, the path to sustainable mobility has to be found, notably by:

- identifying the contribution of single measures and whole packages to an environmentally sound situation in urban areas, and their effect on the public;
- identifying the investment and operational costs of such measures and packages, and their effect on public finances and transport operators;
- identifying gains and losses which the measures and packages may bring to users;
- balancing benefits and costs properly in a convincing way;
- optimising policy packages to gain public acceptance.

5.1. Major challenges

Interaction of government levels

Responsibilities, duties and means for transport policy are shared among government levels, though each has limited legal competence to solve problems. The cantonal level has been driven by federal intervention to take on environmental protection, though implementation is difficult because it also involves less environmentally aware municipalities. Urban areas are the most affected by traffic and need large scale cantonal and national measures, covering city centres, suburbs and metropolitan peripheries. Urban areas also need private commitment, for instance firms that increase private parking costs or share the cost of their employees' public transport.

New questions

In the 1970s and early 1980s, conceptual approaches and master plans for urban transport were developed in many cities to solve congestion problems. They focused on infrastructure projects and "hardware": by-passes, parking facilities and public transport improvements. With the growth of environmental problems, the need for innovation in transport technology and behaviour became stronger. Short-term effects were required and policy was engaged in single measures rather than whole concepts. Traffic regulation was a priority in many cities and some thought was given to economic measures (parking fees, road pricing, etc.) to reduce traffic to a tolerable level. Internalisation of external costs became an important issue.

Politicians consider that it is unavoidable that environmental gains have to be weighed against welfare losses. Balancing positive and negative economic impacts has become a key concern: what are the real costs of air pollution? How would drivers react to increased fuel prices or parking fees? The following answers are possible:

- fuel taxes are introduced at national level; urban road pricing, parking fees and local speed limits are local tools and can be locally very effective, though they can shift traffic to other areas, where public transport might not be so good;

- the closer the leverage point is to the emission, the more direct the effect on air pollution or noise; it is thus easier to predict the effect on emissions of a regulatory measure to reduce air pollution such as standards and catalytic converters, than to predict behavioural changes due to a change in prices or speed limits;

- the effect of economic instruments will be stronger the closer the fiscal base is to actual emissions and if it is linked to variable rather than fixed costs;

- the effect of price measures depends on the price elasticity of demand; price measures are generally more efficient than command and control measures because individuals are free to choose their transport pattern, though the effect of regulatory measures is more predictable (despite uncertainty about the acceptance of speed limits for instance).

249|

Counterbalancing negative social and regional effects

Environment friendly transport policy measures can have side-effects for the private sector and municipal budgets. Raising parking fees, road pricing or area access licensing, for instance, entail costs for users and income for the public sector. Here it is important to distinguish between a change in real economic costs and benefits, and transfers from one user group to another. A balance can be made for each actor or by consolidating the effects on all, to assess the politically very relevant issue of who is on the winning and who on the losing side.

An old rule in policy making says: try to solve different policy problems with different policy measures. Thus an environment-oriented transport strategy should not try to (and cannot) solve social or regional problems at the same time, though policy packages have to avoid negative effects such as:

- reduced access in urban areas;
- environmental effects due for instance to increased car traffic in regional shopping centres which have poor access by public transport;
- increased financial burden at regional level.

The integration of the instruments used in urban areas with those used at the cantonal and national level is very important because solving urban emission problems might cause new emission problems at other places. A typical example of this effect is road by-passes.

Thus policy packages should be optimised at an early stage to deal with the regional dimension and therefore collaboration with other municipalities and cantons should be sought, especially with regard to the following elements:

- improved public transport access in suburbs and around urban areas, and improvement of transport chains (*e.g.* park and ride);
- integrated parking policy: simultaneous restriction or concentration of private parking and charging in surrounding areas;
- integrated capacity management;
- getting political partners within other municipalities.

Understanding the dynamics

Transport in every city is imbedded in an ongoing process of changing infrastructure, city character, behavioural patterns and problem perception. Transport policy assessment has to deal with these dynamics. The better they are understood, the better we can deal with new elements, problems, solutions and attitudes. Attention has to be given to:

- new environmental problems (*e.g.* particulate matter, global environmental problems);

- new technological concepts (*e.g.* environmentally sound technology, introduction of telematics in traffic steering and as an alternative to physical mobility);

- increasingly scarce public financial resources;

- policy cycles (changes in political priorities, government and administration);

- changes in economic conditions and demographic development.

Understanding these dynamics does not mean intensified forecasting and obtaining detailed information about an uncertain future, but dealing with uncertainty and applying stepwise thinking. A coherent monitoring system is essential in this respect.

Policy packages

Transport policy practice shows that individual instruments can be helpful to improve environmental performance, but none has the power to achieve the objectives of sustainable development. Particularly in urban transport, the interaction of individual measures, the interests of different user groups and the scarcity of space require optimised policy packages. The combination of reinforcing measures, avoiding counterbalancing effects, is essential for gaining public acceptance.

5.2. Getting partners – and political acceptance

In a situation where changes in habits and privileges are required to reach political goals – such as environmentally sound mobility – participatory approaches can smooth the path to public acceptance. Participation becomes a stage in project development and implementation.

Leverage points and participation outreach

A broad participatory process can involve several leverage points:

- participation in problem identification and assessment, to identify different perceptions and narrow the spectrum of assessments;

- participation in the definition of goals, with a broad interpretation of sustainability involving mainly environmental quality, accessibility and equity;

- participation in defining strategies and measures, when the discussion might turn back to the definition of problems and goals. If earlier stages of participation have been well structured, the search for strategies and measures is easier;

251

- participation in implementation: the participatory process can guarantee continuous support, as arguments pro or against measures have been put on the table;

- participation in effectiveness monitoring.

Participation in problem assessment provides a common (though not fully binding) basis for discussing policies and measures, and getting broad acceptance. The outreach of participation should be as comprehensive as possible: it makes little sense to restrict involvement in the problem identification stage to those who suffer directly from traffic nuisances. Those who are most likely to be affected by negative side-effects of the measures should also be involved and both parties should learn to acknowledge each other's point of view, while engaging in a process of negotiation on problem perception, goal setting and the design of measures.

At the same time all involved in the participatory process should see themselves as potential actors in transport policy, where solutions do not depend entirely on public authorities, as most every inhabitant and business is engaged in transport. For instance businesses can raise private fees and lower the cost of public transport for their employees.

An important condition for fruitful participation is that the process should be clear. Those involved should understand the dialogue and negotiation and should be able to convince those they represent in subsequent and separate meetings. Such a participatory process represents a challenging exercise in communication.

The involvement of the private sector and the benefits of public/private partnerships

Companies have long considered themselves as potential losers in an environment-oriented transport policy, and their political representatives have opposed such policies, especially with the emergence of the polluter-pays-principle. As they had earlier in other areas (such as water pollution and waste disposal), companies have found ways to support environmentally friendly transport. Several firms charge for parking and use the money for reducing the public transport costs of their employees. There is a widely-accepted name for such endeavours: mobility management, which gives the company with a greener image as well as it limits parking. Mobility management creates a channel for dialogue with the private sector in the difficult area of environment-oriented transport policy. Of course for transport operators mobility management will bring more clients.

Getting along with neighbouring communities

Communities of the inner suburban belt often face environmental problems similar to those of the city centre, as they are under pressure from traffic originating in outlying areas. Thus they have a similar perception of urban transport problems, even if the emphasis can be different: a suburban community being crossed by traffic flows, while the city centre suffers from congestion but is at least the destination of these trips.

Yet the relation between the city centre and suburban communities can be antagonistic. The more the centre restricts private transport (through high parking fees or road pricing) the more car drivers will look for new destinations for their commuting or shopping trips. This geographic shift of demand is the origin of location decisions for businesses, providing momentum for urban sprawl. But car restraint measures should not necessarily be extended to the suburbs because:

- many suburban communities tend to be liberal or right-wing, whereas city centre residents are often more left-wing or green and are much less motorised; though the perception of traffic problems may be similar, the policy approach may be different;

- suburban communities are sometimes still growing, and new businesses or retailers bring in additional local taxes; these decentralised businesses make use of their competitive advantage over city centres in terms of cheaper parking and access;

- it is more difficult to raise parking fees and apply road pricing in areas where the road network provides ample possibilities for alternative parking or routes.

There are examples of regional transport policy co-operation, but they are largely due to the need to join forces to improve regional public transport systems. There are substantial difficulties with car restraint policies. Bilateral rather than multilateral negotiations between the city and neighbouring communities suffering most from environmental pressure might be preferable. On the other hand, there is a need to engage cantonal and national levels in transport policies covering whole metropolitan areas.

Shared responsibility with cantonal and federal government

It is in general terms easy to assign the right measure to the right level. Setting fuel and vehicle import taxes is clearly a national matter. Speed limits are set according to different road types. Parking fees are determined by municipalities or private firms. It is also easy to identify the leverage points for measures. Assessing local impact, *i.e.* regional distribution effects and geographic equity, is more difficult. What do, for instance, higher fuel prices mean to the inhabitants of a densely populated city, a rich suburban community, a village at the edge of the agglomeration and a mountain region? Yet practice shows that the most ambitious step towards shared responsibility at different government levels is political harmonisation. Not all levels are equally concerned by environmental issues (urban areas and populations are

253|

generally under most pressure) and may therefore not be interested in addressing them. This means that higher government levels may not always want to take measures appropriate for their level, and may not want to allow urban authorities to take measures affecting other levels, such as traffic management on highways in urban areas. Furthermore there may be situations in which the national government does not financially support environmental protection measures taken by local communities. Cities under environmental pressure therefore have to carry out information campaigns and create multilevel taskforces.

Notes

1. Blöchliger H. *et al.*, (1999) Finanzierung des Verkehrs von morgen. Bericht D9 des NFP 41, Bern.
2. Gotthard, Lötschberg.
3. For a few years the cantons have also been allowed to do so, under federal control.
4. For an overview, see: DETEC (1998), Transportation – yesterday, today, tomorrow.
5. BUWAL – Bundesamt für Umwelt, Wald und Landschaft (1997), Parkplatz-Massnahmen in Schweizer Agglomerationen. Bern.
6. DETEC (1999), Aktionsprogramm Energie 2000, 9. Jahresbericht.
7. DETEC (1998), Transportation – yesterday, today, tomorrow.
8. For scenarios of the ecological and economical consequences of either version, see for example ECOPLAN (1999a), Ökologische und wirtschaftliche Auswirkungen der neuen Finanzordnung mit ökologischen Anreizen.
9. The approval of the energy tax and accompanying measures would make the CO_2-tax redundant.
10. Re-structuring of inhabitants.
11. In Bern and Zurich new counting methods for passengers were introduced in 1997/98.
12. Including public transport fares in entrance fees to football matches and other events.
13. Kanton Zürich (1999) Die Luftreinhaltung in der Schweiz, Cercl'Air. Luftqualität im Kanton Zürich, Jahresbericht 1999 der städtischen und kantonalen Fachstellen.
14. Not to be confused with a consultation of inhabitants and businesses along the road, which has to be carried out later in the process.
15. This section and the following section on Bern are to a large degree taken from reports by ECOPLAN, a leading Bernese consultancy.
16. For a description of objectives and measures for public transport, cycling and walking see also Gemeinderat der Stadt Bern (1995), Räumliches Stadtentwicklungskonzept, Verkehrskonzept.
17. Hoppe K. (undated), The importance of Public Transport in a Strongly Ecological Orientated Traffic Policy: The Case of Bern.
18. See ECOPLAN (1994), Parking policy, and ECOPLAN (1997), Kombiniertes Road Pricing-/Parkplatzabgaben-System für die Stadt Bern.
19. Gemeinderat der Stadt Bern (1998): Massnahmenplan Verkehrssicherheit der Stadt Bern, Dezember , Bern.
20. See Amt für Statistik der Stadt Bern (1997) and Stadt Bern: Einwohnerbefragung (1996).

255

21. See Gemeinderat der Stadt Bern (1983), Kurzbericht zur Parkraumplanung der Stadt Bern, p. 3.

22. See Volkswirtschaftsdirektion des Kantons Bern, Kantonales Amt für Industrie, Gewerbe und Arbeit (1992), Massnahmenplan zur Luftreinhaltung in der Region Bern.

23. In fact the reduction targets should have been met by 1994 but no Swiss canton did (see Volkswirtschaftsdirektion des Kantons Bern, Kantonales Amt für Industrie, Gewerbe und Arbeit (1992), Massnahmenplan zur Luftreinhaltung in der Region Bern, Schlussbericht: Allgemeiner Teil, p. 9).

24. 84% of total NO_x emissions in the urban area of Bern are emitted by transport. In the case of VOC the share of transport amounts to 21%.

25. The slogan can be translated as "to put more air into transport".

26. The winner of the commuter trophy was a cyclist.

27. See KIGA (1993), Parkplatzmassnahmen, p. 55 and KIGA (1993), Parkplatzmassnahmen Zentrumsgemeinden Rahmenkonzept, p. 38.

28. See ECOPLAN (1993), Strukturelle Auswirkungen von Parkplatzmassnahmen, p. 116.

29. Volkswirtschaftsdirektion des Kantons Bern (2000), Lufthygienischer Massnahmenplan für den Kanton Bern (Vernehmlassungsentwurf).

30. This number takes into account pollution control measures as well as the most recent forecasts for improvements in engine technologies.

31. Amt für Gemeinden und Raumordnung (2000), Abstellplätze für Fahrzeuge.

United States*

I. Introduction

Key sustainability trends and issues in urban travel in the United States are outlined below.

The trend toward devolution in transport decision-making, from federal to state, metropolitan area, and local levels, continues. States and local governments have wide discretion to invest federal transport funds to meet locally identified priorities. Long term sustainability goals such as air pollution and greenhouse gas emission reductions with national or even international dimensions have to compete with immediate local priorities to solve traffic congestion and repair roads.

The national surface transport law, the Transport Equity Act for the 21st Century (TEA-21) defines a challenging, innovative and flexible participatory transport planning framework that states and local areas are expected to follow. TEA-21 encourages a balance among economic, environmental, and social equity goals and a shift from fragmented jurisdictional and modal decision-making toward a more integrated and systematic approach.

Under the Clean Air Act Amendments (CAAA), air quality is a national transport goal with broad public and political support. In combination, TEA-21 and the CAAA strongly encourage states and local areas to incorporate air quality goals into their transport planning.

Air quality has been improving largely due to vehicle and fuel technology, and retirement of more polluting older cars, though this improvement is being offset by trends in increased vehicle use and consumer shifts to light duty trucks (sport utility vehicles and vans) with lower fuel economy.

The low cost of owning and operating a car, particularly low fuel costs relative to those in Europe, contribute to the growth in car travel and to the difficulty in attracting drivers to alternative modes. The Bureau of Transport Studies estimates

---

* Prepared by William M. Lyons, Volpe National Transport Systems Center Research and Special Programs Administration, the United States Department of Transportation. This paper has not been formally reviewed within the United States Department of Transportation, and it does not therefore necessarily represent the official positions of the Department.

257|

---

that the inflation adjusted cost of owning and operating an automobile declined from US$0.47 per mile in 1975 to US$0.39 in 1995.

TEA-21 and the CAAA encourage active public involvement in all stages of the urban transport planning process. Public consultation and transparency of decision-making are important national themes.

There are major opportunities to improve co-ordination and integration of land use and transport planning. Typically, zoning and other land use decisions are made by cities and counties, while transport decisions are made by state departments and regional transport planning agencies with responsibilities defined under TEA-21, and transport providers.

Title VI of the United States Civil Rights Act and Environmental Justice Orders protects citizens, specifically minority and low income populations, from the adverse impact of federally funded transport investments. State and local transport planners are facing a major challenge in taking into account this equity dimension in transport decisions.

Integration of energy, environment and transport planning at state level could be improved.

The national framework for balanced transport planning presents great opportunities for metropolitan planning organisations and their partners to further sustainability goals in transport decisions. At the same time, states and urban areas face the challenge of meeting large expectations placed on their transport planning processes to integrate many complex dimensions, from air quality to environmental justice, welfare reform, economic development, and planning for intelligent transport technologies. These challenges are technical and institutional.

2. Institutional Framework

2.1. *Transport decision-making*

Responsibilities for transport planning and decision-making are complex and overlapping. They are shared by Federal, state, metropolitan area or regional, county, and city authorities. The United States Department of Transportation is the major source of funds for interstate highway construction and maintenance, and a major source of funding for public transport in urban and non-urban areas. Under devolution trends, decision-making for urban transport investments in all modes continues to evolve toward increased state and local discretion. Under TEA-21, states and local authorities have the flexibility to shift federal funds from highway and public transport programs to locally selected investments. Increased local flexibility is accompanied by federal expectations for a locally defined but comprehensive, co-operative and participatory planning process that balances economic, environmental and social equity goals (see Policy Framework section).

2.2. Air quality

Under the CAAA of 1990, the United States Environmental Protection Agency (EPA) works with the Department of Transportation to assure that states and local areas meet their formal commitments to select transport investments that contribute to progress toward legally defined standards for air quality.

2.3. Land use planning

Cities and counties have primary responsibility for land use planning. In general, land use and transport policies are not strongly co-ordinated, though there is much variation from community to community. States such as Washington and Florida encourage co-ordinated transport and land development. Other urban areas, such as Houston, do very little land use planning, in contrast to other communities, such as Portland, with growth management co-ordinated with transport planning. Several urban areas, such as Houston, Salt Lake City and Hartford, Connecticut are undertaking creative public and private partnerships to co-ordinate long term development and transport (additional information is available at *www.fhwa.dot.gov/tcsp/*).

3. Policy Framework

3.1. Integrated urban transport policy framework

The United States has an innovative integrated policy framework for urban transport.[1] Transport and environmental policy involve complex roles and responsibilities for the national, state, regional and local governments. The Federal Government provides major subsidies for highways and public transport. Although there is national funding for many transport investments, other levels of government and transport providers exercise a great deal of discretion over how federal funds are spent. A major TEA-21 principle is to encourage flexibility for state and local agencies to determine transport investments and strategies. Along with encouragement of local decision-making processes, TEA-21 and the CAAA define clear roles and responsibilities for local, regional and state public agencies. TEA-21 defines a comprehensive transport planning process for states and metropolitan areas. States and local areas have considerable flexibility in tailoring that approach to local conditions and in determining how federal transport funds are invested.

In addition, the CAAA mandates that all states and metropolitan areas reach measurable and enforceable air quality targets. TEA-21 includes directions for transport planners and decision-makers to meet air quality and other goals – transport planning must emphasise system efficiency, and for cities with severe air pollution, transport projects are expected to contribute to cleaner air.

259|

Each urban area can apply this planning framework to reflect its priorities and solve its problems. TEA-21 and the CAAA each involve formal federal oversight to assure that expectations are met; if necessary, federal transport funds can be withheld to provide incentives for compliance with requirements for the planning process and progress toward improved air quality.

The main aspects of the integrated TEA-21/CAAA approach are the following:

- the policies are reinforcing; reinforcement involves clear and complementary institutional roles and responsibilities for planning agencies and transport providers in the planning process;

- the two laws strengthen urban transport planning and decision-making, with federal leadership, combined with flexibility to accommodate different local conditions, goals and priorities;

- air quality is both a national and local transport goal; in combination, the two laws set a priority for improvement of air quality relative to other national and local concerns; this approach combines a national framework for urban planning with high priority national goals with performance targets;

- a comprehensive, co-ordinated transport planning process is required; TEA-21, supported by the CAAA, defines an ideal or model planning process, then monitors progress to ensure that the expected process occurs and air quality is improved; this combines a "top-down" federally led process, with a "bottom-up" state and locally led process;

- responsibility and accountability; federal agencies monitor how successfully the planning process is applied and whether legal commitments toward air quality targets are met; both TEA-21 and the CAAA provide for accountability of responsible state and local agencies.

3.2. Other policies

Promotion of public transport

The United States Department of Transportation uses an incentive formula to allocate over US$3 billion a year to urban public transport for capital expenses, including maintenance. In addition, there are other federal programs that fund capital projects, including new fixed guideway rail projects. States and local governments provide grants for operating deficits and some capital purchases using a range of revenue sources, including sales, gas and income taxes. Over 500 urban public transport operators promote public transport through marketing, fare strategies and other techniques. Metropolitan areas can use the transport planning process to select public transport and other projects that reduce congestion and improve air quality for funding under the TEA-21 Congestion Management and Air Quality Program or to transfer federal funds from the highway program.

Minimising car use in urban areas

Initiatives to minimise automobile use are primarily developed by urban areas and can be funded in part through United States Department of Transportation's transport programs. Under one TEA-21 program, the United States Department of Transportation provides grants for over 200 innovative community development and transport pilot projects in urban and other areas. At a national level, employers are able to provide up to US$60 per month to purchase public transit passes as a business expense deductible from federal taxes. The intent is to provide an alternative to tax deductible discounted or free parking provided to many employees by employers.

Many communities are creating Transport Management Associations whereby employers reduce car use by employees through providing public transit passes, ride-sharing programs, flex-time and telecommute options, or other strategies. Other communities, including those in the Los Angeles metropolitan area, have experienced with Employee Trip Reduction Ordinances where businesses above a certain size commit to reduce car travel by employees, measured in terms of passengers per vehicle-mile.

Traffic management/calming measures

There are a broad range of traffic management and traffic calming measures in place around the country. These are primarily undertaken as local urban initiatives. Although often identified locally as promising strategies for managing congestion, there has been limited experience with road pricing. Exceptions are time of day tolls for bridges and tunnels, and new highway lanes with access limited to high occupancy vehicles and single occupant vehicle drivers electing to pay tolls. These initiatives are primarily for financial rather than congestion control purposes. Several areas have implemented "ozone alert days" when weather forecasts in non-attainment areas indicate a likelihood of extreme air pollution. Citizens are then encouraged to limit car use by riding public transit or other means.

4. National Trends

4.1. Population and land use trends

The population of urban areas is not growing as fast as consumption of land in and around urbanised areas. This indicates a trend towards lower density land use for residences and businesses. For many older cities, particularly in the industrialised

Midwest and Northeast, inner city population is steady or even declining while land consumption in the greater metropolitan area is increasing. In some cities this is the result of population shifts from older centre cities with mature transport and other infrastructure, toward existing or new suburbs, which can involve consumption of open space. These areas of population growth often require new transport infrastructure.

Suburban sprawl is a major concern for residents. According to the Pew Center,[2] suburban sprawl is tied with crime as a top local concern for most Americans. At different times this has reached national political debates primarily over topics such as "congestion and traffic", "time away from families", or "loss of a sense of community". There is political and popular support for a range of strategies involving either "smart growth" or "liveability". These are undertaken by institutions at all levels of transport decision-making.

Overall, land consumption is considerably outpacing population growth. Former mayor of Albuquerque David Rusk studied 213 urbanised areas and found that between 1960 and 1990 population increased from 95 million to 140 million (47%) while urbanised land increased from 25 000 square miles to 51 000 square miles (107%).[3] Data collected by the Department of Housing and Urban Development for its State of the Cities 2000 report (1994-1997)[4] shows a continuation of this trend: urban areas are expanding at about twice the rate of population growth.

A regional breakdown of the data shows significant variations. In some areas, urban sprawl is largely a consequence of flight from central cities, but in other parts of the country, net population growth is playing a larger role in exacerbating sprawl. Population growth is clearly a bigger factor in many parts of the south and the west than in parts of the Midwest and north-east, particularly along the coasts.[5] In fact, according to a recent study of 277 metropolitan areas, between 1960 and 1990 western cities nearly doubled in population, southern cities increased by 70%, and cities in the Midwest and the Northeast grew by a more modest 25% and 12.5% respectively.[6]

Some notable examples of this phenomenon include Detroit, Pittsburgh and Chicago. From 1970 to 1990, Detroit's population shrank by 7% but its urbanised area increased by 28%. Pittsburgh's population shrank 9% in the same period while its area increased by 30%. Chicago's population did increase between 1970 and 1990 by 1%. Meanwhile, its urbanised area grew by 24%.[7]

Southern and western regions are also sprawling for some of the same reasons, but in many of these areas, population growth adds to the other pressures that create sprawl and exacerbates the problem.[8] Good examples include Nashville, Charlotte, San Jose and Phoenix. Between 1970 and 1990, Nashville's population grew by 28% while its urbanised area grew by 41%. Charlotte's population grew by a significant 63% during this period while its urbanised area grew by a staggering 129%. However, San Jose's population grew by 40% during this period, while its urbanised area grew by 22%. Phoenix sprawl provides a similar picture: while its population grew 132% from 1970 to 1990, its urbanised area grew by a similarly significant 91%. Of course, Phoenix has a lot of catching up to do in the growth management realm: between 1950 and 1970, while its population grew 300%, its urbanised area grew by an incredible 630%.[9]

If current trends continue, the United States population will double by 2100.

4.2. Urban transport trends

Urban transport is characterised by high car ownership and pronounced increases in vehicle miles travelled in all forms of passenger travel and freight movement, and greatly increased levels of urban congestion measured using a variety of indicators.

The major shift toward non-work trips demonstrates how difficult it is for transport planners to identify investments and strategies to shift growing car transport demand to alternative modes such as public transport. Transport planners must look beyond the traditional emphasis on centre city-oriented peak hour work trips to consider complex travel patterns involving widely dispersed non-work trips and growth in suburb-to-suburb work and non-work trips. The ability to meet these demands that result from changing family life-styles and work patterns through non-automotive means will continue to be a major challenge for urban areas.

The information on urban transport trends presented below is derived from research by the United States (Department of Transportation Nation-wide Personal Transport Survey (NPTS), the Texas Transport Institute (TTI), Federal Highway Administration, and other sources.[10]

Passenger travel in the United States, measured by local and long-distance trips, has increased during the past two decades (Table 51). The NPTS, which looked mainly at local travel, shows an 82% rise in the number of daily person-miles of travel between 1977 and 1995, and a 79% rise in the number of daily trips. In 1977, the average number of daily trips a person made totalled 2.9, compared with 4.3 in 1995. Average trip distance was about 9 miles in both survey years. Because people took more trips in 1995, individuals averaged about 14 100 miles on local travel or 39 miles daily, compared with 9 500 miles in 1977, or 26 miles a day.

The average number and length of long-distance trips taken per person increased from 2.5 (733 miles) in 1977 to 3.9 (826 miles) in 1995. Totalling long-distance and daily travel shows that Americans averaged about 17 200 miles in 1995, up 53% from 11 300 miles in 1977. About 75 to 80% of this travel is local (trips under 100 miles one way), but long-distance travel grew more quickly.

263

Table 51.   **Population and passenger travel, 1997-1995**

	1977	1995	Change 1977-1995 (%)
Resident population (thousands)	219 760	262 761	20
Annual local person trips (travel day) (millions)[1]	211 778	378 930	79
Annual long-distance person trips, domestic (millions)	521	1 001	92
Local person trips per capita, one way (per day)[1]	2.9	4.3	47
Long-distance trips per capita, roundtrip (per year)	2.5	3.9	56
Local person-miles (millions)[1]	1 879 215	3 411 122	82
Long-distance person-miles (millions)	382 466	826 804	116
Local person-miles per capita[1] (annually)	9 470	14 115	49
Long-distance person-miles per capita, domestic (annually)	1 796	3 129	74
Local mean trip length (miles)	8.9	9.0	1
Long-distance mean trip length, domestic (miles)	733	826	13
Persons over 5 years of age[1]			

1. Data used for local travel are from the travel-day file and include trips of all lengths made by respondents on a single day. About 95% of these trips were 30 miles or less. Per capita calculations are based on population estimates within each survey, and not from Census Bureau estimates reported here.

Source: United States Department of Transportation, Bureau of Transport Statistics, *American Travel Survey Data,* October 1997; United States Department of Commerce, Census Bureau, *National Travel Survey, Travel During* 1977 (Washington, DC, 1979) and *Statistical Abstract of the United States* 1998 (Washington, DC, 1998); United States Department of Transportation, Federal Highway Administration, *Summary of Travel Trends:* 1995 *Nation-wide Personal Transport Survey,* draft, 1999.

Table 52.   **Daily and long-distance trips by mode, 1995**

Daily trips	Percentage of daily trips	Percentage of long-distance trips
Personal-use vehicle	89.5	79.2
Public transport	3.6	18.0
Bicycle/walking	6.5	2.1
Rail	0.01	0.5
Other	0.3	0.2

Source: United States Department of Transportation, Bureau of Transport Statistics, *American Travel Survey data,* October 1997; United States Department of Transportation, Federal Highway Administration, *Summary of Travel Trends:* 1995 *Nation-wide Personal Transport Survey,* draft, 1999.

Several factors account for the growth in travel, most importantly greater vehicle availability and reduced travel cost. People could afford to buy more vehicles and travel services in 1995 than in 1977, especially since the cost of the most widely used transport (cars and planes) fell in real terms. The inflation-adjusted cost of owning and operating an automobile declined from US$0.47 per mile in 1975 to US$39 per mile in 1995. The average airfare declined from US$100 in 1975 to US$70 in 1995 (both measured in constant 1982–1984 dollars),[11] while trip lengths increased. Furthermore, both intercity bus and train fares increased slightly more than inflation over this period, which affected lower income persons who use buses more often than other people.

Other factors influence travel growth in a less obvious manner. With a total population nearly 20% higher in 1995 than in 1977, comparable travel growth might be expected if no other factors changed. Some growth can be attributed to greater labour force participation: the workforce rose 36% during this period as baby boomers (those born between 1946 and 1964) took jobs and more women joined the workforce. In addition, the number of households rose 34%, resulting in more trips to buy groceries and other household items. Notably, disposable personal income per capita rose 34% in real terms.

Although household size declined by 7% between 1977 and 1995, the number of vehicles per household increased from 1.59 to 1.78. Households with two vehicles rose by 54% from 26 million to 40 million, and households without vehicles declined from 11.5 million to 8 million. The number of licensed drivers increased by nearly 50 million from 128 million to 177 million and the proportion of the population 16 years and older licensed to drive rose from 81% to 89%.

Trip purpose

Data from the Bureau of Transport Statistics' American Travel Survey and the NPTS can illustrate not only how people travel, but why. Family and personal business made up the greatest share of local trips (55%). Long-distance trips to visit friends and relatives held a 33% share, while business-related trips (including commuting and business travel) accounted for just over 20% each of both local and long-distance trips.

Between 1977 and 1995, the most growth in daily travel per person took place in trips for family and personal business, which more than doubled, and trips for social and recreational purposes, which increased 51%. Trips to or from work per person grew by 33%, while school or church-related trips grew only by 9%. Over the same period, long-distance trips for personal business, business and leisure experienced the most growth. Trips to visit friends and relatives also grew, albeit more slowly than other types of trips: their share declined from 37% of all long-distance trips to 33%.

Public transport and alternative modes of transport

Most passenger trips (nearly 90% of daily trips and 92% of miles travelled) are made in cars or other private motorised vehicles (Table 52). The share of other modes was considerably smaller: cycling and walking accounted for 6.5% of local trips and 0.5% of miles, and public transport's share was about 4% of trips and

265|

3% of miles. The NPTS shows that local private vehicle trips grew more rapidly than overall local trips (111% compared with 79%). In 1995, the average household made 6.4 local private vehicle trips, up from 4.0 in 1977. Households averaged 57 local miles daily in private vehicles in 1995, 24 more miles than in 1977.

Table 52 also shows a ranking of modes used for long-distance travel. Although travel by bus ranks a distant third and rail maintains an even smaller share, between 1977 and 1995, long-distance person-trips by bus increased by 43% and those by train increased by 23%. The per capita number of bus trips increased by 20%, while those by train remained constant.

Public transit service increased between 1991 and 1998, the most recent year for which data are available, measured in terms of vehicle revenue miles supplied and passenger trips. Overall, transit increased revenue miles increased by 19% and ridership by 5%. The number of light rail/streetcar systems increased from 15 to 20 and vehicle revenue miles increased by 59% and 49% respectively. For the dominant mode in use nationally, fixed route bus, revenue miles increased by over 6% while ridership declined slightly, by 1%. Rail rapid transit (metro) had a service increase of 8% and a ridership increase of 10%. Urban commuter rail service increased by over 20%, with ridership increasing by 17%.[12]

Congestion trends[13]

Growth in travel and dispersed land use in urban areas have contributed to major increases in time spent commuting and congestion of urban areas. Commuters spent, on average, 21 minutes travelling to work in 1995, an increase of 13% since 1983. The average work trip rose from 8.5 miles in 1983 to 11.6 miles in 1995. Research on trip chaining suggests that commuting time and distance are underestimated, because only the last leg of a trip chain to work is measured.

Average commute speeds rose from 28 miles per hour (mph) in 1983 to 34 mph in 1995 (a 20% increase). Average speed varied from 40 mph in rural areas to 24 mph in urban areas. Longer but faster commuting trips are partly a reflection of continued decentralisation of metropolitan areas and a switch from slower modes of transport such as carpools to the faster single-occupant vehicle trips. In 1995, most people travelled to work by personal-use vehicle, with 1 out of 10 carpooling. Carpooling has declined by about 15% since 1977. In 1995, about 5% reached work by transit and another 4% by other means (*e.g.* walking and cycling). These proportions have been reasonably stable since 1977.

The TTI produces annual mobility reports with indicators and evaluation of the levels of mobility and congestion in United States cities.[14] In more than half of the cities studied, the amount of time drivers spend stuck in traffic has grown by at least 350% over the past 16 years. One measure, the Travel Rate index, shows the difference between a trip taken during peak travel times and the same trip made in uncongested conditions. The study shows that drivers in more than half the cities studied needed anywhere from 20 to 50% more time to complete the rush-hour journey in 1997. This peak hour penalty has more than doubled in 68 urban areas between 1982 and 1997. This includes a 260% increase in areas between one and three million population and a 240% jump for cities between 500 000 and one million population. Researchers also calculated the amount of delay each driver experiences. Drivers in roughly one third of the cities spent more than 40 hours over the course of a year stuck in traffic. The amount of delay has nearly tripled since 1982. The financial cost of congestion exceeds US$72 billion per year, up from US$66 billion in 1996. Almost half the urban areas studied had congestion costs of more than US$500 million per year, and congestion costs per driver ranged from US$50 in Brownsville, Texas to US$1 370 in Los Angeles. The congestion cost is comprised of extra travel time and wasted fuel.

4.3. Air quality trends

The 1990 CAAA require progress toward national standards for healthy air quality for emissions of the six criteria and related pollutants: CO, nitrogen oxides (NO$_X$), volatile organic compounds (VOC), sulphur dioxide (SO$_2$), fine particulates, and lead. According to the United States Environmental Protection Agency (EPA), as stated in the Bureau of Transport Studies 1999 Annual Report, sizeable reductions in most emissions categories since the early 1980s are apparent even though vehicle-miles-trips have increased appreciably. For 1997, in comparison with all sources for which EPA estimates emissions, mobile sources contributed 62% (53.842 million tons) of all CO, 36% (8.573 million tons) of NO$_X$, 32% (6.138 million tons) of VOC, and 13% (522 tons) of lead. Mobile source lead emissions have declined significantly since 1970 when they were represented 82% of all lead emissions.

The decline in emissions of pollutants from road transport has played a major role in improving the nation's air quality over the last three decades. Between 1975 and 1997, concentrations of CO declined by 69%, those of nitrogen dioxide (NO$_2$) by 40%, ozone by 31% and lead by 98%. PM$_{10}$ has declined by 26% since 1988, when monitoring began. While the long-term downward trends are unmistakable, for 1996 and 1997 the concentration levels of NO$_2$, ozone, and lead remained the same with PM$_{10}$ declining only fractionally. Measured concentrations for CO continued to decline in 1997.

The following information on transport and air quality trends is provided by EPA.[15] The Clean Air Act of 1970 gives primary responsibility to state and local governments for regulating pollution from power plants, factories and other stationary sources. EPA has primary responsibility for regulating mobile sources which include cars, trucks, buses, and aircraft. The EPA vehicle emission control program has achieved considerable success in reducing both nitrogen oxide and hydrocarbon emissions. Cars coming off today's production lines typically emit 70% less nitrogen oxides and 80% to 90% less hydrocarbons over their lifetimes than their uncontrolled counterparts of the 1960s. The improvement came about in response to stringent regulations, which required auto manufacturers to develop systems capable of capturing excess gasoline vapours and cleansing tailpipe emissions.

Ozone levels in many cities have come down with the introduction of lower volatility gasoline and improved emission control systems on cars. But although there has been significant progress since 1970 in reducing emissions per mile travelled, the number of cars on the road and the miles they travel almost doubled in the same timeframe.

EPA believes that control of hydrocarbon and nitrogen oxide emissions is the most promising strategy for reducing ozone levels in most urban areas. Toward that end, the federal government will establish more stringent limits on gasoline volatility, control hydrocarbon vapours that evaporate during vehicle refuelling, tighten tailpipe emission standards, and require improvements in Inspection and Maintenance programs. EPA also is developing requirements for warning systems on all cars to alert drivers when the emission controls malfunction. Because of continued growth in the number of vehicles and miles travelled, hydrocarbon emissions from conventional gasoline vehicles will begin to increase after 2005, despite continued improvements in emission control systems.

4.4. Climate change and greenhouse gas emissions[16]

Transport emissions grew by 9.5% between 1990 and 1997, which was less than in the residential and commercial sectors but more than in industry. In absolute numbers, however, transport emissions grew the most: about 41 million tonnes of carbon more in 1997 than in 1990 reaching 473 million tonnes in 1997, or about 32% of all energy-related carbon emissions. In 1997, the transport sector contributed about 26% to US emissions covered by the Kyoto Protocol.

Notes

1. See Lyons, William, M. (2000) The United States Transport Equity Act for the 21st Century and the CAAA – An Innovative Framework for Transport and Environmental Policy, United States Department of Transportation, Volpe National Transportation Systems Center, paper presented at the ECMT/OECD workshop on innovative institutional frameworks in Madrid, December 2000.

2. The information on urban population and land use trends is compiled from the United States Census Bureau, United States Department of Housing and Urban Development, Pew Center for Civic Journalism, Brookings Institute, and other sources, as presented by the Sierra Club (*www.sierraclub.org/sprawl/population.asp*).

3. See *Debate on Theories of David Rusk*, The Regionalist, Fall 1997.

4. United States Department of Housing and Urban Development (2000), *State of the Cities*, 2000.

5. Diamond and Noonan (1996) *Land Use in America*, Island Press, p. 87; Benfield, Raimi and Chen, *Once There Were Greenfields*, Natural Resources Defense Fund, p. 5; Porter (1997) *Managing Growth in America's Communities*, Island Press, p. 4; See also Bartlett, Mageean and O'Connor (2000) *Residential Expansion as a Continental Threat to United States Coastal Ecosystems*, Population and Environment, Volume 21, Number 5, May.

6. Janet Rothenberg Pack (1998) *Metropolitan Areas: Regional Differences* Brookings Review, Fall 1998, p. 27.

7. United States Census Bureau.

8. Bartlett, Mageean and O'Connor (2000) *Residential Expansion as a Continental Threat to United States Coastal Ecosystems*, Population and Environment, Volume 21, Number 5, May.

9. United States Census Bureau.

10. As presented in the Transport Statistics Annual Report published by the United States Department of Transportation, Bureau of Transport Statistics (*www.bts.gov/transtu/tsar/tsar1999/*).

11. United States Department of Transportation, Bureau of Transport Statistics, 1998.

12. United States Department of Transportation, National Transit Database (*www.fta.dot.gov/ntl/database.html*).

13. The source for this section is the *Transport Statistics Annual Report* published by the United States Department of Transportation, Bureau of Transport Statistics (*www.bts.gov/transtu/tsar/tsar1999/*).

14. See the TTI's 1999 Mobility Report (*mobility.tamu.edu/news_release/*).

15. United States EPA, Office of Transport and Air Quality (*www.epa.gov/otaq/04-ozone.htm*).

269|

16. The information on national transport trends and greenhouse gases is from *the Transport Statistics Annual Report* published by the United States Department of Transportation, Bureau of Transport Statistics (*www.bts.gov/transtu/tsar/tsar*1999/).

OECD PUBLICATIONS, 2, rue André-Pascal, 75775 PARIS CEDEX 16
PRINTED IN FRANCE
(75 2003 08 1 P) ISBN 92-821-0305-6 – No. 53115 2003